MW01122507

Humber College Library
3199 Lakeshore Blvd. West
Toronto, ON   M8V 1K8

The Contemporary Piano

The Contemporary Piano

A Performer and Composer's Guide to Techniques and Resources

Alan Shockley

HUMBER LIBRARIES LAKESHORE CAMPUS
3199 Lakeshore Blvd West
TORONTO, ON.   M8V 1K8

ROWMAN & LITTLEFIELD
Lanham • Boulder • New York • London

Published by Rowman & Littlefield
An imprint of The Rowman & Littlefield Publishing Group, Inc.
4501 Forbes Boulevard, Suite 200, Lanham, Maryland 20706
www.rowman.com

Unit A, Whitacre Mews, 26-34 Stannary Street, London SE11 4AB

Copyright © 2018 by Alan Shockley

All rights reserved. No part of this book may be reproduced in any form or by any electronic or mechanical means, including information storage and retrieval systems, without written permission from the publisher, except by a reviewer who may quote passages in a review.

British Library Cataloguing in Publication Information Available

Library of Congress Cataloging-in-Publication Data

Names: Shockley, Alan Frederick, 1970– author.
Title: The contemporary piano : a performer and composer's guide to techniques and resources / Alan Shockley.
Description: Lanham : Rowman & Littlefield, [2018] | Includes bibliographical references and index.
Identifiers: LCCN 2017048671 (print) | LCCN 2017049518 (ebook) | ISBN 9781442281882 (electronic) | ISBN 9781442281875 (hardcover : alk. paper) | ISBN 9781442281899 (pbk. : alk. paper)
Subjects: LCSH: Composition (Music) | Piano—Instruction and study. | Piano—Performance.
Classification: LCC MT40 (ebook) | LCC MT40 .S56 2018 (print) | DDC 786.2/193—dc23
LC record available at https://lccn.loc.gov/2017048671

∞™ The paper used in this publication meets the minimum requirements of American National Standard for Information Sciences—Permanence of Paper for Printed Library Materials, ANSI/NISO Z39.48-1992.

Printed in the United States of America

Contents

Figures

Acknowledgments

In some ways this book, like my study of the piano, began when I was a toddler. My father had an incredible musical ear. He played the piano and organ well and worked as a professional gigging musician as a young man, and there was always a piano at home. One of my favorite childhood photos shows the three-year-old me seated on the floor between an old floor-standing phonograph and the even older Lexington upright that was my childhood piano. Visible in a reflection in the mirror fronting the top of that piano is my father's face. Long before I started taking piano lessons, I was in the habit of sitting beside him on the piano bench and following his hands with my own.

I learned a lot about the inside of the piano before entering my teens—my godfather, a registered piano technician, sometimes took me with him on the job. From him, I learned how to dismantle and reassemble the cabinet of a piano, as well as how to do some repairs to the action and pedal mechanisms and a bit of the art and science of regulation.

Unlike a lot of my composition work, much of the work of this book has not been solitary. So many pianists, composers, technicians, and piano makers have given generously of their time and their expertise. In particular, my hearty thanks to the following people:

My own piano teachers, Connie Mitchum, Mrs. Joe Argo, Ivan Frazier, and Donald Gren. And though I did not study individually with them, pianists Richard Zimdars and Martha Thomas also contributed much to my piano studies as an undergraduate student. Margaret Leng Tan, for staying up late several times (once while running a fever) to chat with me about Cage, Crumb, prepared pianos, and toy pianos. Thanks to George Crumb for his advice to me as a young composer and pianist and for his warm support of this project. Pianist Vicki Ray, who took time out of her busy schedule to comment on my work. Pianist Sarah

Cahill had many useful suggestions of composers and other pianists I should contact, in addition to providing lots of advice herself. David Smooke, my fellow toy piano devotee, who encouraged me in this work early on and is continually uncovering new sounds from the toy piano. Pianist Adam Tendler generously gave of his time to chat about marking and preparing pianos and shared with me scores and insight into several recent works, some of which were unpublished and in some cases performed with only a protoscore, thereby giving me access to works that otherwise would've been entirely inaccessible. Piano technicians Alan Eder, Sue Babcock, and Ed Whitting lent to me so much technical expertise. Pianist and musicologist and dear friend Benjamin Binder, for reading and feedback.

Piano makers Carl Ulrich Sauter, Udo Steingraeber, and Wayne Stuart, for sharing with me innovations in the beautiful instruments made by Sauter Pianofortemanufaktur, Klaviermanufaktur Steingraeber & Söhne, and Stuart and Sons Pianos.

George Wheeler and Alex Miller for great conversations concerning this project, and to Carolyn Bremer for encouragement throughout the work. My student research assistants Julian Esparza (for the 2016–2017 school year) and Victor Fu (for 2017–2018) for running down many leads for me. My theory and composition students who push me to be a better teacher and composer, and who teach me so much each day.

So many other composers and pianists made suggestions and shared works with me, including Mark Ainger, Stacey Barelos, Elizabeth A. Baker, Aron Kallay, Mu-Xuan Lin, Guy Livingston, and Mark Uranker. Bert Turetzky, one of the original editors for the New Instrumentation Series books and the author of *The Contemporary Contrabass*, the very first book in the series, was encouraging from the very start.

My mom, for driving me to lessons for all of those years and for tolerating all of the piano banging.

Zola and Harper for joyfully filling my every day with music, for inspiring me, and for making me laugh—both at them and at myself.

Huge, truly incalculable thanks to Jessica Sternfeld, for encouraging me to start this project in the first place, convincing me to keep going, serving as a sounding board for all of my ideas, and being my first and best editor. And for being my partner.

Introduction

This book is designed as a resource for composers writing for the piano and for pianists interested in playing repertoire that makes use of techniques and implements unfamiliar to them. In the appendixes I also provide some information and images that steer both composers and performers to the individual characteristics and physical layouts of various instruments. Despite modern pianos sharing many elements, there remains a surprising diversity of string layouts, brace structures, bridge components, and even variance in number of keys for a few models and in the number and type of pedals across instruments of different sizes, designs, and makers.

I do not label the various approaches to playing and preparing pianos as "extended" techniques, even though most pianists, at least as of this writing, would themselves think of many of the techniques I discuss as extended—and perhaps even experimental. Fortunately, today's extensions of technique often become tomorrow's standard and expected practice. One day Saint-Saëns is storming out of the concert hall because of Stravinsky's "misuse" of the bassoon (his asking the solo bassoonist to play a melody very high in the bassoon's range). A few years later, that work is widely considered a classic, and young student bassoonists think nothing of playing that solo. So, the following pages outline dozens of techniques for use on the piano and consider them all as viable approaches to the instrument.

When I began this work, I planned on spending some pages warning against techniques or preparations that have a high potential for damaging the instrument. But, as I continued this work, I began to feel that I did not want my own respect for the piano (and fear of damaging one) to be a limit to the creativity and invention of others. So, I warn about techniques and preparations that may damage the instrument, but I also describe and discuss at least a few approaches (and some works that employ these) that damage or even destroy pianos. I have no immediate plans myself to destroy any pianos, but if that is where your art takes you, and you can afford to repair or replace the instrument you damage, I hope that some of the information in this book will help you in blazing new paths.

No work like this one exists in a vacuum. I discovered Gardner Read's reference works on extended techniques as an undergraduate composer. I don't remember exploring what these books covered for the piano, probably because I felt like I knew the piano. But, I do remember being excited to read about multiphonics for woodwinds and unusual uses of percussion instruments, and I immediately planned new works that would take advantage of these "new" devices. A few years later, I pored over Bertram Turetzky's *The Contemporary Contrabass* and copied pages from John Schneider's *The Contemporary Guitar*, borrowing a device here or there from these and then running down performers to demonstrate them to me, so I could make sure that I understood each one. I hope this book inspires composers and pianists as those books did me.

I must also acknowledge at the outset that there are limitations built into the very nature of a study such as this one. As exhaustive as any author's attempt at cataloging the many techniques available on an instrument might be, there's always tomorrow! Tomorrow, somewhere, a pianist will discover yet another new technique. As a composer, I find the adventurous spirit that leads to these discoveries exciting, and I look forward to much more pushing at the limits of the piano's—and pianists'—capabilities.

Most but not all the techniques detailed in these pages are practical on grand pianos (of most any size, make, and model), with their horizontally oriented strings and gravity-assisted actions. Many of the techniques covered are also possible—and a few even more practicable—to perform on upright pianos. The text mentions and explains when these exceptions are the case. Otherwise, the text defaults to the grand piano, and any directional descriptions refer to a grand piano's architecture. So, the text refers to hammers as striking upward (as on a grand) not away from the player (as on an upright) or to releasing the damper pedal as lowering the dampers onto the strings (again, as on a grand), not the pedal's releasing the dampers to their at-rest position pressed laterally against the strings (as on an upright).

Chapter 1 goes over the basics of the instrument as well as conventions of notation. Here are brief descriptions of the pedal mechanisms of both upright and grand pianos, as well as information on ways of notating for the keys and pedals, use of ledger lines and octave signs, and articulations and slurs.

An overview of the history and mechanism of the piano occupies chapter 2, describing many developments that piano makers adopted, a few that never caught on, and some recent innovations, including some computer- and sensor-enhanced pianos.

Chapter 3 is divided into two sections. The first covers various techniques performed on the keys of the instrument, discussing many types of cluster and glissando, as well as playing silently on the keys to set up sympathetic vibrations and various "underpressure" techniques on the keys. The chapter's second section covers various techniques as performed on the pedals.

Chapter 4 starts by giving a basic protocol for playing inside the piano without damaging the instrument and gives some ways to assist the player in orienting herself inside the instrument. Then the chapter discusses strumming on the strings, pizzicato techniques, scraping and rubbing the strings, and using various electrical devices to excite the strings.

Chapter 5 covers muting with the fingers and hands, as well as ways of utilizing various objects and materials for muting. The chapter also includes instructions for constructing weighted cloth-covered mutes.

Chapter 6 very briefly outlines the basic physics involved in harmonics and then launches into practical considerations for producing harmonics on the piano, with instructions on how to mark nodes safely, as well as ways to make harmonics more resonant. Ways in which harmonics make microtones readily available on the piano appear here as well.

Chapter 7 is in two large sections. The first of these covers ways of hitting the instrument and implements to use for this; this section addresses percussive techniques as used on the strings and other surfaces of the piano, both interior and exterior. The second section discusses ways composers have found to employ the pianist to make noises into or near the instrument.

Chapter 8 details various devices that can be used for bowing the strings of the piano and gives instructions for making and prepping some of these. Because the bowed piano has become a kind of instrument in its own right, there's a good amount of repertoire, and there are several pieces for an ensemble of players all bowing a single instrument; the chapter acknowledges the work done by Stephen Scott and the Bowed Piano Ensemble over the past few decades in this regard.

The expansive chapter 9 details preparations, looking at rooting these in experimentation in the early days of the piano that morphed into unusual timbral stops for some pianos and, once makers abandoned those, back to preparations. I have divided preparations into "families" or classes, including surface preparations, string preparations, hammer preparations, hammer-wrap preparations, double preparations, una corda preparations, key preparations, and pedal preparations.

The last chapter, chapter 10, leaves the piano to discuss the toy piano, a separate instrument that has been adopted by many contemporary pianists as a part of their touring rig and that is experiencing a boom in new works written for it. The chapter covers the history, materials, range, action, many techniques that transfer well from the piano to the toy piano, and some techniques to be played both inside and outside the instrument, as well as some that require preparations.

1

Basics of the Piano and Its Notation

Whether you are an experienced composer or pianist or just beginning to learn the instrument, it is helpful to understand how this big beast of an instrument works. There are many elements of the piano that have become standardized, though there are a few makers challenging even the most foundational elements of the instrument.

RANGE

The standard compass for pianos built from the late 1880s to the present is eighty-eight keys, running from A0 to C8 (see figure 1.1).[1] Steinway expanded the compass of their pianos from eighty-five keys to eighty-eight in the 1880s, and most other piano makers, beginning with Steinway's other American competitors, quickly followed suit. There have been, and currently are, a few outliers. Some makers of the past century have offered modern pianos with fewer than eighty-eight keys, marketing these instruments as easier to move, requiring less space in a home, and being less expensive. Among other makers, Wurlitzer, Gulbransen, and Melodigrand (Aeolian) all have offered smaller-compass pianos in the twentieth century, stressing that these instruments had the same piano actions and other components as their other pianos but required less space (and were less expensive). After the eighty-eight-key standard took over, piano makers have produced very few instruments with fewer keys. Most pianists will have never played on an acoustic piano with eighty-five, seventy-three, or sixty-four keys. I have never seen one in a concert space or music department.[2]

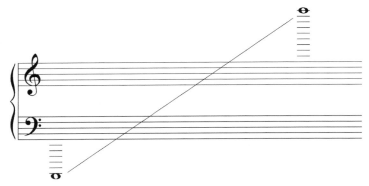

Figure 1.1.   Standard range of the piano

EXPANSIONS OF RANGE

There are also a few piano makers offering instruments with more than eighty-eight keys (see figure 1.2). The renowned Viennese maker Bösendorfer offers a few grand piano models with an added four subcontra keys, taking the range down to F0 and taking the piano's number of keys to ninety-two. Bösendorfer's flagship concert grand piano, the 9'6"-long Model 290 "Imperial" Grand adds nine additional subcontra keys (each single-strung), taking the instrument's range down to C0, for a total of ninety-seven keys. The Australian boutique piano maker Stuart and Sons, founded in 1990, offers pianos with both additional subcontra keys like the Bösendorfer and a few additional treble keys. Because Stuart and Sons makes very few pianos (about ten a year) and makes most of its pianos to order, it is possible to get one of their grand pianos with a compass from C0 to F8, yielding an instrument that adds nine keys below the typical low A and five additional high treble keys above the typical C8, for a total of 102 keys. Wayne

Figure 1.2.   Grand piano expanded ranges

Stuart is currently developing his next generation of concert grands and plans to offer these with an additional four treble keys, giving these instruments a range from C0 to B8 (108 keys)! Pianos with these expanded ranges are definitely not available to most pianists, and there are very few works that use notes beyond the eighty-eight standard keys.

Until more makers adopt such expansions as standard, composers may need to create alternate versions of works that call for these extra notes (or resign themselves to serious limitations on where their pieces can be performed), unless they are writing for a particular venue and know that the hall has an "Imperial" grand or a Stuart and Sons instrument.

THE GRAND PIANO'S PEDALS

Upright pianos and grand pianos differ on their standard pedals and may even differ in the number of pedals. For grand pianos, all modern instruments have a damper pedal, which lifts all the dampers from the strings. All grands also have an una corda pedal, which slides the key frame laterally so that the hammers strike the strings differently—on modern instruments it is not a true una corda, which would move the hammers so that they struck only one string from each unison set. Instead, the modern una corda moves the hammers so that, at least for the triple unisons, the hammer strikes two of the three strings. For the bass notes that are single-strung or have only two unisons per note, the una corda may not reduce the number of strings struck at all but instead moves the hammers so that a different portion of the hammers' faces come into contact with the strings.

Almost all modern grand pianos also have a third pedal placed between the una corda pedal and the damper pedal. For grands with this third pedal, it is a sostenuto pedal, which allows selected dampers once raised to be held away from the strings. The sostenuto pedal on grand pianos can be used to affect the dampers throughout the range of the piano—the dampers merely need to be raised by pressing the keys, and then the dampers can be suspended off the strings by using the sostenuto pedal.

THE UPRIGHT'S PEDALS

For upright pianos, the pedal configuration is slightly different. All upright pianos have a damper pedal, which functions in much the same way as the damper pedal on the grand piano—engaging the pedal moves all the dampers away from the strings. For upright pianos, the second standard pedal is not the una corda but a "soft" pedal, also called a half-blow pedal. The half-blow pedal mechanism tilts the action closer to the strings, so that the hammers are closer to them and thereby reduces the volume of the instrument. Most, but certainly not all, uprights constructed today have a third pedal, but what this third pedal does is not uniformly standard. A very few upright pianos have a sostenuto third pedal. However, it is more common for this third pedal to be a bass damper pedal, moving the dampers off the strings for the lower half of the instrument only. It is also fairly common for the third pedal to mute the sound by lowering a curtain of felt between the hammers and the strings (a sordino pedal).

NOTATION

Most piano music is notated in a similar fashion—the score is parsed into two staves, connected together with a brace to form a grand staff (see figure 1.3). Usually the top staff uses the treble clef, and the bottom staff uses the bass clef, though when a work makes use of extreme registers, moves quickly between different registers, or features a lot of hand crossing, the clefs may vary in the two staves. Some works also make use of additional staves—a composer adding a third staff is quite common, and the composer usually does this to clarify the component voices of a work, which might become jumbled together if packed into the grand staff.

Orchestral reductions for piano, polyphonic works consistently using multiple registers, and some other scoring situations may occasionally call for a solo piano work with four or even more staves (see figures 1.4 and 1.5). Occasionally a composer may also reduce the page footprint and give the piano a bit of music notated on a single staff (see figure 1.6). This is especially common in works or passages to be played by a single hand alone.

Within the staves, the score can separate different voices through stem direction. Typically, scores use upward stems to show an upper voice in either staff and downward stems to indicate a lower voice.

When a composer desires a particular fingering or when a passage is only practical with a fingering that the composer fears may be difficult for the performer to

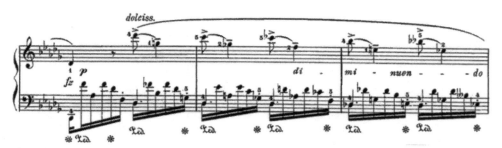

Figure 1.3.   The grand staff, excerpt from Chopin, Nocturne in D-flat, op. 27, no. 2

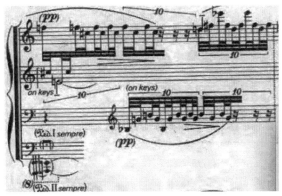

Figure 1.4.   Additional staves, four-stave excerpt from Crumb, *Gnomic Variations*, p. 20, m. 5

Copyright © 1982 by C. F. Peters Corporation. Used by permission.

Figure 1.5 Additional staves, five-stave excerpt from Takemitsu, *Rain Tree Sketch II*, Schott, p. 7, m. 1

Takemitsu RAIN TREE SKETCH II. Copyright © 1992 by Schott Music Co. Ltd., Tokyo, Japan. All Rights Reserved. Used by permission of European American Music Distributors Company, sole U.S.and Canadian agent for Schott Music Ltd. Tokyo, Japan

Figure 1.6.   Single-staff piano excerpt, Finnissy, Sonata for (Toy) Piano (Ricordi), p., mm. 1–3

Music by Michael Peter Finnissy. Copyright © Ricordi G-Co. Buehnen Musikverlag GmbH, Berlin—Germany. All Rights Reserved. Reproduced by Kind Permission of Hal Leonard MGB S.R.L.

uncover, the score can indicate fingering. Fingering indications for the piano (and for other keyboard instruments) use the Arabic numbers *1* to *5* and the same for corresponding fingers on each hand: *1* indicates the thumb, *2* the index finger, *3* the middle finger, *4* the ring finger, and *5* the pinky. Some scores indicate which hand should play a particular passage and, as in indicating which finger, this is usually done to clarify fingering for performance. Brackets can indicate which hand should take a passage or the score may list abbreviations for the hand: commonly *l.h.* or *r.h.* in English for "left hand" or "right hand," *M.S.* (mano sinestra) or *M.D.* (mano destra) in Italian.

Barbara Kolb's 1976 piano solo *Appello* concludes with a series of quickly sounded thirty-second note chords (see figure 1.7). Kolb's score provides fingering for every note of these chords (and even provides alternate fingerings in a couple of instances), thus aiding the performer in approaching this passage.

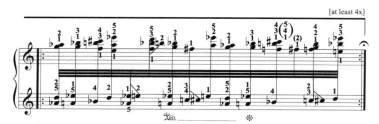

Figure 1.7.   Fingering indications, Barbara Kolb, Appello "And I Remembered the Cry of the Peacocks—Wallace Stevens" last page, last system.
Replicated by author.

NOTATING PEDAL INDICATIONS

Beneath the bass staff, many composers add pedal indications. For Romantic-era composers, these are usually minimal. Many nineteenth-century composers relied on pianists to refer to the then-prevailing performance practice concerning pedaling. They reserved pedal indications for exceptional circumstances, giving an indication to depress the damper pedal over multiple measures to blur several harmonies together or to play senza pedal to confirm a secco sound.

There are basically two typical ways for a composer to indicate pedaling. One is marking "℗." for the place where the player should depress the pedal and * to indicate the pedal's release (see the pedal indications in figure 1.8). In the second, the composer gives a horizontal line beneath the staff to indicate where the pedal should be depressed. If the pedaled passage is an isolated event, then the line appears as a bracket; if two or more pedaled passages are required in sequence, then

Figure 1.8. Pedal indications, excerpt from Liszt, *La campanella*

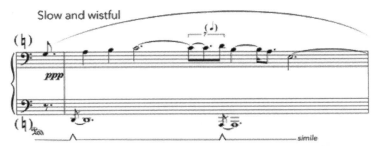

Figure 1.9. Pedal indications, excerpt from Finnissy, *English Country Tunes* (United Music Publishers, Ltd.), p. 13, m. 1. Replicated by author.

the clearing of the pedal between the two passages is indicated by lines forming an inverted V (see figure 1.9). Joseph Banowetz, in his book *The Pianist's Guide to Pedaling*, calls the use of "℔" "cumbersome" and notes that both this and its accompanying release symbol are often "too large . . . [and] imprecisely placed."[3]

Music written after the Romantic era tends to give more specific directions to the performer. Specifically in the realm of piano music, many twentieth- and twenty-first-century composers include more pedal indications. For some works this also involves the composer giving details not only for when the damper pedal should be depressed and released but also for half or quarter pedal (and for rhythmic or pulsed pedaling or flutter pedaling) and for the use of the other two pedals of the instrument.

In figure 1.10, Sciarrino indicates using the damper pedal and qualifies the pedaling with "tenuto" and "press." He also indicates using the sostenuto pedal, here abbreviated "Th.P." from the German *Tonhalte-Pedal*. Sciarrino, in a work for violin and piano (see figure 1.11), includes indications for all three pedals in the course of only a few gestures, notating pedaling for the damper pedal, the una corda, and the sostenuto (again, using an abbreviation for *Tonhalte-Pedal*, here "Th Ped."). He also includes a half release of the damper pedal. For clarity's sake, before showing the una corda pedaling, the composer indicates "tre c." (for tre corde, or three strings). Some composers cancel an una corda marking with tutte corde (all the strings).

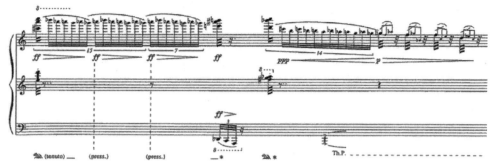

Figure 1.10. More detailed pedal indications, excerpt from Sciarrino (Ricordi), *Due notturni crudeli,* **p. 10, beginning of second system**

Music by Salvatore Sciarrino, Copyright © 2001 Casa Ricordi S.r.l., Milan—Italy. All Rights Reserved. Reproduced by Kind Permission of Hal Leonard MGB S.R.L.

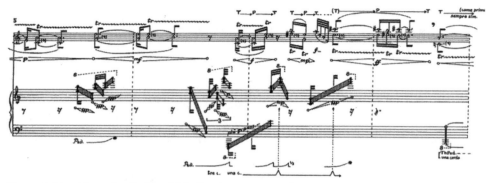

Figure 1.11. More detailed pedal indications, excerpt from Sciarrino, Sonatina for Violin and Piano (Ricordi), p. 7, first system

Music by Salvatore Sciarrino, Copyright © 1976 Casa Ricordi S.r.l., Milan—Italy. All Rights Reserved. Reproduced by Kind Permission of Hal Leonard MGB S.R.L.

LEDGER LINES AND OCTAVE SIGNS

Pianists regularly read ledger lines both below the bass staff and above the treble staff. However, if a note with four or more ledger lines is approached in an angular fashion or if there is a single note in an extreme register, potentially requiring several ledger lines, that is surrounded by notes within the staff, then it may be clearer to notate that exceptional note using octave signs. If an entire passage sits well above or below the staff, then octave signs may again be easier to read than notating using lots of ledger lines. For these, the usual indications are 8va (ottava alta) for a note to be played an octave above the notated notehead and 8vb (ottava bassa) for a note to be played an octave below the written note. There are similar indications for the double octave or fifteenth above and below: 15ma (quindicesima alta) and 15^{mb} (quindicesima bassa). Indications for the octave or fifteenth higher should appear *above* the staff. Indications for the octave or fifteenth lower should appear *below* the staff (see figures 1.12 and 1.13).

Figure 1.12.   Octave above, octave below, and double octave above indications, Shockley, *bristlecone and pitch*, **mm. 62–64**

Figure 1.13.   Further example of octave above, octave below, and double octave above indications, Rzewski, *The People United Will Never Be Defeated!* **(ZEN-ON Music Co., Ltd.), p. 22, mm. 5–6**
Replicated by author.

Using one, two, or three ledger lines between the two staves of the grand staff—such as writing a note attached to the bass clef staff using two ledger lines above that staff—is common, but usually a composer can and should avoid notating extended passages using ledger lines between the two staves or using more than three ledger lines for notes between the two staves. It is usually easier and tidier for the player to read if the composer changes the clef or moves the passage that would otherwise require ledger lines to the other staff, eliminating the ledger lines.

Though the notation for figure 1.14 is mostly clear, the notes in the top staff in the first measure all require multiple ledger lines, and the notes in the lower staff in the second measure demonstrate the same difficulty, with their notes given above the bass clef staff using lots of ledger lines. In both cases, moving the notes to the other staff would enable the player to read them much more quickly and easily. Another notation solution for this particular passage is to

Figure 1.14.   Example of how *not* to use ledger lines between the staves

Figure 1.15. Renotated version of the passage from figure 1.14

switch clefs for the staves containing all of the ledger lines. Figure 1.15 is the same passage demonstrating both of these solutions, with the clef changed in the first measure to eliminate the ledger lines and the notes moved from the bass clef (where it required lots of ledger lines originally) to the other staff (now requiring no ledger lines at all).

ARTICULATIONS AND SLURS

The whole range of articulations and slurs are common in piano music. Early in the twentieth century, for example, composer and pianist Béla Bartók used a wide variety of articulation indications. In his 1911 piece *Allegro Barbaro*, in addition to slurs, Bartók uses eight different articulation signs, as well as sforzando (*sff*), an indication that combines a fortissimo dynamic indication along with an accent. And, the piece uses both the accent and the marcato indication in combination with notes at the beginning of slurs. It also asks the player to play combinations of multiple articulations in simultaneous musical statements between the two hands, including accent-with-tenuto simultaneously with tenuto, marcato-staccato simultaneously with marcato, and marcato-tenuto simultaneously with marcato (see figure 1.16).

Figure 1.16.   Some of the articulations Bartók uses in
Allegro Barbaro

More recently, other composers have built an even larger palette of articulations. In particular, composers applying serial principles related to pitch to the organization of articulations have made regular use of several additional articulations. Olivier Messiaen's *Mode de valeurs et d'intensités* provides a ready example (see figure 1.17), as does a Pierre Boulez score (see figure 1.18). Messiaen's piece in many ways led to composers like Boulez and Stockhausen (who both studied with Messiaen) to experiment with serializing other musical elements in addition to pitch, and having a twelve-member pitch series, led them to expanding dynamic levels from *ppppp* to *fffff*, and to add to their palette of articulation signs to build twelve-member series for these musical elements, too.

Figure 1.17. Messiaen, *Mode de valeurs et d'intensités* (Durand et cie), p. 7, first three bars

Replicated by author.

Figure 1.18. Boulez, *Structures* (for two pianos; Universal Edition), section Ic, mm. 4–7

Universal Edition

2

The History and Mechanism of the Instrument

Sometime in 1700 or thereabouts, Bartolomeo Cristofori invented the pianoforte. It is possible that he had been experimenting with this new instrument for a few years by that date. We know that in 1700 he successfully constructed a piano because a 1700 inventory of the Medici instruments in the court at Florence lists Cristofori's newly invented "*arpicimbalo,*" and his "*arpi cimbalo del piano e'forte*" is mentioned by court musician Federigo Meccoli (like Cristofori, an employee of the Florentine court). Meccoli says that Cristofori invented his new instrument that year. There is also a mention of a Cristofori instrument, a "*gravicembalo col piano e forte*" by writer Scipione Maffei in a 1711 description.[1] The most significant aspect of Cristofori's invention was the piano's action itself, as this is the thing that most set this new instrument apart from the harpsichord or clavichord, which were by then familiar keyboard instruments. The earliest surviving Cristofori escapement action is from 1726 and is part of the collection of the Muzeikinstrumentenmuseum of the University of Leipzig. Though there have been many innovations in piano construction since Cristofori's instruments, the basic principles of his action remain: The player starts the lever action by depressing a key, which sets a wooden hammer in motion toward striking a string or strings and also moves a damper from an at-rest position against the strings away from those same strings, thereby allowing the strings being struck to ring freely.

Cristofori's design includes a so-called single-escapement action: The last bit of hammer travel takes place without the governance of the key's motion; the hammer "escapes" from its attachment to the key. If the key were still connected to the hammer's motion at the string (without the escapement), then the key would hold the hammer against the string and thereby also dampen the string, reducing its resonance. Judging by the extant Cristofori instruments, the hammers for his new instrument struck double-strung unisons, and as would remain true for most pianos of the succeeding hundred years, he equipped his instruments with an una corda mechanism, though rather than a pedal-activated mechanism, Cristofori's pianos had a hand stop that shifted the action to the right so that only one of the two unisons per key would be struck by the hammers.[2]

SILBERMANN'S ADDITIONS

Just a few years later, German instrument builder Gottfried Silbermann copied much of Cristofori's action in his own pianos and added to those designs a mechanism that could release all of the dampers from the strings, allowing all the strings of the instrument to ring freely. This idea was to be developed later into the damper pedal, but like Cristofori's una corda stop, Silbermann's damper mechanism was tied to a hand stop that required the player to remove a hand from the keyboard to raise the dampers from the strings. It was an effect to be applied to a whole passage rather than a pedal-activated effect that could be applied to individual notes or chords.[3]

THE DOUBLE-ESCAPEMENT ACTION

By 1821, piano maker Sébastien Erard had developed the double-escapement action, and that year his nephew Pierre registered the patent in London.[4] This action prevents the action parts from returning to their at-rest position if the key is only partially released and allows for a note to be restruck more quickly because the key does not have to wait for the action to reset before setting the next hammer throw in motion. The young Franz Liszt arrived in Paris just a few years after Erard had begun implementing his new action, and Liszt performed his first Paris concerts on a double-escapement action on one of Erard's new pianos in the Erard salons in early 1824.[5]

AGRAFFES

In 1808, Sébastien Erard was also responsible for inventing and patenting metal agraffes, which would later be adopted by many other piano makers.[6] The agraffes form individual bridges near the tuning pins that keep the end of the vibrating portion of the string close to the metal plate and resist the force caused by the hammer hitting the string.

OVERSTRINGING AND EXPANDED RANGE

Early grand pianos were straight-strung instruments, with all of the instrument's strings running essentially parallel to each other. The extant Cristofori instruments have a range of about four octaves (forty-nine to fifty-four keys), but through the eighteenth century, the range of the instrument steadily increased, with Steinway settling first on eighty-five keys and then on eighty-eight as the standard. As the instrument's compass increased, piano makers modified the scheme for stringing the instrument, fanning the bass strings at an angle and running them partially above some of the midrange strings. This new configuration required two levels for the strings and a separate bass bridge. Jean-Henri Pape is credited with the first use of this design change of overstringing in pianos. Pape worked in Paris with Pleyel and created the first piano with overstringing (also sometimes called cross-stringing), with the bass strings at an angle overlapping the tenor strings. Pape's first use of this configuration was in a small upright piano (a "console" instrument) in 1828, but this string configuration was quickly adapted for many other piano designs.[7]

Pape also switched the hammer-covering material from leather to wool felt, the material used for the hammers in all modern pianos. Pape first used felt-covered hammers in 1826, but it was a number of years before the quality of the felt attracted other makers to switch their hammer materials and several years more before the industry as a whole adopted felt-covered hammers as the standard. About ten years after Pape's change to felt, the first of several inventors' machines for covering hammers with felt appeared, but most European makers who had switched to felt-covered hammers continued to cover them by hand until the 1867 Paris International Exposition, when American pianos showcasing various innovations, including felt-covered hammers covered by machine, made a big impression on attendees and the press.[8] (Both Chickering and Steinway pianos received gold medals at the exposition, both had invested heavily in advertising campaigns leading up to it, and both began touting their awards in the press immediately after the exposition.)

THE CAST-IRON FRAME

Though the essential elements of the action were in place in most pianos by the first third of the nineteenth century and the damper pedal and the una corda pedal also widely adopted by makers at this time, the instrument's sound and overall delicateness remained limited until piano makers—after much resistance by some—adopted a full metal frame. Piano makers from early on understood that stronger framing for the instrument would permit thicker strings and strings under greater tension, both elements that would lend a bigger sound and an overall larger dynamic range to the instrument. Scholar Denzil Wraight, in examining the three extant Cristofori pianos, sees in them a steady progression to heavier, sturdier wood framing from the 1720 instrument currently in the Metropolitan Museum of Art in New York City to the 1722 instrument in the Museo Nazionale degli Strumenti Musicali in Rome to the 1726 one in the Muziekinstrumentenmuseum of Leipzig University.[9]

Initially, many piano makers resisted any framing or plate material made of iron. They learned much of their trade by studying the craft of woodworking as cabinetmakers and other furniture makers. But, as more and more makers adopted full metal plates for their instruments, the piano became much heavier and sturdier. Pianos with full metal plates could support beefier strings and strings under higher tension, which made them louder and with a more forward and forceful tone. This is the direction that pianos generally moved through the late nineteenth century.

Alpheus Babcock registered a patent for a full cast-iron frame with a plate for mounting the hitch pins in late 1825. This and many other patents (including two other piano-related patents by Babcock) were destroyed in a fire at the U.S. patent office in December 1836. Babcock resubmitted all three destroyed patent applications a few years later.[10] He joined the Steinway competitor Chickering in 1837, and the company built on his earlier patent for a full cast-iron frame for square pianos. Chickering applied for a new patent for a full iron frame and plate for square pianos in 1837 and, more importantly, another patent for a full iron frame and plate for grand pianos in 1843.[11]

In the early 1800s, there were many piano makers working in parallel, constructing pianos to new designs and in some cases registering patents at the same time for very similar innovations. Theobald Boehm said in a letter from 1867 that he had recommended overstringing to a piano maker in London in 1831, and A. J. Hipkins in his book *A Description and History of the Pianoforte and of the Older Keyboard Stringed Instruments* says that he discovered that the maker that Boehm advised, Gerock and Wolf, constructed at least three different models of piano (two different sizes of upright pianos and a square) using Boehm's overstrung design. At about the same time, the New York piano maker Bridgeland and Jardine, following a design by John Jardine, created at least two square pianos with overstrung bass strings and exhibited those in 1833. Hipkin's 1896 study mentions several other early adopters of overstringing, including an 1836 English patent by John Godwin and another English patent of 1835 granted to Pierre Frederick Fischer with a design used soon after by Fischer's associate Jean-Henri Pape for the pianos Pape was making in his workshops in Paris.[12]

In 1859, Henry Steinway Jr. patented an overstrung plate for grand pianos, allowing makers to use longer bass strings in the same size cabinet. In addition to accommodating longer bass strings, angling the bass strings over the tenor ones moves most of the vibrating length of those strings and the bass bridge away from the stiffer edge of the soundboard and closer to the middle. Because the middle of the soundboard vibrates more freely than the edge, these moves promote a more resonant sound from the bass strings.[13]

History is messy; it does not follow a straight-line trajectory. It would take just shy of a hundred years from the 1726 Leipzig-held Cristofori instrument before a full iron frame would be patented and even more time before metal frames were widely adopted. The slowness of piano makers to adopt a full cast-iron frame is not an anomaly in the ways makers adopted new technologies into the piano. Scholar Edwin Good actually makes this theme central to his study of the piano, showing how, when one maker adopted wool-felt-covered hammers, others continued (for decades) using leather-tipped hammers. Babcock patented a full iron frame in 1825 but was the only maker to adopt them for several years. Even local builders who were aware of Babcock's patent resisted adopting the full iron frame. It was twelve years later and after hiring Babcock in 1837 (and probably because of Babcock's hands-on work) before Chickering (also of Boston) began developing full iron frames.[14]

As with the slow adoption of the full iron frame, there were plenty of makers who resisted overstringing. The highly respected Paris piano maker Erard did not even offer an overstrung grand until 1901![15]

THE SOSTENUTO PEDAL

Xavier Boisselet, a Marseilles maker, patented a *"pédale tonale* (exhibited 1844), similar to the sostenuto pedal" mechanism later patented by Steinway.[16] In 1874, Albert Steinway patented a modified design for the sostenuto pedal, and this mechanism was soon to become standard on most American grand pianos.[17] Yet again, not everyone adopted this innovation. Many European makers were still issuing very fine grand pianos without a third pedal well into the twentieth century.[18]

DUPLEX SCALING

Some piano makers also began examining the string lengths beyond the speaking segment of the string. On most grands there is a very small portion of the string between the agraffes or capo d'astro and the bridge pins. There is also a slightly longer portion of the string between the bridge pin (the termination of the speaking segment of the string) and the hitch pin. The duplex scale refers to these nonspeaking segments of string. Duplex scaling involves taking advantage of either (or both) of these leftover string segments, most usually the portion of the string between the bridge pin and the hitch pin. Theodore Steinway's original idea, which he patented in 1872, was for individually adjustable duplex bridge points so that each note of the rear duplex scale could be tuned to an octave or fifth or some other interval above the tuning of the corresponding speaking string length. The idea is that modifying the bridge so that these usually ignored lengths of string could be tuned to ring in sympathy with the portion of the string being struck by the hammer would produce a much richer and more resonant sound. But, correctly positioning these individual bridge points proved quite time-consuming (and, therefore, expensive), and Steinway began casting bars fixing whole sections of duplex scale bridge points.

Recently, Mason and Hamlin, Petrof, and Fazioli have returned to Theodore Steinway's original idea for fully tunable and adjustable duplex scale strings. Mason and Hamlin uses individually adjustable duplex bridge points (called aliquots) to allow fine-tuning of the rear duplex scale. Both Fazioli and Petrof have instruments that facilitate tuning both the front and the rear duplex scales.[19] Fazioli has added to the piano's cast-iron plate a stainless-steel track. The aliquots slide on this track, allowing the maker—and later the piano technician maintaining the instrument—to adjust the individual aliquots and tune the duplex scale string lengths. These solutions allow the duplex scale string lengths to be tuned for individual strings, thereby adding lots of string lengths that cannot be struck by the hammers to contribute, nevertheless, to the sound of the instrument. Tuning the duplex scale string lengths to overtones of the struck portion of the string adds these string lengths, which otherwise would be damped with felt and contribute nothing to the instrument's sound, as resonating strings, always ringing along with the struck strings.

ALIQUOT STRINGING

Another solution for adding string lengths not for striking but for resonance is to add entire strings just for the purpose of vibrating in sympathy with the struck strings. An aliquot string is an entire string separate from the speaking strings (the ones that are struck by hammers). Typically, these aliquot strings have their own hitch pin and tuning pin and may have their own separate bridge as well. The German maker Blüthner's aliquot stringing was patented in 1873, and their pianos are the only modern pianos made with these aliquot strings. These strings are tuned either in unison with the struck strings (for the highest register notes) or an octave higher than the struck strings (for the middle register notes that also receive aliquot strings).[20] These aliquot strings vibrate in sympathy with the struck strings, contributing their additional resonance to the overall sound of the instrument.

A FEW (MOSTLY NOT ADOPTED) INNOVATIONS TO THE PIANO KEYBOARD

There have been many attempts at innovation to the piano's basic controls or design that have not been widely adopted by makers. Paul von Jankó designed a keyboard in 1882 that fits multiple rows of shorter keys in place of the single row of keys on the ordinary piano keyboard. On the Jankó keyboard, each note can be played on any one of three small keys that are in a line perpendicular to the player. With a smaller key size and each note accessible from three different rows, this keyboard allows even pianists with small hands to grasp much larger spans than on the ordinary keyboard. It also allows scales and chords to be transposed but played using the same fingerings no matter the key. Blüthner Pianos has custom-made pianos as recently as 2008 with a Jankó keyboard but other than a few custom-order instruments, no current maker has adopted Jankó's special keyboard.[21]

Hungarian composer Emmanuel Moór developed a double-manual piano in the 1920s and '30s. This is essentially an ordinary piano with an ordinary mechanism but with an enhancement of an added upper keyboard. The lower keyboard functions exactly as the keyboard does on any other piano. The upper keyboard uses the same action and moves the hammers to strike the same set of strings, but the keys are linked to strike the strings an octave higher than the corresponding keys on the lower keyboard. This places octaves (and larger intervals, such as tenths and twelfths) within much closer proximity than on a single keyboard. Some double-manual pianos also allow the player to couple the two keyboards and thereby play a note and its octave by depressing a single key. There is only a single Steinway double-manual piano, constructed in 1929 and housed at the University of Wisconsin, Madison. The Metropolitan Museum of Art in New York City has a Bösendorfer double-manual piano. Pianist Christopher Taylor has performed Bach's *Goldberg Variations* on each of these two instruments.[22]

A specialized version of the piano, the pedal piano, was developed alongside the piano and adds a pedalboard much like that found on an organ. Mozart and several nineteenth-century composers were enthusiasts of the instrument. Mozart's pedal piano was built for him by Anton Walter in 1785. Robert Schumann had an upright pedal piano, with a twenty-nine-note pedal span. Charles-Valentin Alkan had an Erard pedal piano and wrote several works for it.

In 2000, Venetian piano maker Luigi Borgato developed his Doppio Borgato, a double concert grand piano, with the lower piano played by a thirty-seven-note pedalboard. A few composers have written for this particular modern incarnation of the pedal piano, including Charlemagne Palestine and Ennio Morricone.

In 2012, organ builder Claudio Pinchi developed the Pinchi Pedalpiano System, using a pedalboard much as one would find on an organ, attached to a set of sixty-one felt-covered wooden "fingers." The Pinchi Pedalpiano System allows the user to combine two ordinary grand pianos with the pedalboard and the linked "fingers" mechanism to have a piano played by hand and a second piano played solely with the feet.[23] Because Pinchi's pedalboard attaches to an ordinary grand piano, it is much less expensive to produce than other pedal pianos, and it allows users to attach and remove the pedalboard and attach it to another instrument.

MORE RECENT INNOVATIONS

Innovations in piano design so far in the twenty-first century seem to be coming a bit slower than in the middle of the nineteenth century, but they definitely continue. Kawai has reexamined the piano action and specifically its materials. Working from the principle that a lighter action is necessarily faster, Kawai has begun incorporating some lighter, modern materials in their actions. In the 1980s they began substituting a new composite material they call ABS Styran, which is lighter than wood, for some of the wood components of their piano actions. Now, Kawai's Millennium III action with carbon fiber replaces some components of the action with a new composite material, adding carbon fiber to the ABS Styran from their previous generation of actions. Kawai claims that infusing their earlier material with carbon fiber increases their strength by 90 percent and that their actions with ABS-carbon components are 25 percent faster than a conventional wooden action.[24] Because Pinchi's pedalboard attaches to an ordinary grand piano, it is much less expensive to produce than other pedal pianos, and it allows users to attach and remove the pedalboard and attach it to another instrument.

In the first part of the nineteenth century, Conrad Graf equipped his grand pianos with a felt rack that could be used to mute the sound, calling his device a muffler. In this same period, Erard in Paris used a buckskin rack in his grands as a mute, calling his effect a "celeste." In recent years, Steingraeber & Söhne, following pianist Jura Margulis's suggestion, began working on creating a similar effect on a modern piano. They now offer their "sordino," a very thin felt strip that moves between the hammers and the strings with a mechanism, as an add-on option to their grand pianos that they can install to be operated by a fourth pedal or a knee lever.[25]

In 2006, Steingraeber began working with English engineer Richard Dain to redesign bridge agraffes to improve the energy transfer from the player to the strings. Their continued work together led to incorporating adjustable hitch pins, reducing the pressure of the bridge on the soundboard, which the maker says increases acoustic efficiency. Steingraeber calls this whole set of changes the Phoenix system, which they now offer in their 168, 205, D-232, and E-272 grand pianos.

Steingraeber has also worked with Richard Dain on new materials for their soundboards and now offers a carbon fiber soundboard on several of their grand pianos. Carbon fiber is light and strong but, even more importantly, is resistant to climate changes in a way that traditional spruce soundboards are definitely not. Studies conducted by Dain show that the typical energy transfer from pianist to soundboard is woefully inefficient (passing along only about 4 percent of the energy); Dain claims that his Phoenix system pianos and their modified bridge components and carbon fiber soundboard double this efficiency.[26]

At first, Steingraeber & Söhne offered Phoenix system pianos under the Steingraeber & Söhne name. Pianos are now available with these features, with many components still made by Steingraeber, but issued with the Phoenix Piano nameplate. The folks at Phoenix Pianos have also scrutinized the component action parts and created an action that uses some parts composed of composite materials, such as carbon fiber hammer shanks and water-repellent bushings in place of felt ones. They also offer bass strings wound with stainless steel rather than copper, a change that they say produces the "classical but now 'lost' purity and clarity of sound of historical iron strings" while keeping the best characteristics of modern copper wound ones.[27]

Several makers have experimented with offering a half-blow pedal mechanism on their grand pianos. The half-blow pedal (or "soft" pedal) is a familiar mechanism on upright pianos, and on uprights, it is the typical pedal found rather than the una corda found on grand pianos. It is, however, very unusual to find this pedal on a grand piano. Such a mechanism allows softer dynamic playing by moving the hammers closer to the strings, reducing the force of their strikes. Where the una corda mechanism reduces volume but also changes the timbre of the sound (by reducing the number of unison strings struck by the hammers), the half-blow mechanism is just about changing dynamics.

Steingraeber & Söhne offers a half-blow mechanism controlled by the same pedal as the una corda—depressing the pedal further engages the half-blow mechanism. They also offer a special-order Mozart Rail mechanism. The Mozart Rail combines a half-blow mechanism with a reduction of key depth. Engaging a hand stop on a piano equipped with the Mozart Rail reduces the touch depth of the keys from approximately 10.1 millimeters to 8.1 millimeters and simultaneously moves the hammers to only 36 millimeters from the strings.[28] These two adjustments change the key action's feel, making it closer to a period instrument from Mozart's time, make for a very fast action, and reduce the volume of the instrument.

Fazioli offers an option of a fourth pedal that is a half-blow pedal (see figure 2.1). Fazioli designed this fourth pedal so that the pedal itself is shaped differently from the other pedals and the pianist can easily distinguish the additional pedal

Figure 2.1.   Four pedals on a Fazioli grand piano

from its near neighbors by touch. Stuart & Sons Pianos has offered a fourth pedal as a half-blow pedal on their instruments since they began to make pianos in 1990.

Pianist and piano maker Stephen Paulello has been working for a number of years on improving the design of the piano. Paulello has, in particular, made several innovations concerning the materials and construction of the wire for piano strings. He has developed hybrid materials wire, as well as electrolytic nickel plating for wires, creating wires to replace the strings of antique instruments as well as in modern instruments. His newest piano strings have allowed him to expand the viable range of the piano upward. Both Stephen Paulello Pianos and Stuart and Sons Pianos, making use of Paulello's strings, offer grands with a range expanded to 102 notes. From his small workshop in France, Paulello creates custom pianos that include concert grands with an expanded range to 102 notes (from C0 to F8), which are straight-strung (see figure 2.2). He is now making pianos without any interruptive bars, giving pianists much greater access to the inside of the instrument. Wayne Stuart of Stuart and Sons Pianos, by using Paulello's strings, has also made expanded-range instruments, and as mentioned earlier, the next generation of Stuart and Sons Pianos will feature a further expanded range, offering 108 notes, from C0 to B8, and will also have a plate with no interruptive braces.[29] Stuart and Sons Pianos are constructed not only with front agraffes but also with bridge agraffes, with the goal of transferring energy from the strings to the soundboard more efficiently.

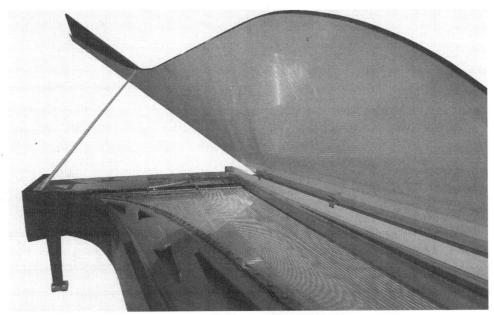

Figure 2.2.   Stephen Paulello straight-strung grand without interruptive braces
Photo by Charly Mandon for Stephen Paulello Pianos

Also working toward efficient transfer of energy, Evert Snel and Hans Velo have developed the Magnetic Balanced Action, which involves installing magnets in the keys of the piano. The action allows the position of the magnets to be changed, thereby harnessing the force of the magnets to adjust the touch weight of the keys. Both Fazioli and Petrof have offered the Magnetic Balanced Action as an option on their instruments.

Wendl and Lung, a brand begun in Vienna in 1910 and since 2003 produced by the Ningbo Halium Musical Instruments Company, Limited, in Ningbo, China, also offers a fourth pedal on some of their piano models, calling it the *pédale harmonique*. Because Feurich pianos are also produced by this same company, some models of Feurich also feature this option. This pedal when fully pressed works like a typical damper pedal, keeping the dampers off the strings and allowing the strings to ring freely. When the pedal is half-pressed, all dampers are raised from the strings; however, only those dampers linked with released keys return to rest on the strings. With the pedal half-pressed, it behaves like the sostenuto pedal and keeps the dampers off the strings of keys that were depressed when the pedal is depressed. All other keys behave as if no pedal is depressed, allowing some notes to ring freely (those that were depressed when the *pédale harmonique* was depressed halfway) and other keys to be played in a variety of ways, including staccato and secco notes.[29]

The piano makers Sauter and Steingraeber & Söhne now make models that include markings inside the piano to assist players playing inside the instrument. For Sauter, their Omega 220, a 7'3" semiconcert grand, includes painted lines on the soundboard to indicate the first three overtones. The Omega 220 also includes white inlays for all the dampers corresponding to white-key notes. Similarly, Steingraeber & Söhne offers a custom option of a "damper keyboard," with each damper painted white or black to match its corresponding key for their various grand piano models.

Some innovations catch on and are adopted by multiple makers and eventually become standard on the instrument; the sostenuto pedal is a good example of one such nineteenth-century innovation. Others, despite receiving support and even public endorsements from well-known artists, languish and mostly disappear. The Jankó keyboard, once praised by several nineteenth-century piano virtuosos, seems to be one of these, for, even though Blüthner has made one custom piano with a Jankó keyboard in the past ten years, schools are not training pianists to play using this interface, and very few pianists have pursued relearning their technique in order to play on this alternate interface.

BEYOND THE EIGHTY-EIGHT: ELECTRONIC AUGMENTATION OF THE PIANO

Several engineers and a few piano makers have worked at expanding the piano's capabilities through augmenting the traditional instrument with physically installed electronic extensions. Player pianos first appeared in the nineteenth century, with electrically powered player pianos and reproducing pianos appearing in various designs in the first few years of the twentieth century. With the advent of the radio at the end of the 1920s, the public quickly lost interest in player and reproducing pianos, and the companies that made them mostly discontinued production in the 1930s. In the latter part of the twentieth century, a few designers have revisited the idea of a reproducing piano, marrying the piano and computer technology.

COMPUTER-DRIVEN REPRODUCING PIANOS

In the 1970s, engineer Wayne Stahnke worked with Bösendorfer to integrate computer-controlled reproducing piano technology with some models of the Bösendorfer grand piano. Stahnke created the first Bösendorfer reproducing piano in 1978, and the SE reproducing system was licensed to Bösendorfer. Thirty-seven Bösendorfer instruments were constructed with this technology (including several 290SE "Imperial" grands and smaller reproducing grands 225SE and the 275SE).[30]

In 2006, Bösendorfer received their trademark for the Bösendorfer CEUS reproducing piano system, a collaboration between Bösendorfer and TVE Electronic Systems working with the Vienna University of Technology. The CEUS system senses and digitally records data from the movements of the hammers, keys, and pedals, and then the player mechanism of the instrument can reproduce the recorded performance. CEUS-equipped pianos include sensor buttons and a small display installed in the fallboard. Bösendorfer lists the system as recording 250 levels per millisecond of both key and pedal movements.

The Yamaha Disklavier, which first appeared in 1987, includes electronic sensors that record key movements, as well as the hammer motion and pedal moves. The Disklavier also includes solenoids to move the keys and pedals to reproduce performances recorded on the instrument or to play other data entered into the computer "brain" of the instrument. In 1999, Yamaha expanded the degree of increments for the sensors from the limits of MIDI, a velocity range of 0 to 127, to a new range of 0 to 1,015. In 2016, Yamaha introduced the latest generation of the Disklavier, the Disklavier ENSPIRE. These latest Disklaviers use noncontact optical sensors to record data generated by each key and hammer, as well as that generated by the motions of the three pedals.

OPTICAL SENSOR SYSTEMS

The Moog Piano Bar

A collaboration between Don Buchla and Moog Music Inc., the Moog Piano Bar combines a set of optical sensors and a CPU, which allows the user to send MIDI information from performance on any piano's keyboard and pedals to control any MIDI instrument. The Moog Piano Bar has the advantage that it does not need to be installed but instead includes a sensor bar that the user rests on the cheek blocks and an additional bar that sits underneath the pedals. Both of these can later easily be removed and installed on other instruments. Production on the Moog Piano Bar ceased in 2007, but there are still people using it as the basis for further development of optical sensors for use with the piano.

QRS Music Technologies produces the PianoScan II, another optical sensor used to read information from performance on a standard piano and again send to any MIDI instrument. Story and Clark pianos now come equipped with the PNOscan MIDI record strip already installed, and QRS says that it can be installed by users on any standard piano.[31]

TouchKeys

In 2010, Andrew McPherson began developing TouchKeys key overlays. The user attaches these very thin sensor overlays that are packaged with mated software to the keytops of any keyboard instrument—including a regular acoustic piano's keys. Much like many smartphones, these overlays use capacitive touch sensing to determine the finger positions on the keytops, allowing the player to add timbre changes and other changes of expression to performance on an acoustic piano. A user can send and process the data recorded from the sensors to dedicated TouchKeys hardware or to the user's own computer. McPherson has integrated this interface into the latest generation of his Magnetic Resonator Piano, discussed below.

Groven Piano Project

Composer-researcher David Loberg Code was looking for ways to make additional pitches available on a piano without the necessity of retuning the instrument. The Groven Project networks multiple pianos to a master controller piano. The controller instrument has additional controls that allow the performer to select from among the other instruments, similar to the way an organist selects different stops. The Groven Piano premiered in 2001 in Norway. For this performance, the three upright Yamaha Disklaviers were tuned to three different tuning systems, allowing the performer at the controller piano to access a thirty-six-tone scale rather than merely a twelve-tone one as would be available in an octave on any one of these instruments.

Kawai AnyTimeX Pianos

Kawai has also developed pianos that include integrated digital technology. Their AnyTimeX pianos are acoustic upright pianos with installed optical sensors. These instruments also include a way of muting the hammers' action on the strings and sending the sensor data to an included sampler that includes the sounds of various pianos and other instruments. The user can plug headphones into this sampler, play on the piano's keys, and hear the samples as triggered by ther performance, thereby hearing the performance in headphones while generating next to no sound in the space.[32]

ELECTROMAGNETICALLY PREPARED PIANO

Edgar Berdahl, Steven Backer, and Per Bloland have developed the Electromagnetically Prepared Piano, an acoustic piano whose action functions in the ordinary way but is equipped with a set of electromagnetic actuators that are mounted on a rack that rests inside the piano and allows the actuators to be moved to vibrate different strings. There are twelve actuators, and by vibrating the string with notes other than the fundamental or with more complex material than a simple sine wave (such as noise), each actuator can access more than just a single note on each string, allowing the twelve actuators to sound many more than twelve pitches, even without moving them to other strings. The actuators also can maintain vibrations in the strings, bringing access to steadily sustained notes on the piano, an impossibility without such augmentation.

MAGNETIC RESONATOR PIANO

Andrew McPherson's Magnetic Resonator Piano (MRP) is a hybrid instrument, with electromagnetic actuators for each of the eighty-eight keys of an acoustic piano, each with its own amplifier (see figure 2.3). In addition, a MIDI keyboard can be added to the piano setup, giving the pianist the power to make additional control changes "live" while continuing to play on the piano's keyboard. The electromagnets add some unusual capabilities to the piano's sound. The pianist can silently depress keys, and the electromagnets can vibrate the relevant strings, bringing forth sound from nothing. The pianist can start notes on the keys *ordinario* and then have those notes sustain far longer than any piano note could naturally last. The actuators can also crescendo notes whether played on the keys first or sounded by the electromagnets from the start.

McPherson has written several works for the MRP, including *d'Amore* (2009), a work for solo viola and the MRP. He has recently refined the MRP, adding touch sensors directly to the key surfaces of the acoustic piano. This new generation of MRP no longer requires the pianist to double on a MIDI keyboard, as the mounted sensors give the performer access to the same sorts of controls directly from the piano's keys.

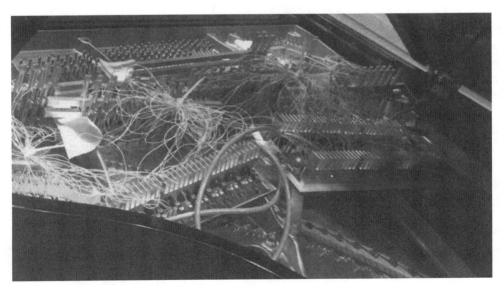

Figure 2.3. Magnetic Resonator Piano
Photo by Alexander Elliott Miller

TRANSDUCER GRAND PIANO

In spring 2017, Steingraeber & Söhne introduced a specially modified version of their D-232 semiconcert grand piano, a D-232 Transducer Grand Piano (see figure 2.4). This instrument has two transducers mounted on the soundboard, allowing transmission of sounds from a computer to the piano's soundboard. Steingraeber touts the ability of this technology to allow a pianist to play on the piano but have the computer send those notes in an alternate tuning to the transducers. Using piano notes (in whatever tuning) to vibrate the soundboard bypasses the usual method of hammers vibrating strings and then the strings transferring their sound through the bridge to the soundboard. This alternate route to the soundboard, using the natural resonance of the piano, sends the sound to the listeners from the piano, not from speakers away from the instrument. This system gives the player the ability to coax differently tuned notes from the piano without retuning it.

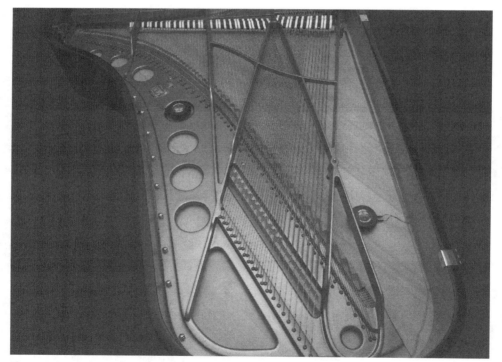

Figure 2.4.   Steingraeber Transducer Grand Piano
Copyright Steingraeber & Söhne, Bayreuth

On the Keys and on the Pedals

There are at least a few techniques on either the piano's keys or on the pedals that stray from traditional technique or are regularly classified as "extended" techniques. Some of these have been a part of piano technique since the eighteenth century, while pianists have devised others much more recently.

TECHNIQUES ON THE KEYS

Clusters

Secundal harmonies—harmonies built of stacked seconds—certainly make appearances in works long before the twentieth century. Many such clusters require no unusual techniques from the pianist, as many chords built of closely spaced notes may be fingered as usual. However, sometimes composers also ask for clusters built of more notes than the fingers can handle and specify clusters to be played with the open hand, the closed hand or fist, the forearm or forearms, or with special implements. Luk Vaes in his dissertation on historical extended piano techniques locates the first published instance of cluster writing for the piano in 1793 in Claude-Bénigne Balbastre's *Marche des Marseillais et l'air Ça-ira* arrangement for fortepiano. This work includes a scalar passage that builds to a measure with a cluster built of a full octave of white keys in the left hand and labeled with the French "*Canon*" (as in the sound of a cannon firing).[1] Vaes goes on to trace many other battle pieces of the late eighteenth and early nineteenth centuries (most of them by French composers) that also exploit the cluster as a similar special effect.

Leap ahead to the twentieth century. Henry Cowell coins the term *tone cluster* for such harmonies and makes use of a huge variety of different cluster techniques in his writing for piano. Writing about his *Antinomy* for solo piano, composed about 1914, Cowell relates the public reaction to his use of forearm clusters to be played as loudly as possible in that work, saying, "[I]t was about this [passage in *Antinomy*] that the *London Times*, which is always right, said that this was the world's loudest piano music and that I was the world's loudest pianist, but of course that was a lot of years ago and I don't suppose I am now."[2]

Some time in the first few years of the twentieth century, pianist-composer Jelly Roll Morton (Ferdinand Joseph LaMothe) began playing rolled clusters by pressing his left elbow on the keys.[3] Leo Ornstein's *Danse sauvage* dates to December 1913 and uses clusters throughout the piece, mostly using four-note or five-note sonorities in a single hand and alternating these smaller clusters between the two hands but expanding at times to ten-note or eleven-note clusters managed by both hands. Charles Ives makes prominent use of clusters in his "Concord" Sonata (written 1904–1919 but first published in 1921), even specifying the pianist use a 14¾-inch-long board to play these. But, it's still Ives's friend Henry Cowell with whom the "cluster" is most closely associated.

As Cowell himself explains, in 1912, as a fifteen-year-old, he was asked to write music for a play. For this, Cowell needed music to go with the Irish legend of Manaunaun, controller of the tides. Cowell tried out low octaves on the piano, then chords, but then "had the idea of having all thirteen of the lowest tones of the piano played together at the same time."[4] He played these with his palms and says he took great care in balancing the sound of all of the notes. Cowell continues directly, "In other words, I was inventing a new musical sound later to be called tone clusters."[5]

Clusters of a very small span can be played with the pianist fingering the individual constituent notes; three, four, five, and even more notes, depending on where the individual notes lie on the keys, can be fingered in one hand—with the thumb taking two or more notes, for instance. It is easy for the pianist to control fingered clusters of this sort, to play them at any dynamic, to roll (arpeggiate) the cluster, and to release constituent notes individually or slowly or both. Composers often choose to notate such smaller clusters to show each individual note on the staff (see figure 3.1).

Figure 3.1.   Cluster with individual notes all shown on the staff, Ornstein, *Danse sauvage*
Ornstein *DANSE SAUVAGE*. Used with kind permission of European American Music Distributors Company, sole U.S. and Canadian agent for Schott Music Ltd., London.

Cluster Notation

Cowell tried out a few different ways of notating larger clusters. A couple of his solutions, rather than showing every constituent note, show only the boundary notes for the cluster and then connect those notes in some way. For the clusters in *Tides of Manaunaun*, Cowell gives each of the boundary notes its own stem, extending this stem past the other boundary note and touching the edge of its notehead (see figure 3.2). Cowell applies this same notation to multiple kinds of cluster, adding an accidental above the two boundary notes, with this two-stems notation, to allow him to specify chromatic, white-key, and black-key clusters with minimal change to his symbol (see figure 3.3).

Cowell's notation for these remains clear, but it works better for passages with clusters of longer durations than for eighth notes or fast, rhythmically charged passages including clusters. In his piece *Antinomy*, for instance, Cowell retains

Figure 3.2. Clusters notated with only boundary notes, each note given its own stem connected to other boundary noteheads, Henry Cowell, *Tides of Manaunaun* (Associated Music Publishers), mm. 1–3

THE TIDES OF MANAUNAUN by Henry Cowell. Copyright 1922 (Renewed) by Associated Music Publishers, Inc. (BMI) International. Copyright Secured. All Rights Reserved. Reprinted by Permission.

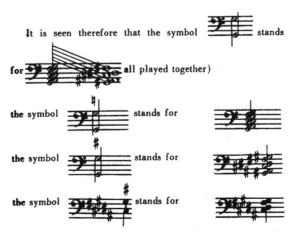

Figure 3.3. Cowell's notation key for chromatic, black-key, and white-key clusters in his *Three Irish Legends*

THE TIDES OF MANAUNAUN by Henry Cowell. Copyright 1922 (Renewed) by Associated Music Publishers, Inc. (BMI) International. Copyright Secured. All Rights Reserved. Reprinted by Permission.

the two-stem notation for the long note values (half notes, whole notes), but for clusters with shorter note values, he finds another solution. For quarter notes and any shorter durational notes requiring beams or flags, Cowell again notates only the two boundary notes, with standard noteheads. He gives one of these notes a normal stem (adding a flag or beam as needed for the particular rhythmic value) and connects the two noteheads to each other with a black line, thicker than a stem and running from the center of the bottom edge of the top notehead to the center of the top edge of the bottom notehead (see figure 3.4).

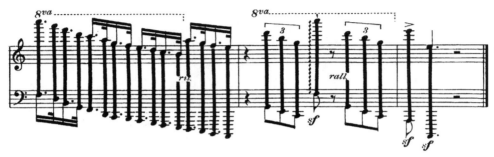

Figure 3.4. Cluster notation, boundary notes with thick center vertical line connecting their noteheads, Henry Cowell, *Antinomy,* **last three measures**
ANTIMONY by Henry Cowell. Copyright 1922 (Renewed) by Associated Music Publishers, Inc. (BMI) International. Copyright Secured. All Rights Reserved. Reprinted by Permission.

George Crumb's notational solutions for clusters mostly follow Cowell's *Antinomy* devices; Crumb notates individual noteheads for smaller compass clusters. For larger compass clusters, he gives noteheads for both boundary notes, connecting the noteheads with a vertical line, just as Cowell does for his shorter rhythmic value notes in *Antinomy*. Whereas Cowell runs a stem from the edge of a single boundary note (leaving the thicker black vertical line to connect the noteheads), Crumb runs his stems from the middle of the noteheads, so the stem, though not as thick as the vertical line connecting the boundary noteheads, continues that line. Crumb differentiates between white-key and chromatic clusters using this same notation, very slightly modifying Cowell's addition of an accidental above or below the cluster; Crumb's idiosyncratic solution is to add a greatly oversized natural sign before the cluster to mean a white-key cluster and an oversized sharp or flat sign before a cluster to indicate a black-key cluster (see figure 3.5).

This passage begins with smaller compass clusters, with Crumb using ordinary notes and stems. The pianist's right hand has white-key diatonic clusters, alternating with the left hand's black-key clusters. The passage continues with alternations of larger-span clusters played with the forearms. For these, the composer gives only the boundary notes and connects those with a thicker black vertical line, which then extends as the stem for those. Crumb adds text in a few places in

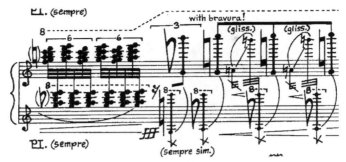

Figure 3.5. Black-key and white-key cluster notation, George Crumb, *Makrokosmos*, vol. 1, no. 10 (Peters Edition), "Spring Fire," p. 17, second system

Copyright © 1974 by C. F. Peters Corporation. Used by permission.

this same passage to confirm that some of the clusters should be played with the forearms, and he even in one place indicates that the quick alternation of smaller span clusters should be played "with the side of the hand."[6] Any of these cluster notation techniques would be clear to a pianist, possibly with a note of explanation in the score; a few other notational approaches have become common.

More composers using shorter duration clusters, especially chromatic ones, has led to a widespread adoption of rectangular noteheads stemmed together as a vertical column as standard notation for a chromatic cluster. These columns of noteheads can use open or filled noteheads and carry stems or not and any number of beams of flags, so they can easily be used for any rhythmic unit the composer desires. The composer can fix the boundary notes with the placement of the noteheads and by adding an accidental as needed to the bottom or top or both boundary notes of the cluster.

Kurt Stone's *Music Notation in the Twentieth Century* suggests using the notation of two ordinary noteheads connected to each other by a vertical bar running from the center of one notehead to the center of the other whenever the composer wants to set specific boundary notes for the cluster and to use the thick (rectangular) black bar notation when the register is fixed but the boundary notes indeterminate. This solution works fine, but I believe boundary notes can also be fixed with the thick bar notation as long as the boundary notes are within a staff or within one ledger line of the staff (see figure 3.6). To specify the boundary notes,

Figure 3.6.　Black rectangular bar cluster notation

the composer needs merely to place the ends of the bar covering the appropriate staff line or space and add an accidental to the left of the top or bottom of the bar if the corresponding boundary note should be on a black key.

This column or bar cluster notation generally indicates chromatic clusters, but should a composer wish to specify a diatonic (white-key) cluster, she could use the same notation and simply add a note that specifies "white-key cluster." Or, the notation can combine the bar notation with Cowell's solution for differentiating white-key or black-key clusters: Simply add a natural sign above or below the cluster to indicate a white-key cluster and a sharp or a flat sign to indicate a black-key cluster. The default cluster symbol without adding an accidental above or below indicates a chromatic cluster.

Stockhausen in his *Klavierstück X* writes palm and forearm chromatic clusters and also asks the pianist to block a cluster with the palm and then slide the hand across the keys horizontally, resulting in glissando clusters. In the performance notes, he recommends that the pianist wear fingerless woolen gloves to make playing these easier and to enable the player to perform the cluster glissandi more rapidly. Note that Stockhausen's clusters and those in the Crumb excerpt in figure 3.5 resemble each other and are both similar adaptations of Cowell's notation as used for shorter-duration notes in *Antinomy*: Stockhausen again gives only the boundary notes, with a thick vertical line connecting the noteheads.

Cowell writes many different variations on the cluster technique. Many of these appear in his early work *The Tides of Manaunaun* mentioned earlier. In ad-

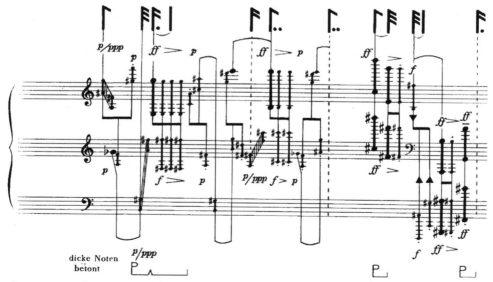

Figure 3.7. Palm glissando clusters (along with forearm clusters), Stockhausen, *Klavierstück X* (Universal Edition), p. 11, part of the first system

KLAVIERSTÜCK X by Karlheinz Stockhausen. Copyright 1961 Universal Edition. All rights reserved. Reprinted by Permission.

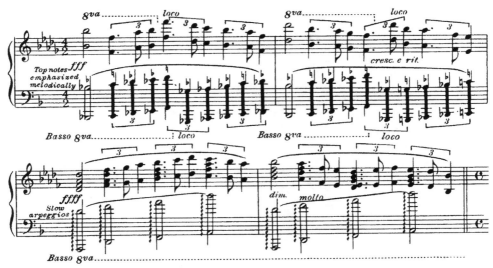

Figure 3.8. Arpeggiated clusters and clusters linked with emphasized melody notes, *Tides of Manaunaun*, p. 2 of score, p. 45, second and third systems

THE TIDES OF MANAUNAUN by Henry Cowell. Copyright 1922 (Renewed) by Associated Music Publishers, Inc. (BMI) International. Copyright Secured. All Rights Reserved. Reprinted by Permission.

dition to black-key, white-key, and chromatic clusters and palm and forearm and double-forearm clusters, this piece also specifies rolled or arpeggiated clusters and clusters with a specific note at the top that the pianist needs to bring out as an emphasized melodic line (see figure 3.8).

In many works, large clusters also include a small amount of aleatory, such as the score specifying only one boundary note or giving a large bar of noteheads over the approximate span to be played rather than specifying each and every note of the cluster. This sort of limited freedom acknowledges that register and range of a cluster may be more important to the effect of some clusters than specific notes. This sort of freedom in notation also acknowledges that some types of clusters (forearm clusters and double-forearm clusters, for instance) necessarily work differently with different pianists' physical builds (including arm length and hand size). At times composers go even further with incorporating freedom with their clusters. Earle Brown's *Corroboree* for three or two pianos notates clusters in a few places, in some instances asking for palm clusters giving only approximate pitches and in other places specifying forearm clusters while giving only one specific pitch, either the top note or the bottom note of the cluster. Brown uses open rectangles to indicate forearm clusters and open horizontal brackets for the smaller clusters. For each symbol, the open side indicates the fingers. For the forearm clusters, Brown gives a note on the staff to indicate the placement of the elbow but does not specify the exact span of the cluster. Brown does not indicate a note for the heel of the hand and gives only approximate pitches and spans for

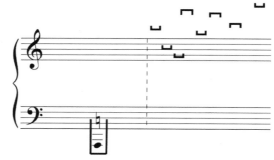

Figure 3.9.   Cluster symbols found in Earle Brown's
***Corroboree*. Notated by author.**

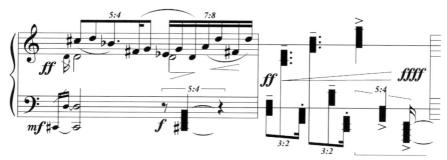

Figure 3.10.   Example with graphic showing several clusters notated by register and approximate span

these. Like both Cowell and Crumb, Brown adds to his (forearm) cluster symbol a natural sign to indicate a white-key cluster and a flat sign to indicate a black-key cluster (see figures 3.9 and 3.10).

Composers quite early in the twentieth century chafed at playing clusters while limited in their span by human hands and arms or the limitations of playing larger span clusters with great speed and accuracy. Charles Ives, as we have seen, specified using a cluster board in his Piano Sonata no. 2, asking the pianist to use a section of wood "long and heavy enough to press the keys down without striking" the keys. Ives asks for a very specific 14¾-inch length of wood for this cluster board.[7]

Composer William Russell incorporated the piano in several percussion ensemble works in the 1930s, and these works embraced the piano as percussion instrument and included using cluster boards.[8] This idea of constructing a device to depress a chromatic cluster definitely predates Russell's or Ives's use in the first third of the twentieth century—Charles Blanchet, in his 1889 organ piece *Scènes Pastorales et orage dans les Alpes*, details a board needed for this piece to depress the five-note chromatic span of the lowest major third on the pedal board to assist in the work's depiction of a storm.[9]

Lou Harrison calls for the pianist to play using an "octave bar" in several of his scores. Harrison and William Colvig created the octave bar to enable the pianist to play clusters within rapid passages. The bar is a specialized cluster board that not only sounds all the notes within its span of an octave but also emphasizes the octave comprised of the two boundary notes of that cluster. As Harrison biographers Leta Miller and Frederic Lieberman describe it, the octave bar is a:

> flat wooden device approximately two inches high with a grip on top and sponge rubber on the bottom, with which the player strikes the keys. Its length spans an octave on a grand piano. The sponge rubber bottom is sculpted so that its ends are slightly lower than its center, making the outer tones of the octave sound with greater force than the intermediary pitches.[10]

Evidently, at one time, pianists or ensembles could even order octave bars directly from Harrison and Colvig.[11]

After reading Henry Cowell's book *New Musical Resources*, Harrison was inspired to write some very large clusters. His *Variations for Violin and Piano*, written when Harrison was just nineteen, has some clusters that, by the length of the black bars on the staves, appear to ask the pianist to play a three-octave span with each arm simultaneously (for six octaves in all).[12]

With several composers specifying forearm and double-forearm clusters, and Ives, Russell, and later Harrison making use of cluster boards, it was only a matter of time before a composer specified larger or even full-compass clusters on the piano. Johanna Beyer's *Suite for Piano* (1939) includes a glissando cluster over all eighty-eight keys of the piano. Peter Garland's *The Three Strange Angels* (1972–1973) for bass drum, piano, and bullroarer calls for a cluster board that the player can use to depress all fifty-two white keys at once and instructs the player to fashion a board so that she can play these large clusters using only one hand; in the second part of the work, the player sounds this large cluster every eight seconds and uses the other hand to play a C$\sharp$ in octaves, barely audible in the context of these big clusters. Simon Steen Andersen's *Pretty Sound (up and down)* (1976) asks the pianist to use a cluster board to sound all eighty-eight keys at once. Joseph Schwantner's song cycle for soprano and orchestra *Magabunda* also asks for an eighty-eight-note cluster in the piano part.

When I was writing my set of pieces *black narcissus* for one pianist and Bösendorfer 290SE reproducing piano, I experimented with ways of taking advantage of this instrument's expanded compass and using ninety-seven-key clusters on it. I eventually opted for large chords with notes in all registers of the piano but with far fewer than ninety-seven simultaneous notes because I found that sending MIDI information for all the keys at once immediately bottlenecked and, instead of a nice sharp simultaneous attack of every piano key at once, the instrument would play a ripple of attacks—definitely not the effect I had been looking for at the time. It's possible that, in the years since my attempts, the technology (and especially the electronic component of this player mechanism) has improved enough that someone could get a reproducing piano to play a simultaneous attack of every piano key. Certainly it is possible for a live performer to play this using a cluster board.

There are more theatrical ways to play clusters besides with the hands, arms, or cluster bars. Karlheinz Stockhausen asks the pianist to sit on the keys in *Klavierstück XIII*. Rock-and-roll pianist Jerry Lee Lewis, who often played the piano standing up, sometimes played treble clusters with the heel or side of his right foot. He sometimes wore cowboy boots with a broad heel for this purpose. He was also known to play with hands and fists and to sit on the keys. (He sometimes climbed on top of the piano and stood there singing, which doesn't produce a cluster, of course, but did allow him to tower over the rest of the band.)

Briana Harley asks a pianist to lie down across the keys of the piano at the opening of her *Hella Hyped: The Reigning Piano* (2016) for piano duo. John Zorn in his *carny* (1989) has the pianist play a cluster with both hands and then add an additional note with her nose. In Nathan Hall's *Tame Your Man* (2012) for piano, electronics, and bondage artist, the bondage artist ties ropes on the piano and on the pianist. Close to the end of the piece, the pianist's movements are so restricted by the bonds that she must play clusters with her torso.

Glissando

I have already mentioned glissando on the keys used in conjunction with clusters; a one-key-at-a-time glissando on the keys is a very old keyboard performance device that certainly predates the development of the piano itself. The glissando took a while before appearing in the notation of a published keyboard score. But, there are at least a few keyboard works published in the middle of the eighteenth century that ask the performer to play several keys with a quick glide of a single finger across the keys.[13] And, composers have continued asking pianists to perform a gliding across the keys ever since. Even though this is a very old technique, it does ask for a different technique from the pianist than typical.

Glissando on the keys of the piano is a lateral gliding across the keys. Any length glissando is possible, from a short glissando over a few adjacent keys to a full-compass glissando from the bottommost key to the highest or vice versa. A pianist can also perform both an ascending glissando and a descending glissando simultaneously. Glissandi in various intervals between the hands or even within a single hand are also possible.

Glissandi can apply some lateral force on the keys in addition to the usual vertical force. As the instrument is designed to accept vertical force but not so much horizontal force, this can wear some of the delicate parts of the instrument: The felt lining the key pins can be damaged by the compression caused by this lateral force, for instance. A glissando can be played with the back of a finger or fingers, with the heel of the hand, or with a wedge shape formed by pressing two or three fingertips together. Loud glissandi can be played by the pianist turning the hands and arms and even the torso to face perpendicular to the keys and running the fingertips and palms across the keyboard in that orientation rather than facing the fingers straight on along the key lengths as is typical. Jerry Lee Lewis and many other pianists of early rock and roll often played such glissandi while standing rather than seated on a bench.

Comic actor and musician Chico Marx is known for his piano glissandi terminating in a "shot" single note, played by the index finger, with the hand oriented to mimic a pistol shooting the key. See, for instance, Chico performing a medley of a Delibes dance "Pizzicati" (also known as the "Pizzicato Polka") and the Fain/Kahal/Norman song "When I Take My Sugar to Tea" in the 1931 Marx Brothers film *Monkey Business*.

A black-key-only glissando is possible, as is a white-key-only glissando. A performer can play both of these glissandi simultaneously, either in parallel or in contrary motion. Because the spacing between these two sets of keys (as well as the heights of the constituent keys) differs (the black keys are taller than the white keys), it is not really possible to play a glissando with the fingers that presents the notes *exactly* in chromatic order. However, composers often specify that even large-span glissandi be performed quite rapidly, and the constituent notes of a quick glissando may be further blurred with judicious use of the damper pedal, so the listener may not be able to distinguish between the resultant sound and a glissando sounding in exact chromatic note order.

True Chromatic Glissando

Pianist Herbert Henck has uncovered a way to play a truly chromatic glissando on the keys that requires a little prep work to the piano: Just beyond the portion of the keys faced with key tops, all of the keys, either the white keys or black keys, are the same height (see figure 3.11). If you first remove the fallboard to expose the backs of the keys, it is possible to play an exact chromatic scale as a glissando.[14] Performing this glissando does come with some differences from using the normal portion of the keyboard interface. The portion of the keys ordinarily located out of sight behind the fallboard or key lid is not covered in the smooth key surfaces

Figure 3.11.   Level portion of the keys beyond the raised sharps

found in the key tops. Another difference: is impossible to apply the same force on the keys when playing closer to the middle of the key rather than at the ends of the keys; the lever that is a piano key transfers energy from the fingers depressing the key much more efficiently at the front of the keys than when playing closer to the fulcrum. It is more difficult to play very loudly when playing beyond the fallboard than when playing at the fronts of the keys.

Harp Glissando

It is also possible to produce a specialized glissando that sounds only preselected notes rather than the full compass of white keys or black keys. By first wedging keys (a piano tuner's rubber mutes can be used for this; see figure 3.12), it is possible to perform a normal glissando on the keys and produce only select notes. With these wedges in place, it is then possible to perform a single glissando that is a single harmony replicated in multiple registers and to play this glissando of a single harmony very rapidly (much more rapidly than a normal fingered arpeggio of the same harmony). This single-chord glissando is something that we typically associate with idiomatic harp performance, so this could be used to lend a harp-like quality to a piano passage (see figure 3.13).

Figure 3.12. Keys wedged in preparation for "harp" glissando

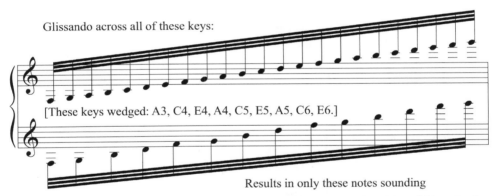

Glissando across all of these keys:

[These keys wedged: A3, C4, E4, A4, C5, E5, A5, C6, E6.]

Results in only these notes sounding

Figure 3.13. "Harp" glissando, with the keys A3, C4, E4, A4, C5, E5, A5, C6, and E6 wedged

Two Fingers on One Key

A very simple on-the-keys technique is perhaps not one that arose through a composer seeking to extend the possibilities of the piano but is something performed by many pianists in various repertoire while also being something that a composer has chosen to specify only recently; this is to ask the pianist to play a single key with multiple fingers at the same time. Bartók in his Suite, op. 14, at the end of the second movement specifies that a few notes marked both *fortississimo* and *marcatissimo* be played with both the thumb and the index finger at the same time (see figure 3.14).

Figure 3.14. Two fingers on a single key, Bartók, Suite, op. 14, II, last system
Replicated by author

Two (or More) Keys, One Finger

Conversely, it is possible to depress two or more keys with a single finger. Even with the other fingers of the hand placed on top of individual keys as in ordinary piano technique, it is quite easy to angle the thumb so that it approaches the top of the keys almost perpendicular to them and to depress two or even three keys with the thumb alone. Many times pianists work out fingerings for works that include this sort of playing, but I haven't yet uncovered any works that exploit this one-finger, multiple-keys technique for any reason other than the convenience of a particular fingering—instances in which the composer wants the performer to play more notes that she has fingers. There are many instances in the Romantic-era piano literature that call for this. Virtuoso pianists-composers Liszt and Alkan both wrote large sonorities to be played by a single hand and include fingering indications showing that the thumb (or another finger) must play two notes at once. In the Alkan example in figure 3.15, a large fingered cluster is given to the left hand, with the thumb, second finger, and the fifth finger each asked to play two notes simultaneously.

Figure 3.15. Single finger covering multiple notes, Charles-Valentin Alkan, op. 55, *Une fusée, Introduction et Impromptu* (1859), third system, last page

On the Keys, Arms Full Extended

Drew Baker's *Stress Position* (2008) requires that the pianist play repeated notes on the keys in both the lowest and highest extremes of the instrument simultaneously for the entire work. This requires that the pianist keep her arms extended for

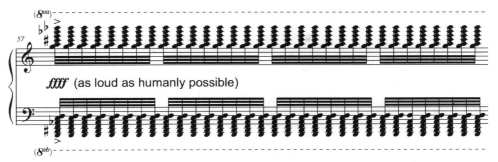

Figure 3.16. Extreme registral separation between the hands, Baker, *Stress Position* (2008)

the duration of the piece. The composer explains that he composed the piece "to address the topic of torture," so the composer has a theatrical reason to force the pianist to play with limbs uncomfortably extended[15] (see figure 3.16).

Underpressure Playing

Without depressing the keys and without activating the strings, the player can make sounds on the keys themselves. Helmut Lachenmann has the pianist play a lateral glissando across the key tops with the fingernails, mimicking the scraping sound of a guiro in his work entitled—what else—*Guero* (see figure 3.17). Lachenmann uses two different locations to produce distinct guiro sounds—specifying that the player run the fingernail across the front of the white keys or across their tops. Either way, it is mostly the movement of the fingernail sliding off the edge of one key and then slapping against the next across the tiny gap between keys that produces the individual clicks of this technique. Lachenmann's idiosyncratic notation for *Guero* uses a three-line staff (indicating C4 with the middle staff line and an octave above and lower with the other staff lines). The lines and curves on the staff indicate a quick slide of the fingertip, with discrete dots along these lines and curves indicating a slowing of the movement across the key's edges or tops. The composer punctuates the end of a couple of these gestures by having the pianist extend the slide into a tap on the keyboard side of one of the wooden cheek blocks that frame the keyboard.

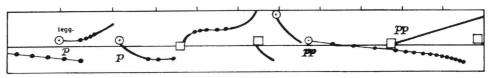

Figure 3.17. "Guiro" effect, Lachenmann, *Guero* (Breitkopf and Härtel, 1969), p. 1, second system

GUERO by Helmut Lachenmann © 1972 by Musikverlage Hans Gerig, Köln
1980 assigned to Breitkopf & Härtel, Wiesbaden

Figure 3.18.   Tremolo of key-top tapping, Shockley, *Hoc florentes arbor*

Just as a person might "drum" with fingertips or fingernails on a desktop, a pianist can do this on the key tops—a tremolo of tapping on the key tops that produces a dry percussive sound (see figure 3.18). The pianist can also play on the keys with underpressure, while focusing on moving the keys and setting the action into motion, rather than in making sounds purely on the surface of the keys. Ken Ueno's *Volcano* (2011) asks the pianist to play on the keys with enough force to engage the piano's action but mostly not enough force for the hammers to sound the strings. The score explains, "Play an aleatoric selection of R.H. and L.H. notes in the highest octave, . . . in a way to highlight the sounds of the key mechanism and hammer noise. It is permissible, even desirable, every once in a while . . . to strike a key just hard enough to sound a pitch."[16]

The guiro effect along with the various sorts of key-top tapping and Ueno's technique of having the pianist press the keys without sounding the strings can be grouped together as underpressure techniques, and one way of notating these effects would be to write rhythm and notes on the staff as usual (substituting *X*-shaped noteheads for this purely percussive effect) and then writing the word *underpressure* near the staff. Alternately the score could specify "guiro" or "key-top tapping/tremolo" for those particular effects.

Composer Charlie Sdraulig in his piece *collector* (2014–2015) gathers a host of underpressure techniques together and assembles an entire piece from these, completely in the absence of any *ordinario* on-the-key-sounding notes. *Collector* also calls for other actions at or on the keys, including asking the player to grasp a key and wiggle it left to right and to scrape a fingernail across the tops and fronts of keys, and includes specifications for hand width and tension.

Though these are all to some degree percussive effects, I have chosen to detail these techniques here with on-the-key techniques rather than with other techniques that involve hitting various parts of the piano. I've done this mostly because the keys are usually tapped in ordinary piano performance, and these techniques are performed in much the same way as "regular" notes and only involve playing the typical activators of piano sounds—the keys—rather than involving parts inside the instrument or parts that are considered furniture and not (usually) as sound-making surfaces. Viewed in this way, a guiro glide across the key tops is just a white-key glissando performed with underpressure, and a key-top tremolo is an ordinary on-the-keys tremolo performed with underpressure.

A composer can also take underpressure a step further and ask the pianist to mime playing the keys, transforming the finger and hand movement from sound producing to purely theatrical gestures.

Key-Lip Plucking

Another on-the-keys technique that Lachenmann specifies in *Guero* takes advantage of the small lip that the white keys on most pianos have. This lip can be plucked from the underside, providing a subtle, quiet, thumping sound. Reasoning that this is a plucking action, Lachenmann labels this as pizzicato in his score. Mu-Xuan Lin in her *Pale Fire* (2015) for piano and tape uses triangular noteheads along with the indication "key pluck" to indicate this same technique (figure 3.19).

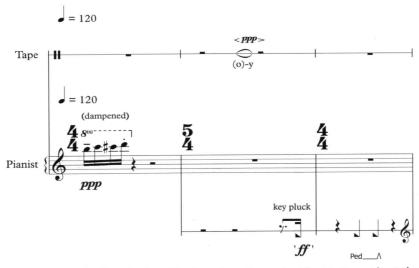

Figure 3.19.   Plucking the lip of the keys from the underside, Mu-Xuan Lin, *Pale Fire*, mm. 1–3

Depressing the Keys Silently

Depressing a key on the piano sets many individual parts into motion. Many of these parts are involved in the transfer of energy from the player's downward motion on the key top to the hammer's motion to the excitation of the string or strings that the hammer strikes. However, for all but the uppermost keys of the piano, depressing a key also sets into motion several parts that mute the strings when the key is at rest and that must be moved away from the surface of the strings in order for those strings to vibrate freely. The primary part of this mechanism is the damper, a piece of wool felt attached to a small piece of wood, which is in turn attached to an arm that the key's action uses to move the damper away from the strings when the key is depressed and to move the damper back against the strings when the key returns to its at-rest position.

It is possible to use a key to move its damper without causing the hammer to strike any strings; the player simply depresses the key slowly or in a very gentle manner, thereby not moving the hammer quickly enough or forcefully enough for it to strike the string or strings. Once the damper is off its strings, those strings can be excited in other ways.

Much of the characteristic sound of the piano is provided by its many strings ringing in sympathy with struck notes sounded on the keys. Engaging the damper pedal frees all the dampers from their strings. By silently depressing and holding select keys while sounding other notes on the piano, it is possible to narrow this bed of sympathetic resonances to a single harmony. Many composers have taken advantage of this.

The first of Schoenberg's *Drei Klavierstücke* published in 1910 has the pianist silently depress the keys for a four-note chord while playing many of those same notes an octave or two below the held ones (see figure 3.20). Schoenberg notates these silently depressed notes in the same manner as natural harmonics for a bowed string instrument and labels them "flageolets." He uses diamond-shaped noteheads. Aaron Copland also uses a silently depressed key in the opening measures of his *Piano Variations* (1930). At about the same time, Béla Bartók centers an entire small piece from his set of teaching pieces, *Mikrokosmos*, entitling the movement "Harmonics."

Though these strings for these keys ring in sympathy with overtones of the strings actively sounded by the player (in these cases on the keys), they are not themselves harmonics—they are full strings ringing. As such, I do not refer to notes sounded in sympathy by releasing the dampers as "harmonics." However,

Figure 3.20. Keys depressed silently for resonance, Schoenberg, *Drei Klavierstücke*, op. 11, no. 1, mm. 14–16

each of these works notates the silently depressed notes are given diamond-shaped noteheads. This is widely accepted as the way to notate these.

TECHNIQUES ON THE PEDALS

Just as musicians have found new ways of using the piano keys and bringing out new sounds simply from the keys, they have also expanded the use of the pedals. One way that some composers have innovated in their use of the standard three pedals found on most modern grand pianos is through greater specificity in the pedals' use and finer divisions of the pedal's range.

Fractional Damper Pedal Indications

Richard Valitutto's "papier-mâché" from his set *assemblages* (2015–2016) includes indications for engaging the damper pedal both halfway and one-quarter of the way down (see figure 3.21). Marco Stroppa's collection of works *Miniature Estrose* divides the damper pedal's distance of travel into even finer gradation, giving indications of ³⁄₅ pedal and ¹⁄₇ pedal and others. *Miniature Estrose* also has the indication for a half una corda pedal (see figure 3.22).

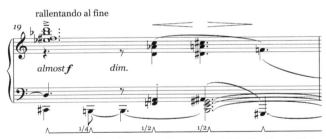

Figure 3.21.   Half and quarter damper pedal indications, Richard Valitutto, *assemblages*, "papier-mâché," m. 19

Figure 3.22.   Fine fractional pedal indications, Marco Stroppa, *Miniature Estrose*, "Innige Cavatina" (Ricordi Print Licensing, licensing@halleonardmgb.it), p. 91, m. 79

Music by Marco Stroppa, Copyright © 1991 Casa Ricordi S.r.l., Milan—Italy. All Rights Reserved. Reproduced by Kind Permission of Hal Leonard MGB S.R.L.

Half Una Corda

Vaes in his exhaustive history of extended piano techniques states that depressing the una corda halfway cannot have any physical effect and "cannot have anything but a psychological effect, however, for the mechanism can only make the hammer strike or not strike a string."[17] However, Stroppa explains in the notes to *Miniature Estrose* that by calling for ½ una corda, he wants to take advantage of somewhat-worn hammers on an instrument that has seen some use. His hope is that, by partially engaging the una corda mechanism but not moving the hammers all the way to the position where many of them would engage one fewer string of a unison set, the portion of the hammer that strikes the strings will be not the usual grooved place on the hammer's face of a well-played instrument but the softer (less-compressed) ridge of felt between those grooves to "produce a somewhat muffled, less definite sound, especially when a hammer strikes more than one string."[18] So Stroppa's goal with this marking is not to have the hammers striking fewer strings but to have them striking with a less-worn (softer) surface of the hammer's face to create a very subtle timbral effect.

In his notes for *Miniature Estrose*, a large set of pieces filled with a high degree of detail and written for pianist Pierre-Laurent Aimard, the composer explains that the importance of the pedals is "equal to that of the keyboard, comparable to the pedals of the organ."[19] The score also includes a call out to piano makers to give to the piano additional "stops" and to improve the pedals. Among his suggestions are a "graduated" sostenuto pedal that would allow the player to raise and catch dampers for new notes and add those to ones already being held by the sostenuto (a great idea), a pedal mechanism that would move the hammers closer to the strings (such a half-blow mechanism is actually now an option on a few high-end pianos), and an una corda mechanism that would allow a wider shift of the action (that would theoretically allow a true una corda shift, with the hammers striking a single string from a set of unisons; this is a mechanism that existed in the nineteenth century, and there are even score examples in Beethoven's sonatas of his asking for one string, two strings, or a gradual transition from one string to all three strings).[20] Stroppa also proposes a mechanism that would allow the performer to "program" various raised damper combinations and preset those, then recall them on demand with a lever. I feel piano makers are a long way from offering an option like this, as many makers still offer many instruments without even a regular sostenuto pedal, and some makers (such as Bechstein and Bösendorfer) until the 1970s or 1980s were still making even very large and very expensive grand pianos with only two pedals (with no sostenuto).

Percussive Use of the Pedals

The pedals can also be used percussively, with the player tapping the pedals for the sound potential of hitting the metal of the pedal. Beyond this, because the damper pedal controls a mechanism that lifts dozens of wood and felt dampers from the surface of the piano's strings and then returns those dampers to their at-rest positions against the strings, rapidly pressing the damper pedal can cause the dampers to excite the strings enough to make an audible sound. Rapidly or violently releasing the pedal can make a dull thump as all of the dampers reseat on their strings.

There is also a resonance effect that can be "played" through specialized use of the damper pedal. First, a large sound should be produced and sustained by depressing the damper pedal as usual. Then, the player should release the damper pedal very, very slowly. As the pedal is released, strings are gradually partially or completely damped as the dampers return to their seats on the strings. As this happens, the illusion of a crescendo of the remaining vibrating strings is created.

Luciano Berio in his brief encore piece *erdenklavier* (1969) suggests rhythms for the damper pedal, adding a note that says that it is unnecessary to coordinate these pedal movements with the keyboard notes (see figure 3.23). Ken Ueno in his 2011 *Volcano* gives the damper pedal its own one-line staff and indicates both accented pedaling and accented pedal releases, exploiting how these sudden motions on the pedal cause the dampers to sound the strings (see figure 3.24).

Figure 3.23. **Rhythms for the damper pedal, Berio, *erdenklavier* (Universal Edition, published in UE33013 "6 Encores"), first system**

Universal Edition

Figure 3.24. **Making sounds on the strings with accented damper pedal movements, Ueno, *Volcano*, mm. 11–13**

Inside the Piano
Plucking, Strumming, Scraping, Rubbing

INSIDE THE PIANO

As long as there have been pianos, there have been folks reaching inside the instrument to make sounds. However, many pianists still face with great trepidation the notion of touching the instrument's guts. I think a part of this stems from the fact that most pianists do almost no tuning or instrument maintenance themselves. Practically all other instrumental players tune their instruments themselves. Most do some tuning and basic instrumental cleaning every day, whereas most pianists hire a professional technician to tune, adjust, and do all repairs on their instrument. Clarinetists assemble and disassemble their instruments every day. Brass players insert timbre-modifying external devises into their instruments on a regular basis. Percussionists often do much of their own repair work, make some of their own mallets and beaters, and even create new instruments. Many pianists have never touched the insides of their instruments. Most pianists have never tuned a piano, never adjusted any part of a piano beyond lifting the lid or sliding the music desk, and certainly never removed or replaced any parts from a piano.

Because of this distance between player and instrument, a pianist may see the inside of the instrument as mysterious and even forbidding. Add to this that many pianists have been told by a teacher or a piano technician or a concert hall manager that touching the inside of the piano or performing extended techniques (of any sort) will damage the instrument, and there may be years of accrued pressure dissuading a pianist from reaching inside a piano.

Composers should be aware of this disinclination when asking a pianist to play inside the instrument or to prepare the piano's strings, and pianists who are inexperienced with many of the techniques covered in these pages or who feel some trepidation about exploring should be cognizant that some of their fear may have more to do with what they have been told and their own inexperience than with physical reality.

Modern pianos are, on the whole, sturdily constructed machines designed to withstand prolonged use. There are certainly ways to damage a piano by playing inside the instrument or preparing it in some way. There are also ways of damaging a piano by playing purely on the keys, by improperly situating the instrument in a room, or by neglecting regular tuning and maintenance. With tuning, maintenance, placement of the instrument, and playing (including traditional on-the-keys performance, playing with preparations, playing inside the instrument, and any other nontraditional performance approach), the pianist must treat the instrument with attention and care in order not to damage it.

Many pianists may hesitate tackling inside-the-piano repertoire because they feel that they just do not know their way around the inside of the instrument, that the learning curve is simply too steep. But, I believe with a little exploration, any pianist can learn the basic inside geography of the instrument very quickly. If the pianist adds to this some additional landmarks within the instrument, either universal ones or work-specific ones, the player can gain speed and facility with locating notes and identifying strings with a minimal outlay of time. And, there are now a few piano makers who are introducing additional markings inside their instruments to assist performers looking to play inside the piano, with some current instruments differentiating white-key and black-key dampers, and indicating string nodal points.

Because most of the energy of instrumental development for the piano has been concentrated on playing the instrument using the action as set into motion by playing on the keys, not a lot of energy has been invested in enhancing the design of the piano to accommodate playing inside the instrument or preparing it. There are certainly parts within the piano that are delicate and can be damaged in performance. However, most of the materials of the inside of the piano are actually quite durable and strong.

BASIC PROTOCOL FOR PLAYING INSIDE THE PIANO

I would caution all pianists to clean their hands just before a performance or practice that will involve playing inside the instrument.[1] Removing dirt and excess oils from the skin is an easy precaution to take. Prolonged contact with moisture, dirt, and skin oils can tarnish, discolor, or even damage some interior piano parts. Once you have finished performing inside the piano, wipe down the hard surfaces that you have touched during the performance with a clean, dry cloth to remove any transferred oils or moisture. Simply make these steps a part of your routine before and after playing inside the piano.

Minimize your contact with the soft materials of the instrument, the piano's felts in particular. Fortunately, there are very few extended techniques or preparations that require you touch the felt of the instrument at all. When marking locations for yourself in the piano, try to find alternates to making any marks that involve the felts. It is easy to crush the fibers of, compress, or even tear the felt, and there is no way to undo this damage.

It is also easy to damage the finish of the surfaces inside the piano. There is a very thin finish on the soundboard and gold leaf or paint on the frame, both of which are easy to scratch or mar. This would probably involve only cosmetic damage but damage nonetheless, so approach how you interact with these surfaces with caution.

For the harder surfaces of the piano, an easy precaution to take is to make sure that any materials put into contact with the piano are always softer than the materials they will touch. Do not use steel on the copper-wound bass strings. The steel strings of the middle and upper register are harder, so you can put harder metals in contact with them. Nevertheless, use detempered steel if you must use steel, and better yet, substitute brass (a much softer metal) for steel if possible for items that will be in contact with the steel strings.

When inserting materials between the strings (string preparations), the first thing that you should always do is depress the damper pedal to release the pressure from the dampers on the strings. This prevents your action of spreading the strings to insert the preparation from compressing or scraping the felt of the damper. Depress and hold the damper pedal again when it is time to remove materials from between the strings.

Before inserting items (bolts, screws, etc.) between the strings, Richard Bunger in his landmark work *The Well-Prepared Piano* recommends inserting the blade of a screwdriver between the two strings involved and rotating the screwdriver so that the width of the blade spreads the two strings a little further apart from each other. This procedure can be repeated to remove the preparation materials from between the strings. This gives you a little more control over spreading the strings apart and allows you to gently seat the preparing object between the strings. It also minimizes finger contact with the strings and is an easy habit to acquire. So far, I have never damaged any strings using a screwdriver in this way, but a steel screwdriver blade is also a very hard surface to press against the strings. Recently, I replaced my screwdriver with a kid's plastic knife. A disposable knife will probably not be sturdy enough for this use, but a thicker plastic knife works nicely.[2] Using a kid's knife as opposed to the average screwdriver has the added advantage that children's flatware pieces are available in bright colors, so it is much easier to spot the tool inside the piano.

The following is a basic protocol for playing inside the piano:

- Wash and dry hands before touching the inside piano surfaces.
- Only touch felt surfaces when absolutely necessary.
- Whenever possible, select preparation materials that are as soft as, or preferably much softer than, the piano parts with which they will be in contact.
- Release the dampers before inserting and again before removing items from between the strings.
- Ease the insertion or removal of items between strings by spreading the involved strings with a child's plastic knife or other thin plastic rectangle. (Do this in addition to depressing the damper pedal.)
- After each performance, wipe down hard surfaces inside the piano with a clean, dry cloth. Leave the piano at least as clean as you found it, preferably even cleaner.

As far as what materials to use for the strings, either for preparations or for playing on the surface of the string, the rule is these materials should be as soft as or preferably softer than the strings. There are two different string materials to consider: the flat steel wire used from the middle register to the topmost note of the piano and the steel wrapped in copper used for the bass register strings. Common materials for string preparations are screws and bolts. First, any bits of metal that you're going to place in contact with the strings should be shiny, new bits of metal. Do not use rusty or grimy screws or bolts. For the steel strings, aluminum, copper, and brass are safer to use than steel. On the wound strings, you definitely should not use steel. The Piano Technicians Guild protocol goes even further, stating, "Only plastic screws/bolts or similar materials softer than metal may be used when inserting between wound strings."[3]

THE DIFFERENT GEOGRAPHIES INSIDE THE PIANO

Certainly in the earliest years of their training and probably continuing for most of their performance life, pianists spend much more time honing their technique for playing on the keys of the piano than they do playing inside the instrument. In addition, the outside interface for the instrument is mostly universal, whereas the inside architecture varies considerably from maker to maker and even from model to model within one maker's instruments: Almost all pianos have eighty-eight keys with the same arrangement of white keys and black keys. Almost all grand pianos have three pedals: una corda, sostenuto, and damper. However, two models of grand piano, even from the same manufacturer, can have very different internal geographies.

All modern pianos have a large cast-iron plate that enables the instrument to withstand the approximately thirty-five tons of pressure exerted by the strings. The plate (also called the frame or the harp) has raised braces cast as part of it that run roughly parallel to the strings. The first of these braces (also called struts or stress bars) runs just to the left of the lowest bass string and on most instruments forms the raised edge of the plate itself. In order to discuss these structural elements across many different models of piano, I have numbered the braces that run roughly parallel to the strings from this bass brace to the corresponding brace that runs along the short edge of the plate to the right of the highest treble strings on the instrument (see figure 4.1). This first brace, forming the bass edge of the plate and sometimes called the bass bar, I number as 0 because it does not interrupt the strings. Most piano models have three interruptive braces; a few models, such as the Bösendorfer 290 "Imperial" Grand, have four interruptive braces. On an instrument with the bass bar and three interruptive braces, I label the bass bar 0, the center bar 1, the lower treble bar 2, and the treble bar 3. (The noninterruptive treble brace, because it is so short and abuts the edge of the frame, appears more like a lip to the frame than an actual strut, so though it would theoretically be brace 4 on these instruments, I never refer to it.) On an instrument with the bass bar and four interruptive braces, the bass bar is again 0, the lower center bar is 1, the upper center bar is 2, the lower treble bar is 3, and the treble bar is 4. On most instruments, there is a diagonal cast brace (sometimes called the diagonal bar) running from the tuning pin end of brace 1 to the bridge end of the bass bar (brace 0). The combination of the diagonal bar and brace 1 resembles a *V* on many instruments or a *U* or even a *Y* on some. No matter what shape these two braces form, I always label the brace running parallel to the bass strings (and forming the right-hand "leg" on the *V*, *U*, or *Y*) brace 1. I do not number this diagonal fixed brace but call it the diagonal brace or bar.

The Steinway models B, C, and D each have, in addition to the braces that are cast as part of the plate itself, a "plate diagonal bar" that is bolted to the braces, running from the tuning-pin end of brace 1 to the bridge end of brace 2 and crossing over a number of middle-register strings on each of these instruments (see figure 4.2). According to Steinway, they add these diagonal bars on these larger pianos with their large plates to reinforce the plate and prevent breakage when the instrument is stored or transported on its side. As the plate diagonal bar provides an additional obstruction when stringing (or restringing) the instrument, Steinway decided not to make these a part of the casting but add them as a removable part. Though some of the technicians I spoke to frown on this, it is possible to remove this bar for performance.[4]

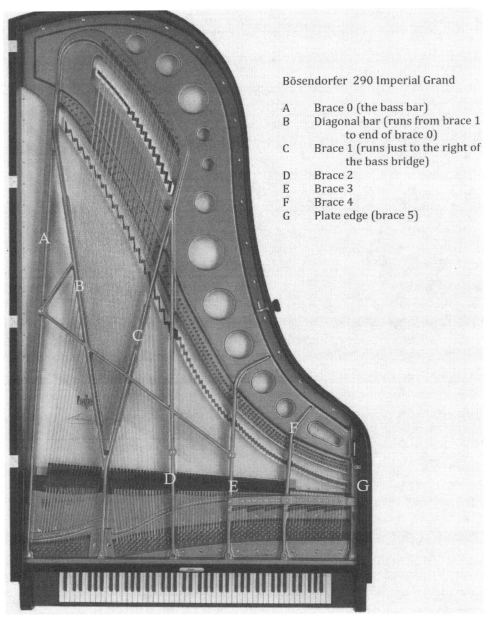

Bösendorfer 290 Imperial Grand

A   Brace 0 (the bass bar)
B   Diagonal bar (runs from brace 1
        to end of brace 0)
C   Brace 1 (runs just to the right of
        the bass bridge)
D   Brace 2
E   Brace 3
F   Brace 4
G   Plate edge (brace 5)

Figure 4.1.   Diagram of plate and brace structure of a Bösendorfer 290 "Imperial" Grand

In addition to the interruptive braces that almost all modern models of grand piano have, most models have horizontal cross-braces running between the interruptive braces just beyond the tuning pins, and most have a capo d'astro bar in the treble section in place of individual agraffes for each set of unisons. These

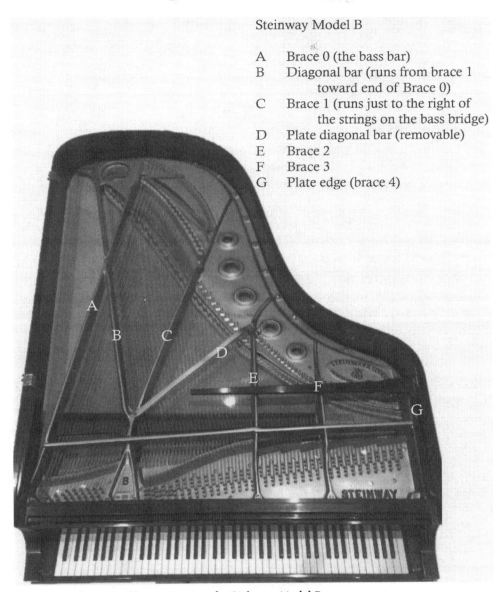

Steinway Model B

A   Brace 0 (the bass bar)
B   Diagonal bar (runs from brace 1
       toward end of Brace 0)
C   Brace 1 (runs just to the right of
       the strings on the bass bridge)
D   Plate diagonal bar (removable)
E   Brace 2
F   Brace 3
G   Plate edge (brace 4)

Figure 4.2. Frame and brace structure for Steinway Model B

horizontal cross-braces and the capo d'astro reduce access to the end of the strings, but on most instruments, there remains enough room for the pianist to pluck sul ponticello or to mute with the fingertips at the end of the strings for all of the strings in the bass bridge section, as well most of the strings on the long bridge up to the second-highest section of strings. Even with a capo d'astro bar obscuring the tuning-pin end of the strings in the highest section of the instrument, because the top eighteen or so unison sets of strings have no dampers, the pianist has easy access to almost the entirety of the sounding length of these strings. There are no dampers covering them, and the strings in the top register of the piano are very short strings, so the pianist can play sul ponticello techniques and easily mute the strings at the bridge end of the string, even if not at the tuning-pin end. On most instruments, this leaves only the second-highest section of strings, with short strings, partially covered with dampers and with, on some models, a thick capo d'astro bar covering the tuning-pin end of these strings. The proximity of the capo d'astro and the dampers severely limits the pianist's access to the end of the strings in this next-to-the-top treble register on some models. In general, without having a particular piano model in mind, a composer could work with the assumption that the pianist will not be able to play sul ponticello techniques on strings in this register (running roughly a tenth or twelfth below F♯6). Appendix C gives more details for several piano models for this.

In addition to the ways that the structure of the plate and braces limit access to the strings in various ways, the overstrung bass strings reduce access to some of the strings on the long bridge. There is vertical space between the overstrung bass strings and the strings below them that allows the pianist to install most preparations, should they be required, on strings of either set. However, it may be difficult to finger harmonics or strum on some of the middle-register strings that are covered by the bass strings. Appendix C gives more information on which strings are mostly covered by overstringing and which ones are only partially covered. If this amount of detail isn't needed, a rule of thumb across makes and models of grand piano is that the first eight or nine sets of strings on the long bridge (the strings immediately above the strings that are attached to the bass bridge) are mostly covered by the bass strings, and an additional five or six sets of strings are minimally covered by the bass strings.

To highlight some of the internal architectural distinctions between different grand piano models, the following are some details of two models by Fazioli, the F228 and the slightly larger F278: On the F228, the strings are interrupted by three metal braces, the lowest eight bass notes have a single string each (all wound), the next fourteen notes have double unisons (all wound), and the remainder of the instrument's notes have triple unisons of flat steel.[5] The F278, on the other hand, has three braces interrupting its strings, plus a gap providing one additional interruption. The string configuration for the larger instrument is quite different from its slightly smaller sibling: In the very lowest bass, it is the same, with the F278 also having eight single-unison bass notes. But, above those eight notes, the two instruments diverge; the F278 has only five double-unison notes (not fourteen) and then seven notes that have triple unisons using wound strings (the F228 has no triple unisons that use wound strings). The two instruments also differ (slightly) in which highest-register notes have no damper, with the F228 having eighteen notes without dampers and the F278 having only seventeen notes without dampers.

All in all, the smaller Fazioli F228 compared to the F278 has one fewer structural interruption to the strings, more double-unison (wound) notes (14 rather than 5), more notes with wound strings (22 rather than 20), fewer overall wound strings used (36 rather than 39), fewer notes with flat steel strings (66 rather than 68; the larger instrument starts the steel strings two notes lower), one more damper-less note (18 rather than 17), and 11 fewer overall strings (234 total strings compared to the F278's 245 strings). There are other obvious physical differences on the insides of these instruments. Though the braces are shaped very similarly, the F278 adds a diagonal brace running from brace 0 (the noninterruptive brace to the left of the lowest bass string) through the *V*-shaped first interruptive brace (brace 1), across the string gap, and all the way to brace 2. Being a longer instrument, it also has a more massive plate and more sound holes in that plate (11 sound holes compared to the F228's 9 sound holes). Each of these distinctions taken alone may not be significant in itself, but this is a large number of differences found between two models of piano near in size and made by the very same maker. You can imagine finding even greater distinctions when comparing instruments made by different makers and when comparing pianos of very different sizes. You would be correct in such imagining.

DISTINGUISHING DAMPERS

Whereas the keys present a pattern that makes it easy to distinguish by touch and by sight any C from any C♯, most pianos present no such distinctions on the inside of the instrument. The most obvious place for a piano maker to mark notes on the inside of the instrument is on the dampers. A very easy way to do this is if piano makers would paint the dampers to correspond with the finish of the key tops rather than finishing all of the damper wood with the same paint (for most makes, black). If Bösendorfer could simply paint white all the dampers corresponding to the white keys and paint black all the dampers corresponding to the black keys, suddenly the dampers would display to the performer a familiar pattern. The fine German piano maker Sauter on one model at least has begun to do something like this, color-coding the dampers by adding a white inlaid strip on each damper that corresponds to a white key. Unfortunately, piano makers as a whole have not adopted this simple solution. Until such time, it is left to the pianist to provide temporary markings inside the piano. For many pieces, marking all of the dampers is not necessary.

The dampers are an obvious place to mark, and it may be necessary to mark a few or even several of the dampers to aid in playing a concert or even a single work. However, the seated dampers rest on wool felt, which is easy to damage, and if you do not need the dampers for finding where you are, there are other locations to mark that are less delicate.[6]

If a composition only includes a few plucked notes or a few glissandi for which the score only specifies register, you may not need to mark more than one or two dampers, or you may be able to place all of your markings in other spots. Some inside-the-piano techniques may require performing quite some distance from the dampers anyway, so you might want to mark the string ends or nodes on the strings or places on the plate rather than the dampers, just to have your markings closer to the performance location.

MARKING INSIDE THE PIANO

- On the dampers

  Use Post-It strips or small self-adhesive dot labels.
  Or use a small dot of Blu-Tack (poster-mounting putty).
  Use great care with pressing on or moving the dampers.
  Do not use chalk.

- On the agraffes, bridge, string ends

  Use Post-it strips, dot labels, or Blu-Tack.

- On the strings

  Use a small dot of Blu-Tack to mark nodes.
  Or loop closely around the string a thin strip cut from the adhesive section of
    a Post-It note, and stick it to itself. (I find this more difficult to do and less
    reliable than Blu-Tack on the strings.)
  Do not use chalk.[7]

- On the felt surfaces

  Rest a small strip of colored paper on the marking spot.
  Do not use chalk.
  Do not use Blu-Tack.
  Do not use any sticky or adhesive substances (including Post-It notes).

THE MUSIC RACK

For many works, the music rack becomes an obstacle to easy access. Some pianists remove the music rack altogether; others take the rack off its guides and rest it diagonally across the inside of the piano. Pianist Danny Holt, whose repertoire includes several works requiring him to play percussion as well as piano, has devised a special music stand that he clips to the lid of the piano, allowing him to remove the standard music rack and place his music outside the piano's interior. Richard Bunger devised a combination music rack–wood clamp device he dubbed the "Bungerack." He made a limited number of these and gifted several of those to friends and published an article in *Contemporary Keyboard* detailing how other pianists could construct their own Bungeracks. Pianist Margaret Leng Tan sees the obstacle of the music rack as one of the reasons that repertoire, such as Crumb's *Makrokosmos* pieces, must be memorized by the pianist.

EXTENDING, SITTING, AND STANDING WHILE PLAYING INSIDE THE PIANO

Playing deep inside the cabinet of a grand piano requires a very different posture from ordinary on-the-keys playing. Playing inside the piano can be very taxing on the back and shoulders, and the performance of some pieces may require the pianist to remain with torso extended over the instrument for an extended period of time. Performers practicing such repertoire should take precautions to prevent injury, including taking frequent breaks to relax the back and shoulders.

One thing a pianist has to consider when performing many works that make use of extensive inside-the-piano techniques is the choreography of moving from on-the-keys playing to reaching inside the piano. In addition, many techniques require the pianist to sound notes on the keys while simultaneously reaching inside the piano. Neither the performer's height nor the length of her arms have that much bearing in playing most traditional piano works, but these can have a serious bearing on just how the pianist is going to coordinate playing a work that requires that she play both on the keys and inside the instrument. Pianist David Burge, who premiered and championed several works that involved inside-the-piano techniques, voices an unequivocal statement on this subject, saying that the pianist must never stand during a performance, recommending that:

> the pianist stay seated at all times. It is rarely, if ever, really necessary to stand. Shorter persons may need to use a somewhat higher bench than usual, but the distracting sight of the performer alternately standing and sitting should be avoided at all costs.[8]

David Burge was a long-limbed pianist. Despite his suggested solution for shorter performers ("use a . . . higher bench"), many pianists will not be able to perform works that require them to play inside the instrument without standing.

Rather than viewing this as a problem, pianist Margaret Leng Tan sees this as part of the theatre of performing such works. Tan carefully maps out her performances, coordinating her movements so that she does not waste movement, and sees her moves from a seated position to standing as part of how she engages the audience with her performance rather than the distraction that Burge warns against.[9]

If the pianist will be standing while playing or will be transitioning from a seated position to standing while playing, then this may very well require an awkward movement involving the right leg; such physical transitions often require that the pianist keep the damper pedal down, using the resonance remaining from the first passage to cover the pause required by the performer's change of position. Keeping the pedal depressed while sitting or standing, especially if both hands are occupied while the pianist is moving, requires deft sliding of the right foot while the pianist repositions it to move her body, and this transition from sitting to standing or vice versa can also place significant strain on the right knee. Margaret Leng Tan recommends taking frequent breaks while practicing inside-the-piano repertoire, and she suggests that the pianist take the damper pedal out of the equation while practicing, suggesting that the pianist can weight or wedge the pedal into position for early practice sessions on a work.[10]

STRUMMING GLISSANDO

There are many other ways to excite the strings beyond actuating the sound with the keys, including plucking individual strings, strumming across ranges of strings, scraping the string windings on lower-register strings, and rubbing strings along their length. It is easy to gain access to the strings on most pianos, and on grand piano models, lifting the lid exposes the full length of all of the approximately 230 strings.

One of the most familiar techniques for sounding notes on the piano without using the keys is the simple chromatic strum across a range of strings. Though a strum like this does not produce the same slide through all of the microtones between two notes as a glissando on the violin would, it has become standard to refer to strumming across a range of piano strings a glissando.

For all but the very highest register of the piano (the dozen or so high notes on the instrument whose strings do not have dampers at all), a ringing glissando requires the pianist to raise the dampers from the strings with the damper pedal before—or just at the start of—the strumming action.[11] Different composers and works provide different levels of specificity for glissando, some indicating only register and some giving specific start or goal notes or both.

Many different plectra are effective for glissando. The flesh of the fingertips produces a dark, subtle sound especially in the low to midregister of the piano. Using the fingernails or a guitar pick produces a brighter sound with a more metallic and distinct onset of the sound. Dynamics for a glissando are mostly determined by the speed of performance and by the plectra materials. Hans Werner Henze in his *Sinfonia No. 6* for two chamber orchestras has the pianist strum the strings using brushes, a natural bristled hairbrush, and (for a forte dynamic) an iron brush.

A pianissimo glissando with the flesh of a fingertip (or with all of the fingers and most of their length) in the lowest register provides an indistinct, complex sound, somewhat resembling a pianissimo tam-tam strike. This effect can be very effectively used in a chamber context—especially if the ensemble doesn't include percussion. A pianissimo low-register glissando across the strings may allow the piano to do double duty as an unpitched percussion instrument. A fortissimo middle-register glissando with the fingernails produces a much brighter sound, with more prominent pitch, and can cut through even a thick texture and add some force to the onset of an ensemble's sound; the same performed with a medium guitar pick can be even brighter and louder. Though, admittedly, it is a very different sound in many ways, such a glissando might be used effectively as a substitute for a glissando on harp to emphasize an arrival or other climactic moment in an ensemble piece (see figure 4.3).

(f.t. on the strings)

Figure 4.3. On-the-strings glissando

Most scores that use on-the-strings glissandi leave the location of the strum (where along the strings' length to strum) up to the performer. The fullest sound is produced away from the string ends, toward the middle of the strings. It is also possible to strum very close to the ends of the strings. The strings are stiffer close to their ends, and the resultant sound has less of the strings' fundamentals and emphasizes the higher partials more. If you desire this sound, specify glissando sul ponticello. (Additional discussion of sul ponticello appears later in the "Pizzicato" section.)

Notation for on-the-strings glissando across several different strings, as in these examples, is mostly standardized at this point. Most composers indicate the glissando with a diagonal line on the staff for the register (or with beginning and goal notes given if the composer wishes to specify these). Before the glissando itself, the composer should write "on the strings" or some similar phrase to differentiate the on-the-strings glissando from a glissando performed on the keys (the on-the-keys glissando, a very different effect, may bring to mind Jerry Lee Lewis or, for that matter, Stravinsky's writing in the solo piano version of *Petruschka* or any number of other works, and you can find details for it in chapter 3).

AEOLIAN HARP OR AUTOHARP TECHNIQUE

Henry Cowell in his piece *Aeolian Harp* is the first person to notate a special subset of strumming across the strings, asking the pianist to finger chords silently with one hand and then strum across the strings for the corresponding register with the other hand (see figure 4.4). For this, rather than strumming so that the full chromatic notes for a register ring, the pianist must depress specific keys silently and either hold those notes with one hand while strumming with the other or "catch" those notes with the sostenuto pedal to keep particular dampers raised off of the strings, therefore allowing only those notes to ring freely. The pianist depresses some notes silently, raising select dampers, then strums across that register of strings (strumming across the full chromatic complement of strings for the register). Though the plectrum comes into contact with all of the strings in the register, only the strings with the dampers raised off of them resonate. Strumming across the other strings (the ones with the dampers resting on them) does contribute a little to the sound—the plectrum or fingers running across those dampened strings adds a little "oomph" to the attack, but the damped strings will not produce any lasting sound. Cowell's notation alone does not distinguish these chords from rolled chords played on the keys. However, he details in his "Explanation of Symbols" that the keys for these notes should be silently depressed with one hand while the strings are strummed by the other hand.

In several pieces, both solo and chamber, composer George Crumb has adopted Cowell's technique from *Aeolian Harp*. Crumb uses this technique in several works. In his 1973 set of solo piano works *Makrokosmos*, volume 2, in "Twin Suns (Doppelgänger aus der Ewigkeit)" Crumb presents a "Hymn for the Advent of the Star-Child" using this technique. Again, in his 1974 *Music for a Summer*

Figure 4.4.   Henry Cowell, *Aeolian Harp* (Associated Music Publishers), mm. 9–11

AEOLIAN HARP by Henry Cowell. Copyright 1930 (Renewed) by Associated Music Publishers, Inc. (BMI) International. Copyright Secured. All Rights Reserved. Reprinted by Permission.

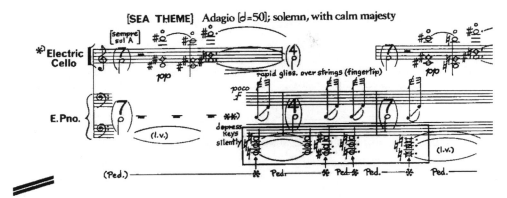

Figure 4.5. On-the-strings glissando, autoharp effect, Crumb, *Vox Balaenae* (Peters Edition), "Sea Theme," p. 8, mm. 1–3
Copyright © 1971 by C. F. Peters Corporation. Used by permission.

Evening [Makrokosmos III], Crumb asks for this technique for a "Hymn for the Nativity of the Star-Child." In each of these instances, Crumb places the silently depressed notes on a staff within boxes and shows the register for the glissando on the strings on a separate staff, with each rapid glissando shown as grace notes. In these works, Crumb does not name the technique. In the first volume of *Makrokosmos* (1972), Crumb also does not specifically label the technique, but the section of the work in which he uses it, he calls "Music of Shadows (for Aeolian Harp)," making clear the connection to Cowell's work.

In the explanatory note of the technique in his 1972 trio *Vox Balaenae,* Crumb again makes the connection to Cowell, labeling the technique the "aeolian harp effect." Because this technique is so closely connected to Cowell's *Aeolian Harp,* many composers follow Crumb's label in *Vox Balaenae* and refer to it as the "Aeolian harp" effect or technique. Using this label is clear. Alternately, and without necessarily discounting Cowell's pioneering work, many composers also call this the "autoharp" technique. Because the Aeolian harp is played by the wind, not by strumming, and the autoharp is played by using one hand to select chords and the other hand to strum a large compass of strings, resulting in just the strings from the chord ringing, "autoharp" better approaches this technique on the piano, so I prefer this label.

When Crumb uses this technique, he usually gives familiar modal or tonal harmonies to be strummed. In his trio for amplified piano, flute, and cello, *Vox Balaenae,* the strummed sonorities in the "Sea Theme" imply major or minor triads but give only the root and fifth of each chord. In both of the Star-Child hymns from the volumes of *Makrokosmos,* Crumb again mates this autoharp technique with major and minor triads.

If the passage calls for strumming chords steadily in succession without pauses between the chords, then the pianist can silently depress the keys for the notes of each chord with one hand and strum across the strings in that register with the other hand. Judicious use of the damper pedal can enable the player to connect each chord in a strummed passage in a legato fashion. The pianist silently depresses the keys for a chord, strums, and then catches the ringing notes by depressing the damper pedal. Then while that chord continues to ring, the pianist silently depresses the keys for the next chord, strums, and immediately releases the damper pedal (but not the keys, for the second chord). Now that that chord is ringing, the pianist catches it with the damper pedal and continues following this pattern. Using the pedal to cover the shifts from one chord to the next also helps to cover mistakes, if the pianist should accidently sound a note from the keyboard while trying to finger each chord silently. At any but the lowest dynamic level, the presently ringing chord will mask the moment when the player fingers the next chord if the player accidently presses one key too assertively and its hammer lightly taps its string or strings. Note that, in figure 4.6, the right hand releases each measure's first chord well before the end of the measure and takes the keys of the next chord two beats *before* the new measure, but this change of harmony does not *sound* until the strum on the strings that is notated in the lower staff just before beat 1 of each new measure. The basic pattern is:

1. finger the chord silently on the keys,
2. strum on the strings,
3. catch the ringing chord by depressing the damper pedal,
4. release the keys of the chord (the damper pedal allows those notes to continue ringing),
5. finger the next chord silently ahead of when it is supposed to sound and then strum on the strings while continuing to hold the new chord's keys down (as in steps 1 and 2),
6. immediately after strumming, release the damper pedal (so that the full chromatic gamut doesn't ring), and then
7. re-press the damper pedal to capture just the new sounding chord notes (which is step 3 again, and the pattern continues).

For autoharp chord passages, the instrument's brace structure and the span that the player can finger (silently) with one hand greatly constrain the notes and voicing for each chord. The passage from Crumb's *Vox Balaenae* in figure 4.5, for instance, keeps each chord within the span of an octave (easily fingered in one hand by most adult pianists). This passage works well on many models of piano, but the brace structure of a Steinway D, for instance, renders three of four chords of this opening of the passage impossible to sound as a single strum. The first interruptive bass brace

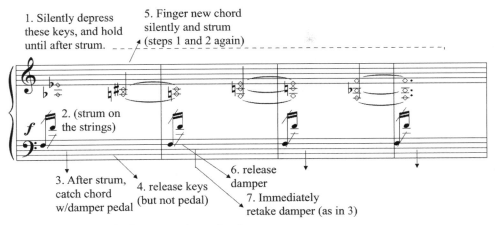

Figure 4.6. Pattern for legato autoharp chords

of this instrument comes right in the middle of this register of strings, as located between E2 and F2. If the chord is not to be rewritten for this model of instrument, then the player must either perform it in two short strums, broken while the performer navigates over the brace that is between them, or by strumming the two regions of strings with the two hands simultaneously, thereby realizing what was notated as a single longer "monophonic" strum played with one hand as a shorter duophonic one played with both hands strumming simultaneously. Such passages as this work better on a smaller model grand, such as the Steinway M. On the "M," the first interruptive brace appears several notes higher, so the strings for the notes in the passage are all together in the lowest section of strings of the instrument, they are all on the bass bridge, and presented without a brace or gap or other interruption.

Discussing performing Crumb's music, especially premiering *The Winds of Destiny* (2004), pianist Marcantonio Barone mentions a few piano specifications, which, at least on the Steinway D that Barone was performing on, either do not work as notated or may not produce the sound the score asks for if performed exactly as notated. As an example of the latter situation, Barone found that a mallet hit to the soundboard through the circular sound hole of the frame did not produce the loud sound required by the score. Barone suggested to the composer moving the mallet hit to a location on the soundboard exposed to the left of the frame and the bass strings, where he found the strike produced a louder sound.[12]

Barone also discovered a brace on the Steinway D that prevented a smooth, uninterrupted glissando as required by the score in a couple of places. In these he substituted a left-hand glissando to one section of the strings and a right-hand glissando to the remaining strings, with these glissandi performed simultaneously in contrary motion rather than a single ascending glissando as notated. This makes for a clear example in which the model piano that is likely to be used for performance physically prevents performing the piece exactly as notated.[13]

Appendix C gives the brace layout for many concert grand and semiconcert grand pianos, so a pianist or a composer can check any individual strummed chord voicing and quickly ascertain which pianos accommodate that chord in a given voicing and which require some sort of adaptation of the written passage to accommodate the individual architecture of a particular piano model.

AUTOHARP TECHNIQUE WITH LARGER CHORDS

If the composition gives the pianist ample time before asking the pianist to strum an individual chord, the composer can write a larger chord to be strummed than the pianist can grasp with a single hand. If the pianist can finger the chord between the two hands and then keep the dampers raised for all of those notes by catching the dampers with the sostenuto pedal, then both hands are free to strum more than one register of strings at the same time. The size of the two-hand chords fingered silently and caught with the sostenuto pedal could be even further augmented with help from a page-turner or other assistant. The assistant and the pianist could both depress keys silently with both hands, and the pianist could catch all of these notes held by the four hands with the sostenuto pedal.

Composers writing for two pianists playing a single piano could also move beyond the one-hand limitation in a strummed passage with steadily changing chords by asking one player to use both hands to finger the chords silently, while the other player concentrates on doing the strumming for each one. HOCKET piano duo made an arrangement of Cowell's solo piano *Aeolian Harp* that takes advantage of this idea—HOCKET divides the responsibilities of this piece, with one player taking over all duties of fingering on the keys and the other doing all strumming, plucking, and other inside-the-piano work.

Composers writing for a Yamaha Disklavier, a Bösendorfer 290SE, or some other modern player or reproducing piano can also write single-player works that expand beyond what a player can finger with one hand (or even with two). The computer controlling the player mechanism can be given the task of silently playing chords of any size, and the player needs only strum each one to sound the notes. The movement "an image in the water" from my *black narcissus* written for the Bösendorfer 290SE—essentially a ninety-seven-key Bösendorfer "Imperial" Grand with a computer-controlled player mechanism installed—divides the responsibilities for strummed chords in this way (see figure 4.7). For this movement, the piano mechanism silently depresses large chords (using a MIDI velocity value of 1 out of 127, which raises the dampers and moves the hammers but does not bring the hammers into contact with the strings). The pianist, using a guitar pick in

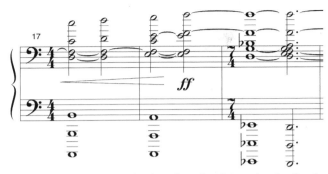

Figure 4.7. **Player mechanism fingering large chords silently for a player who strums with both hands, Shockley, "an image in the water,"** *black narcissus*, **mm. 17–19**

each hand, then strums across multiple registers for each chord, setting the strings into motion for these very large chords.[14]

To follow the notational convention for the autoharp technique, this excerpt would require two additional staves. All of the sounding notes given above would then be given diamond noteheads, as these notes are "fingered" silently by the player mechanism, and the additional staves would show the register(s) that should be strummed and when they should be strummed. In this instance, the score follows Cowell's notation in *Aeolian Harp*, notating the silently depressed notes as normal and including text instructions that explain to strum the strings rather than play these notes on the keys.

SWEEP ALONG THE LENGTH OF A STRING

Just as he explored many types of cluster, composer-pianist Henry Cowell also dug into many of the different sounds that are possible with the pianist playing directly on the strings of the instrument. Cowell's use includes chromatic, on-the-keys glissando, but he also explores the sounds possible by rubbing a single string (or single set of unisons) with the fingertip.

Whereas the on-the-strings glissando explained earlier involves strumming in a perpendicular motion across all the strings within a register, here we have the player creating sounds by playing along the *length* of a string or a single set of unison strings. Because pianos use different string materials in the bass and tenor register than for the remainder of the instrument, running a fingertip along a bass string produces a very different sound from running a fingertip along a middle-register unison set. Rubbing the flesh of the fingertip along a unison set of the flat steel strings of the middle register and above produces a very, very delicate sound, whereas similarly rubbing along the wound strings produces a quiet but more easily audible one. The player can bring out different harmonics in these notes by varying the speed of the movement of her finger on the strings.

Though this technique does involve the finger or fingers gliding along the string—in other words, a glissando—I refer to this as a "sweep" rather than a glissando to differentiate it from a glissando across several strings at once. Cowell uses this sweep technique in *The Banshee* (1925), in which the score directs the player to "sweep lengthwise along the string of the note given with flesh of finger."[15] *The Banshee* presents several variations of this basic technique, including a similar sweep along the string's length, but along three notes at once and along five notes at once (requiring the pianist to do this sweeping motion with all five fingers of one hand, followed by another sweep with the five fingers of the other hand. He also asks for the single-note sweep to be performed with the back of the fingernail rather than with the flesh of the finger in some instances.

The fingernails on the string windings can produce a much louder sound than the one done with the fingertip, and Cowell gets even more volume out of this technique by asking for the player to play five notes together with the backs of the fingernails rather than the flesh of the fingers. And because five notes is not nearly enough, he also asks the player to sweep over the string lengths of a whole range of notes with the backs of the fingernails of both hands simultaneously. In a few places, he also follows the fingernail sweep on a single string with a flesh of the fingertip sweep along the string or strings for that same note, asking the pianist to perform a fingernail sweep and, when that fingernail has reached the middle of the string, to "start a sweep along the same string with the flesh of the other finger, thus partly damping the sound."[16] Though Cowell's instructions say the new sweep with the flesh of the finger dampens the sound, that movement—being the original technique described previously—actually vibrates the string anew, just at a lower dynamic level than the preceding sweep with the fingernail. The effect is that the note first sounded with the fingernail, then echoes at a lower dynamic level with the flesh of the fingertip.

The copper-wound bass strings speak better with this playing technique than the upper-register steel strings, so on the wound strings, it is possible to perform this string-sweeping technique at a piano dynamic (not just at pianissimo or below). Additionally, the copper-wound strings allow the player to dig into the windings with the fingernails or a plectrum of some sort. A short flick of the fingernail along the windings of a bass string (or a tenor unison set) can produce a loud, accented note.

Rather than ringing the string as a whole with such a fast move against the string windings, it is also possible to ring a harmonic from the string. George Crumb calls for this in his *Gnomic Variations*, asking the player to touch with the side of the thumb the node at the middle of the string (to produce the second partial harmonic) and then to use another finger of the same hand to flick quickly across the string winding with the fingernail. This effect speaks loudest in the lowest register of the piano with the very long strings to be found there and with the fundamental or first couple of overtones, which ring the longest portion of those strings.

A medium-slow fingernail scrape across the windings of a copper-wound string produces a steady, sustained sounding of the string's fundamental. A very slow fingernail scrape (or a very slow scrape with a guitar pick or other plectrum) can produce a harsh, guttural sound with little to no discernable pitch. Such slow scrapes can be effective at most dynamic levels, and if the piano is also amplified, this technique can produce a striking sound even at a low dynamic level.

In an ensemble setting, it is easy to hide all of these along-the-length-of-the-string techniques, and depressing the damper pedal and allowing the full range of the instrument's strings to resonate sympathetically with the rubbed or scraped string makes any of these sounds fuller.

Composers and improvising performers can easily combine several of these techniques together in a single passage. It's very easy to transition quickly among on-the-string glissando, fingernail scrapes, and fingertip rubbing along the length of the strings. In a couple of my works, I call this mélange of fingertip and fingernail on-the-string techniques a "scrabbling" on the strings and suggest the performer can move among the techniques ad libitum while following a graphically indicated pitch-register contour.

PIZZICATO

Plucking strings on the piano is one of the simplest techniques to explain and one of the easiest extended techniques to perform. Pizzicato on the piano also lends itself to many variations and is a technique that can speak in many different colors.

Pizzicato with the flesh of the fingertips on the strings anywhere from a few inches from either end of the string to the middle of the string produces a fundamental-rich tone. This pizzicato, which I would label as the "ordinary," the default pizzicato, speaks well from low to moderately loud dynamic levels. In the middle register, plucking strings with the flesh of the fingertip near the middle of the string produces a round, harp-like sound.

Rather than plucking with the flesh of the fingertip, the performer can also pluck with the fingernail. Fingernail pizzicato produces a thinner, brighter sound, which has a little less of the fundamental and a little more of the higher overtones. This sound cuts through a little better, blends with other instruments a little less, and is a little more brittle than the ordinary pizzicato. Adding the indication "(fingernail)" or "(fin.)" after pizzicato specifies this type of plucking.

Typically, single notes are plucked, not multiple ones, but it is possible to pluck two or three notes with one hand at a time. It is possible to pluck even four or five notes with one hand in the midrange to the upper reaches of the instrument, though the strings to be plucked would need to be close to each other, and built of mostly minor or major second intervals. In the bass register and even in the low-tenor register, the string spacing is larger, and the strings are thick and require more force to pluck; consequently, it is more difficult to pluck more than three strings with one hand at a time below the middle register.

It is also possible to pluck strings with both hands at the same time, though most players find this challenging to do either if the notes are not clustered closely together for both hands or if they're not in a simple relationship between the two hands: Giving the same interval to each hand or octave-related notes will be easier to do than "unmatched plucking." So, for example giving a C3 and an F3 to be plucked by the left hand and a C4 and an F4 to be plucked by the right hand simultaneously will not pose so much difficulty.

Just as on the violin, plucking different regions of the string on the piano makes a difference in the color of the sound. Plucking away from the ends of the strings produces a full sound with a prominent fundamental. Both ends of the speaking length of the string vibrate less freely than does the large middle portion of the string. Plucking close to the end of the string reduces the prominence of the fundamental and allows more of the high overtones to speak within the sound. Such plucking on the string instruments is called sul ponticello; this same designation works well for the piano: pizzicato sul ponticello (or abbreviated s.p.).[17] This sul ponticello sound is available by plucking the ringing string length close to the agraffes or capo d'astro located near the tuning-pin end of the string. On grand pianos, this is also available by plucking the far end of the strings, close to the bridge pins that run along the tail and the bent side of the piano.[18] But, to pluck at that end of the string for all but the very shortest high-register strings requires that the pianist leave something—or someone—to keep the damper pedal depressed, and then the pianist needs to walk around to the tail of the piano. Unless the composer desires this additional theatrical element, the pianist will likely choose to pluck the strings sul ponticello simply by reaching in and plucking within an inch or so from tuning-pin end of the strings.

Pizzicato on the piano strings can, of course, be performed with various plectra. Guitar picks are very effective on the piano strings, and there are several works that call for their use. Lois V. Vierk's *To Stare Astonished at the Sea* (1994), for example, asks that the pianist use a guitar pick in each hand throughout much of the piece for individual pizzicato notes and for glissandi of different spans on an amplified piano.

Pizzicato can also be combined with other techniques—plucking a muted note adds a wonderful additional timbre to the palette. It is quite easy to mute a string or a set of unisons by pressing on the string or strings with the side of the first joint of the thumb and then to pluck with the index finger (finger 2) or to mute with the tip of the index finger and pluck with the middle finger (finger 3). I am also particularly fond of muting a string and then simultaneously plucking that string sul ponticello. To do this, mute the very end of the string with the side of the tip of the thumb and pluck with the index finger placed very close to the thumb (and therefore very close to the end of the string).

Plucking strings can also be performed in conjunction with various preparations to varying degrees of timbral difference from sounding those prepared strings by striking a key. If the strings are first prepared by placing paper on them, then the plucked notes have a more delicate attack than if played on the keys, and the paper rattle is the same. Some nice sounds can be produced by preparing individual notes by threading coins between the strings, or placing screws or bolts between them and then plucking those prepared strings rather than the usual key actuation. In these instances as well, plucking produces less force than a hammer strike to the strings, so the sound is somewhat diminished, but this more intimate sound may be exactly what a passage calls for!

It does take most pianists a little more time to locate notes inside the piano, so it may be necessary to give the player a little more prep time to play pizzicato, and fast passages of pizzicato notes or quick alternation between pizzicato notes and on-the-key notes prove very challenging for almost all performers. However, these difficulties can be mitigated somewhat by both the composer and the performer. On the composer's side, a piece that limits the variety of plucked notes and uses notes always in the same register allows the performer to memorize their location: Returning to the same notes later in a piece is much easier than locating different notes. A composer who gives space to the performer before pizzicato notes gives the performer time to locate them and to play them accurately. I'd draw an analogy to writing for timpani—a timpani part that allows each drum to be tuned before the piece begins and then allows each drum to be responsible for producing only one note (requiring no retuning) or only a couple of notes or a piece that gives lots of time to the player before pitch changes (thereby giving the performer time to locate the new note and retune the instrument well before the new entrance) is significantly easier to play than one which asks that the timpani player produce steady melodic material filled with lots of chromaticism.

The performer, too, can install visual aids to assistance in the performance of pizzicato or other inside-the-piano techniques. See the first portion of this chapter for details on marking inside the piano.

STOPPED BASS-STRING NOTES

Cowell in his piece *Sinister Resonance* published in 1930 calls for a difficult-to-produce technique that does not pop up in many other pieces. Cowell asks the pianist to press hard with the third finger of the right hand on the lowest bass string and then sound the string by depressing the key as usual. *Sinister Resonance* has the pianist play a melody in this fashion, stopping the string (and effectively shortening its resonating length), and then repositioning the finger that is pressing against the string to change the resonating length and produce additional notes. Though a pianist might confuse this with playing harmonics on the string, which can be produced by *lightly* touching a nodal point on the string and sounding with the key, this is a different technique, requiring *heavy* pressure on the string, and produces a limited number of pitches (as well as different ones from the overtones available on that string). Pianist Stacey Barelos, a Cowell specialist, says that this effect works best on large grand pianos, but she has been able to produce stopped-string notes on a five-foot baby grand. However, she says that the "ability to do so will depend on the particular piano and how hard you are willing to press on the strings!"[19] Later in *Sinister Resonance*, Cowell asks for this same technique but in a higher register and on a note strung with flat steel strings. Pianists, including Cowell, seem to have great difficulty producing stopped-string notes on any strings other than the very lowest bass strings; Cowell in his own recording of *Sinister Resonance* and pianists Sorrel Hays and Chris Brown each substitute other techniques for these middle-register stopped-string melodies. Hays does not play the written melody notes at all, substituting harmonics available on the indicated string for the stopped-string notes given in the score. Cowell himself substitutes second partial harmonics played on the strings an octave lower than each melody note (so producing the correct melody notes but using a different technique and not playing the melody on a single string set); Brown also substitutes a melody in second-partial harmonics.[20]

There are many other ways to excite the strings into vibration, many more ways than can be catalogued here! However, the following are a few others.

SOME OTHER WAYS TO TOUCH AND VIBRATE THE STRINGS

In addition to setting the strings into motion with the fingertips and fingernails, the strings can be tapped with thimble-clad fingertips. Wen-chung Chou in his *Yü Ko* (1965) for nine players has the pianist imitate sounds of the *qin*, asking her to play on the strings while wearing metal thimbles on the fingertips and requiring this technique simultaneous with hand muting the strings. Crumb also asks for thimbles on the strings in his *Makrokosmos*, book 1, "The Phantom Gondolier" (see figure 4.8).

Ashley Fure's sextet *Soma* (2012) asks the pianist to drag a heavy roll of duct tape across the surface of the length of the strings, producing screeching, high harmonic clusters on strings in contact with the tape. Fure also has the pianist hit the piano's braces with the roll of duct tape, scraping across the bass strings while moving from one brace to the next.

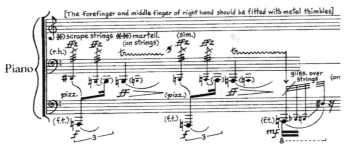

Figure 4.8. Fingers with thimbles on strings, George Crumb, *Makrokosmos*, book 1, "The Phantom Gondolier" (Peters Edition), no. 5, p. 11, beginning of first system (unmeasured)

Copyright © 1974 by C. F. Peters Corporation. Used by permission.

Rolling and dragging balls across the strings can also set them into motion. Annie Gosfield's *Brooklyn, Oct. 5, 1941* (1997), a piece with a program tied to a baseball game in the 1941 World Series, has the pianist strike a bass key while rolling a baseball along the strings. (Gosfield's piece also has the player play with the ball and with a leather catcher's mitt on the keys and ends with the baseball's resonant bounce to the frame.)

Witold Szalonek's solo piano piece *Mutanza* (1968) asks the pianist to pour steel balls onto the piano strings. Clara Iannotta's amplified ensemble piece *Troglodyte Angels Clank By* (2015) has the pianist place fifteen to twenty glass marbles on the strings at the hitch-pin end of the strings and then has the player slide these along the strings.

Stefan Prins's 2010 chamber work *Fremkörper #2* asks the pianist to drag a smooth stone across the strings. Drew Baker's 2005 *Gaeta* for two pianos and water percussion has the pianists produce a high-pitched harmonic screeching by pushing a piece of slate along the length of the strings. Sofia Gubaidulina in her

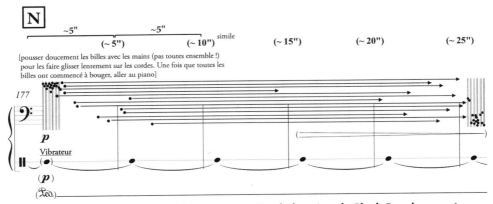

Figure 4.9. Marbles on strings, Clara Iannotta, *Troglodyte Angels Clank By*, piano part, mm. 177–82

1993 *Dancer on a Tightrope (Der Seiltänzer)* for violin and piano asks the pianist to drag a glass tumbler across the surface of the strings, as well as to strike the strings with the edge of the tumbler.

Fure's *Soma* mentioned previously for its duct-tape drag on the strings also has the player scrape the strings in various ways with the edge of a credit card. *Soma* makes use of a variety of different attack strategies with the credit card.

VIBRATING THE STRINGS WITH ELECTRICAL DEVICES

Vibrators (yes, the kind of devices used for personal pleasure), electric toothbrushes, and other low-power vibrating devices can all be used to set the piano strings into motion. Iannotta's *Troglodyte Angels Clank By*, in addition to the rolled marbles, asks the pianist to set the strings into motion using a battery-operated, multispeed vibrator. Voler Bertelmann, who performs under the name Hauschka, has explored using several different items to play on the strings of the piano; his *Mount Hood* from his 2010 album *Foreign Landscapes* among other things also uses a type of vibrator (pocket-sized, in this case).[21] Hauschka in some cases tapes one end of the vibrator near the agraffes and uses the tape to position the other end of the vibrator so that it is in contact with a single set of unisons, thereby providing a drone of a single note. He also transfers the vibrator's motion to the strings in a secondary fashion, first placing a piano tuner's long wooden-handled, leather-faced split mute so that it mutes a triple set of unisons and then applying the vibrator along the length of the split mute. This produces a pitched rattle. Elizabeth A. Baker has also used multiple vibrators on the piano's strings as a way to provide a background bed of sound over which she then improvises on the keys and inside the piano. John Cage uses a more whimsical vibrating device in his *Water Walk* (1959), placing on the strings of a grand piano a powered toy fish. The fish's flapping fin sounds the bass strings of the piano.

Julian Anderson's piano concerto *The Imaginary Museum* (2017) has the harpist vibrate the harp's strings using an electric milk frother. This could also be used to vibrate a piano's strings. Most of the milk frothers I have encountered use a stainless-steel wire head, and though these are very light-gauge steel, I would recommend caution if using one of these on the delicate copper-wound bass-register strings. They should be safe for use on the steel strings.

Electromagnets can also be used to set the piano's strings in motion. Stephen Scott uses a set of electromagnets placed on one chromatic octave's notes in his *Resonant Resources* (1983). Composer/improviser/pianist Cor Fuhler often places magnets and small electrical devices he makes himself on the strings of the piano. His suite for piano, radio, and optional couch, *Love Is Statistic Static* (2015), makes use of flat, cylindrical, and skittle magnets, as well as various electrical devices, some of them newly devised by Fuhler. One piece of the suite, "Andante Heartbeatissimo," has the player place three remote-controlled dog collars on the bass strings; the player activates the collars during the piece to vibrate strings in the bass register to provide rumbling sounds. There are works by several composers that take advantage of the EBow to vibrate the piano's strings. The EBow, designed for use primarily on electric guitars, is a battery-powered electromagnet in a handheld plastic housing. Alvin Lucier's *Music for Piano with Magnetic Strings* (1995) uses five EBows and has the player spend most of her time "listening for harmonics, audible beating, [and] occasional rhythms produced as one or more magnets vibrate against adjacent strings, and other acoustic phenomena."[22] The pianist makes all of the sounds of the piece by placing each of the EBows on strings of the piano, listening, and repositioning the EBows following a prose score.

Maggi Payne uses three EBows to great effect in her *Holding Pattern* (2001), having the pianist surreptitiously set the EBows in place in the instrument before the performance begins. The work opens with a large cluster chord played fortissimo, and as the sound naturally dissipates from this chord, three notes "magically" continue sounding through the use of the EBows. Payne's score recommends modifying the EBows very slightly, removing the guide ridges at the bottom of each device to gain better access to a set of unison strings on the piano with the EBow. Fuhler, in a performance at the 2008 Approximation Festival in Düsseldorf, can be seen using, in addition to cylindrical magnets, at least a half-dozen EBows.

Using electromagnets to vibrate the piano's strings is by no means a new idea. In 1886, Electorphonisches Klavier, a German company, devised a system that used electromagnets to vibrate a piano's strings, introducing the possibility of piano notes with endless sustain.

5

Muting

Muting the strings of the piano is one of the simplest ways to enact a significant timbral change to individual notes while still potentially sounding notes "as usual" by depressing individual keys. The pianist can mute individual notes or whole ranges of notes as a simple preparation, or she can mute notes "on the fly" with the fingertips or edge of one hand while continuing to play on the keys with the other.

Generally, muted notes sound darker and more centered on the fundamental than *ordinario*, unmuted ones. Their sustain is also shorter and can be considerably shorter than corresponding unmuted notes. In the low bass register, the sound can be a bit like a thumpy electric bass. In the register just below C4 (middle C), the sound can be very marimba-like. In the top register, most of the normal strings' sound gets dampened by the muting, and the muting mostly reduces the sound to that of the hammer hitting the strings, with just a little bit of the fundamental coloring that percussive sound.

MUTING WITH FINGERS AND HANDS

To mute with the fingers, press firmly with a fingertip (or two) on the string or strings close to the near end of the sounding span of the string. For wound strings, pressing right at the beginning of the winding or just a little further along the string length is perfect. For the steel (unwound) upper-register strings, pressing a half inch or a little more from the agraffes or capo d'astro (on the near side of the dampers) works well.

If only one or two pitches are needed and they are very close to each other, then muting with the fingertips might work well. Muting with the fingertips works great for a quick alternation between a muted and unmuted sound on the same pitch. Muting with the fingertips also provides a good amount of control over the sound, so a pianist could even sound notes fully muted, sounding normally, and various gradations in between (that mostly would be unavailable when using other strategies for muting). One could even notate a slow transition to and from a fully muted sound. Finger muted notes retain some pitch, but by pressing with more than one fingertip or with the whole hand on the strings, the player can remove almost all pitch from the sound. Again, it is possible to make a smooth transition from *ordinario* to partially muted to more fully muted (but retaining some pitch) to a note fully dampened by the player pressing the strings with the whole hand.

It's also relatively easy to mute with the edge of the hand—the fleshy bit between the wrist and the base of the little finger works well (and the pianist can probably mute a few additional notes with the side of the little finger). Depending on the size of your hand and what register you are muting on the piano, you may be able to mute a perfect fifth or even more. With my own hand, I find muting this way is usually a bit inconsistent—some notes sound fully muted, others have one—or more—of the unisons ringing freely, despite my attempting to apply even pressure to the strings. But, if there is no time to mute the strings using some sort of preparation or if you merely want a brief change of color during a live improvisation and you want more than one muted note at a time or several different muted pitches in quick succession, then muting with the edge of the hand may be the best method for the situation.

FINGER MUTING AND ACCESS TO THE STRINGS

Appendix C contains details on the internal structures of most of the modern concert grands and many semi-concert grands and smaller instruments that pianists are likely to find in concert halls across the world. There you can find details on brace placement and stringing, which may be useful information when thinking about muting with the fingertips and hands. Most large grands divide the even placement of the strings with three braces (sometimes also called struts). There are a few grands that have four interruptive braces, like the Bösendorfer 290 "Imperial" Grand. Almost all of these pianos share some general characteristics of their geographies to consider when planning to mute with the hands near the ends of the strings close to the tuning pins: Most grands give the player access to this end of the strings for the full bass and tenor registers. Many grands have a capo d'astro bar used in place of agraffes for the upper register, and for at least some grands, the combination of the placement of the capo d'astro and the dampers themselves cover much of the ends of the strings, restricting some of the player's access to the near end of some strings.

For grands with three interruptive braces, the notes beyond the third brace are likely to be damper-less. For grands with four interruptive braces, notes beyond the fourth brace are likely to be damper-less. For all of these grands, that means that, for roughly the top eighteen notes, there are no dampers in the way, so even with a chunky capo d'astro bar in the way, it is likely that the player can still access the end of the strings with the fingertips (at least). It is really only the strings for the next-to-the-top section of notes that seriously restrict the player's ability to touch the ends of the strings. This section, running roughly from D5 to G6, contains the strings with the most restricted access on most any grand that I have examined so far. On most grands, from A0 to B4 should be safe, and from A6 to C8 should be safe to ask for pizzicato sul ponticello or muting with the fingertips. Even the remaining more restricted range is fairly accessible to pianists on some models of instrument while being almost impossible to access on a few other makes and models.

SQUEEGEE (AND OTHER OBJECT) MUTING

In addition to muting with the fingertips and the edge of the hand, there are also ways of muting by applying objects to the strings. The following ways of muting with objects rather than with the hands or fingertips essentially present different varieties of surface preparations (or, in a few cases, string preparations), but I group muting techniques together and separate muting techniques using preparations from the other preparations covered in chapter 9 for a couple reasons. For one, muting crops up in many works that use no other preparations, so forms to my mind a special class of preparations. For another, there are many works that call for muting without specifying how the player should mute the strings, so in performance one player might use surface preparations to mute the notes, while another might choose to mute with the fingertips. Because muting and harmonics are both so common and because these techniques display so much variety of technique, dedicating separate chapters to these both gives them the attention they need and does not overburden the already-lengthy chapter on preparations.

The objects used for muting may be handheld—a player can mute the strings by pressing a tennis ball to the end of the strings or by pressing a balled-up piece of notebook paper. An artist's squeegee intended for use with screen printing can be used to mute several notes at once. I have a wooden-handled, neoprene-bladed squeegee that I use for this. It covers a larger span than the edge of my hand, and because it has a thick square-edged blade, it also more consistently mutes all the notes it's applied to than I am able to cover with the edge of my hand. The squeegee can be wielded with one hand while the other hand plays on the keys as normal, so this may be a good solution if the pianist temporarily needs several notes in the same register muted.

WEIGHTED CLOTH-COVERED MUTES

Composer Stephen Hartke has devised another mute that is easy (and inexpensive) to make at home and can be customized to cover just about any number of notes at once. This mute sounds very similar to muting with the hand but is more consistent than hand muting and easily covers more notes at once than muting with the fingertips or side of the hand. The basic idea for this mute is that it needs to have enough weight to dampen the strings and to stay put, and it needs a soft exterior and some malleability to help it to mold to the various sets of strings and so that the mute does not add any extraneous noise to its application and removal. Hartke made his mutes with BBs and old socks. Fill a sock with BBs, and tie the end of the sock to close it. Then, place that whole (heavy) sock inside another sock (tied-end first), and then tie that sock closed. Depending on the thickness of the socks, you may want to add one more sock outside the first two. I made my own weighted cloth-covered mutes following Hartke's design by sewing a cylindrical sleeve of cotton jersey T-shirt fabric, filling the sleeve with BBs, and sewing it closed. Then I enclosed that pouch with another sleeve of the same T-shirt material. Sewing these rather than knotting them closed allows creating a mute that mutes along its full length and allows easily made mutes of lengths both shorter and longer than the socks you may have available to you. BBs work well as the weight for these, but dry (uncooked) beans or rice could also work. For these lighter materials you will most likely need a larger-diameter soft wrap to give the mute enough weight for accurate muting. With BBs as the weight, I've made mutes that work consistently and are only about two inches in diameter.

Short-length mutes are very easy to handle, so the pianist can place the mute on the strings quite quickly and remove it quickly as well. However, a longer mute may prove very useful. A two-foot (or longer) mute, one not over-packed with weighting materials, can mute a lot of strings with it, and the pianist can fold the unneeded length, and drape it off of the strings and onto the plate or tuning pins. A longer mute might also allow muting strings on both sides of one of the piano's braces with a single mute, with some of the mute arcing over the brace (see figure 5.1).

A pianist can mute strings and release them with the hand very quickly, and it's relatively easy to position and remove squeegee and weighted cloth-covered mutes quickly. There are also ways to mute notes of the piano that take a little longer to get into place and longer to remove. These are methods of muting that are types of string preparations. My experience with these mutes is that each has its own sound, and all of them sound different from muting with fingertips or the side of the hand, but there may be passages or works in which one of these muting techniques give the best sound or proves the easiest for the performer.

Figure 5.1. Weighted cloth-covered mute in place

PIANO TUNER'S MUTES AND FELT MUTING

You can mute with piano tuner's mutes. These are rubber wedges, with or without a handle, applied to the wide end of the wedge. These can be inserted and removed quickly, but you may need to use more than one mute just to mute a single note, as triple unisons require inserting two wedges. With piano tuner's mutes, you can play with the differences in timbre achieved by different placements of the mutes along the length of the strings.

You can also mute notes with a length of felt. This is a device of the piano tuner, who may take a lengthy bit of wool felt and press small loops of the felt between every pair of strings for the whole piano. Some tuners use a screwdriver blade or another tool to press a loop of the felt down between pairs of strings. Others simply press the felt loops down by gripping the felt tightly and pressing with the tip of the thumb. Either way, this preparation takes time and is the sort of preparation that probably needs to be done before the performance and works best when used for notes that need to be muted for an entire composition rather than for a section or movement. In *The Well-Prepared Piano*, Richard Bunger discusses using felt for muting and recommends specifically what he calls "safety muting." Because his book is focused on piano preparations, Bunger discusses running long strips of felt over the strings, arcing the strips over strings that won't be muted, and muting all the strings for notes that won't be used for a performance. Muting all of the notes surrounding prepared notes ensures that the performer won't accidently sound an *ordinario* piano note and break the illusion that she is not playing a piano at all.

POSTER PUTTY MUTING

Poster putty (such as Blu-Tack) can also be used to mute individual notes of the instrument.[1] Poster-putty-muted notes sound quite different from muting with the hand or fingertips, but using poster putty has some advantages. The notes can all be muted before the performance, and many notes can be muted throughout a piece. The putty *can* theoretically be removed during the performance and even put in place during the performance, but even muting a single note would take a few seconds to retrieve a ball of putty placed on the frame for the proper moment, and then the player would need to press it into place and hope that it works properly. Using a tiny bit of putty does not affect the timbre of the strings at all (and therefore is effective as a marker to indicate a harmonic node on a string, for instance). A larger ball of putty placed on the string in about the same spot that the player would use to mute with the fingers mutes the sound of that note. You should experiment with what amount gives you the best effect, but I have found a pea-sized ball, or maybe slightly larger, works well (see figure 5.2).

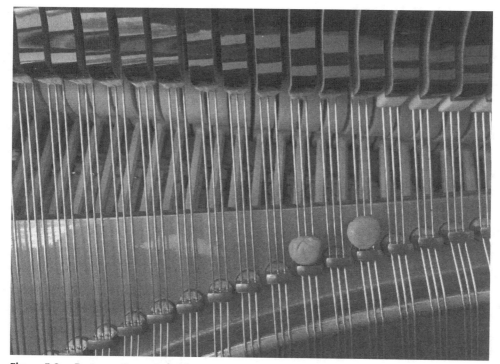

Figure 5.2.   Poster-putty-muted strings

KEY-FRAME SLIDE MUTING[2]

There's another method of muting that does not require the pianist to touch the strings or to use any extraneous objects but does require some setup time. At the moment, as far as I know, one short étude (Shockley, *thunk* [2018]) is the only work that exploits this method of muting. On a grand piano, this method of muting is made possible first by removing a bit of the cabinetry to gain access to the full key action (this is something that every tuner or technician would do to regulate or adjust the hammers or to make any other adjustments to the action that are necessary on a grand piano). On most instruments, there are two long hand screws underneath the keyboard that need to be removed, and then the key slip and the fallboard also need to be removed. Then the cheeks should be lifted out, and one can pull the key frame (with the entire keyboard and action assembly attached to it) out of the piano. For the purposes of muting the instrument in this manner, the key frame does not need to be removed from the piano but slid a very slight amount (only about nine millimeters on one semi-concert grand on which I have experimented) forward, toward the player and out of the piano. The adjustment can be about that distance for the bass end of the key assembly, and the treble end can be slid even less or not at all. In other words, rather than sliding out the whole keyboard, the movement can be to pivot it on the back corner of the treble so that the bass swings out a very slight amount (see figure 5.3).

The keys need to come forward just enough that the spoons at the back do not engage the dampers. This means that the keys engage the hammers as usual, but the dampers remain seated on the strings, effectively muting most of the notes of the piano. The notes of the topmost octave and a half or so of the instrument are produced by strings of such short lengths that their natural decay is quite brief and they have no dampers—they ring freely all the time. If you'd like to mute those strings as well, they will need to be muted in one of the other ways outlined previously (perhaps by threading the strings with wool felt, such as a strip of felt used for regulating). For the rest of the piano's range, the strings are muted with the dampers comfortably seated on them, and all the keys can be played as normal. This produces a lovely muted sound, and it's consistent over all the notes of the piano that have dampers. And, here's the truly magical aspect of muting the piano by disengaging the keyboard from the damper mechanism: The damper pedal is still engaged! This means that every note (at least every one that has a damper) that is played on the keyboard delivers a wonderful muted sound. Playing those very same keys with the damper pedal depressed, produces an ordinary piano sound—completely full and unmuted. The player can quickly alternate between the dry, dull, even woody muted sound and the full, unmuted, ordinary piano sound simply by playing completely without the damper pedal engaged or keeping it engaged.[3] I will be surprised if a composer does not use this muting technique immediately after this book hits the bookstores!

Figure 5.3.   Key slip, key blocks, and fallboard removed, action pulled out for key-frame slide muting

MUTING WITH OTHER TECHNIQUES

It may be obvious, but muted notes can be played in many ways other than with the keys, so muting can be combined with lots of other extended techniques. Pizzicato muted notes are very effective, and a pianist can mute a string and also pluck that same string with the same hand. Muted harmonics work well (at least for the lower, fuller overtones of the bass-register strings), and yes, muted pizzicato harmonics are also possible. The player can also mute a string or strings with a fingertip of one hand and scrape the windings of that same string or strings with a fingernail on a finger of the other hand.

Another nice effect that can be produced while muting with a fingertip: The timbre can be gradually and continuously changed by sliding the muting finger along the length of the string, thereby pressing different nodes of the string and muting and emphasizing different partials.

FULL DAMPENING OF STRING SOUND

Whereas all of the muting techniques I've covered so far involve muting the strings of the piano to produce a darker sound, one that's less rich in high overtones and has a slightly shorter overall decay than an *ordinario* note in the same register, there are also "extreme" muting effects. These involve dampening the strings in such a way that striking the key produces no truly pitched sound. The strings are not allowed to ring as they normally would. One way to produce this sort of sound is to press the strings with the whole hand or with the whole forearm. I have also used a large phone book (of the old-fashioned yellow pages sort), and other heavy items can be used, such as a heavy hardcover book or a brick wrapped in a towel. Once the strings are muted in one of these ways, the keys can be struck as usual to produce the dull sound of the hammer hitting the string. Another very nice sound, a sort of bass drum thud, can be produced by muting the string with a phone book or with some other large heavy object, holding the damper pedal down to allow other strings in other registers to ring freely, and then hitting several of the muted strings with the palm of the hand.

MUTING NOTATION

Though there are a few composers who have tried alternate ways of notating muted notes, a standard is now mostly in place. Muted notes for the piano are notated just as hand-muted ("stopped") notes for the horn are: with the + sign placed above or below the notehead (on the opposite side as the note's stem; see figures 5.4 and 5.5). I suggest that the score include a key that explains that the + sign indicates mute, or on the score page itself the composer can include an explanatory note the first time the indication appears. If the only muting is single notes muted with the fingertips, then the plus sign along with one explanatory note is probably sufficient. If the score uses any other form of muting or if it uses multiple muting

Figure 5.4. Muting notation

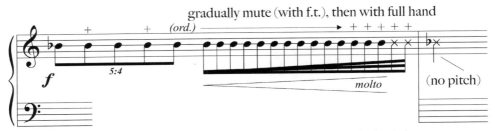

Figure 5.5. Gradual transition from open sound to fully muted on a single pitch

techniques, then the score should explain the muting techniques and implements; most of these are not standardized. The + sign should be used for all muted notes, but a composer who is using multiple types of muting may want to create modified + signs for secondary and tertiary muting techniques (placing the + sign within a box for one, the + sign within a circle for another, the + underscored for a third, and so forth).

Composer Nicholas Deyoe's *Ashley, Christopher, Andy* for cello, piano, and percussion with two assistants assigns one assistant to the piano (the other assists the percussionist). The pianist's assistant has a separate line on the score and controls the placement and pressure applied to towels that are positioned over specific ranges inside the piano. The assistant also does some muting by hand to smaller ranges of notes (and at one point even assists on the keys, playing the topmost C on the instrument in a passage, that keeps the pianist busy with playing clusters).

As mentioned previously, finger muting is quite a flexible technique and can easily be combined with others. Figure 5.6 is a score example with finger muting in combination with a pizzicato performed right at the end of the string.

Figure 5.6. Muted *sul ponticello pizzicato*, Shockley, *wndhm (1785)*

6

Harmonics

Harmonics on the piano, especially on the bass strings where they can speak very loudly, are among the easiest nontraditional techniques to perform. Harmonics also lend themselves to combination with various "off the keys" techniques.

UNDERSTANDING HARMONICS

Every note on the piano sounded by striking a single key is a complex entity of partials, composed of each individual string resonating as a whole and in many component parts all at once, along with lots of sympathetic resonances produced by other strings of the instrument. The string vibrating as a whole produces the fundamental frequency of each string, and for the piano, the fundamental is the most prominent frequency each string produces when set into motion by the hammer's strike. However, if the pianist lightly touches a node on the string with a fingertip of one hand and sets the string into motion by striking the corresponding key with the other hand, the fundamental is dampened, and one of the many overtones that that string also produces rises to prominence.

First, some of the basic terms: *Partials* refer to all of the component vibrations of a resonating body. *Overtones* are any of those component vibrating frequencies that are *above* the fundamental. *Harmonics* are kinds of partials not including the fundamental—*harmonic* is an abbreviation of the term *harmonic partial*, and both of these terms refer to partials with whole-number ratios with the fundamental. The first partial is the fundamental. The first harmonic (or harmonic partial or overtone) can be explained by the ratio of 1:2, with the first harmonic vibrating at double the frequency of the fundamental. The ratio of the fundamental to the second overtone is 1:3, and so forth (see figure 6.1).

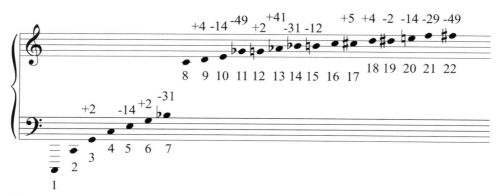

Figure 6.1.   The lowest partials of a low-C string on the piano

The longer the vibrating string length, the louder the harmonic, so harmonics ring better on bass strings than on tenor or treble strings, and they are louder on the longer bass strings of concert grand pianos than on the much shorter bass strings of baby grands and upright pianos. In addition, generally, the lower a particular overtone is in the harmonic series, the louder and easier that overtone is to produce, again mostly because a lower overtone means a greater vibrating length of that particular string.

The first overtone, produced by the string vibrating in two halves, is the loudest harmonic produced on any one of a piano's strings. When striking a key and sounding a piano string *ordinario*, the first overtone is part of the composite sound but does not speak nearly as loudly as the fundamental. With the string vibrating as a whole, it has two nodes that correspond to the two fixed ends of the speaking length of the string. At those nodes, the fundamental has zero amplitude. At the halfway point between those nodes is the antinode, where the fundamental has maximum amplitude. This halfway point on each string is also the node for the octave harmonic, the first overtone. If you lightly touch this node, you dampen the fundamental, bisect the string, and make the first overtone ring most loudly from each half of the string.

Though this tends to be a very loud and resonant harmonic on the lowest bass strings of larger grand pianos, reaching the node on these strings requires most pianists to stand and extend well over the inside of the piano. On most concert grand pianos, the octave harmonic easily sounds from the lowest string all the way through the strings of the tenor register of the piano and well into the treble register as well. Other than a few specialized straight-strung instruments, all modern pianos are overstrung, with the bass strings overlapping some of the tenor strings. This means than the bass strings obscure the octave node (along with nodes for several other of the lower overtones) for some of the tenor-register strings, making some overtones in the tenor register mostly unavailable to the player.[1]

Figure 6.2. Fifth partial harmonics, George Crumb, *Gnomic Varia-tions*, "Var. 6—*largamente, retoricamente*," p. 11, end of first system
Copyright © 1982 by C. F. Peters Corporation. Used by permission.

HARMONICS INTRODUCE MICROTONES

Because harmonics ring the string in whole-number ratios with the fundamental string length, these overtones naturally are in just intonation. Especially higher in the overtone series, many harmonics are quite distant from the nearest equal-tempered note produced normally by striking a key and sounding the full string or strings with the hammer. There are also a few prominent lower overtones that happen to be quite distant from the corresponding note in equal temperament. Harmonics open up some beautiful just intonation notes, or they can allow interplay with the microtonal differences between these notes and near-frequency, conventional equal-tempered notes.

On the keys (in equal temperament)

Bb3: 233.08 Hz
Gb4: 369.99 Hz
Ab4: 415.30 Hz

As harmonics over low C (32.70 Hz)

Bb3 (flatter than on the key): 228.9 Hz
Gb4 (flatter than on the key): 358.7 Hz
Ab4 (sharper than on the key): 424.1 Hz

MARKING NODES

Locating nodes on the strings in performance can be nerve-wracking. The common method of marking nodes used to be to mark lightly on the strings with chalk *near* the node needed for each harmonic. I specify *near* the node because if you mark with chalk *on* the node, then the first time you touch that node to play a harmonic, you are likely to rub off most or all of the chalk, making locating that same harmonic later in the piece challenging. If you are marking with chalk, I suggest marking the string a finger thickness before or beyond the node's actual placement. Then, you simply practice touching that finger thickness short of the marks each time.

Several piano technicians have told me that they detest finding chalk inside a piano and that cleaning away all of the chalk dust takes a lot of time and is tedious work. The Piano Technicians Guild says that chalk may be used for marking the steel strings, but it must never be used for the wound strings. I recommend simply avoiding chalk entirely. In addition to chalk (on the steel strings), pianists have tried many different materials for marking directly on strings, including grease pencils, china markers, nail polish (on steel strings only), permanent marker (steel strings) or with white correction fluid, such as White-Out (steel strings). Though it is possible to remove such marks after performance by using something abrasive on the strings, doing so is generally a very bad idea, so I don't recommend any of these methods of marking.

Fortunately, there are a few other effective ways of marking nodes on the strings that require minimal cleanup work. One is to attach a thin strip of painter's tape perpendicular to the string and across the node (painter's tape is better than most other varieties of tape for this purpose as it leaves no residue; see figure 6.3). Painter's tape also comes in a variety of colors, which may be helpful in performance by allowing the player to mark different nodes or strings needed for different phrases of a piece and differentiating them by using strips of different colors of tape. If the composition calls for lots of different harmonics or multiple harmonics on the same string, the player may very well want to differentiate the harmonics by using different colors or sizes of the strips of tape placed on the strings.

One method of marking the bass strings favored by pianist Herbert Henck is to tie and knot a piece of colored thread around the string and then slide the loop into position with the knot directly over the appropriate node.[2] The windings of the bass strings can help to keep the thread in place when the strings vibrate. This marking method does not work on flat steel strings.

Another method of marking nodes that I recommend is using a tiny ball of poster putty (such as Blu-Tack) on or very near the nodes. Press a tiny ball for each marker lightly onto the string so as not to press any of the putty into the windings on a bass string, where it may be difficult or impossible to remove later.

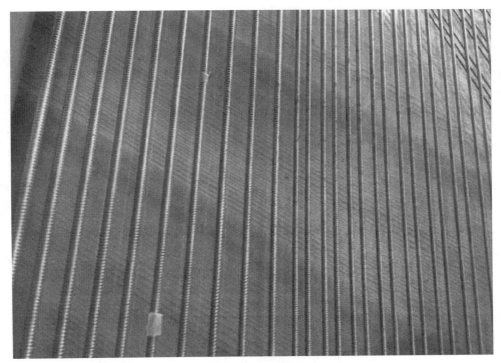

Figure 6.3.   Various nodes marked with painter's tape

Use a small pinch of the putty (about half the size of a standard pencil eraser—or even less) because a larger amount (the size of a full pencil eraser or larger) will likely change the tone of the string at least slightly. If you manage to press the putty securely into place, in performance you may be able to touch the putty very lightly to sound the harmonic. The putty is easy to spot visually and easy to find with the fingertip, so I prefer marking with poster putty to marking with strips of tape. Marking with poster putty, thin strips of painter's tape, or (on the wound strings) knotted loops of colored thread are better methods than marking with chalk, especially because they leave no residue in or on the piano, which will keep your piano technician happier. They are also all better methods than any of the pencils, liquids, or markers, as each of these has the potential to damage the finish of the steel strings, to dull the exterior of the copper-wound strings, and in some cases to drip onto other even more delicate internal piano parts.

Two piano manufacturers have modified designs of their instruments to assist pianists playing harmonics. Steingraeber & Söhne has designed a grand piano with indications cast into the plate to help the pianist locate some of the harmonic nodes. Sauter now makes its Omega 220 (a 7'3" semi-concert grand) with what it calls an "extra register." This consists of curved lines painted directly on top of the sound-board showing the nodes for three prominent harmonics in three different colors.

PLAYING HARMONICS

Almost all harmonic techniques require touching the string with a fingertip at the appropriate node. There is one node for the first overtone (second harmonic partial) at the midpoint of the speaking string length. For the second overtone, as the string is divided into thirds, there are two nodes that could be stopped: One—that a performer at the keyboard is likely to use—is located a third of the string length beyond the bridge near the tuning pins, and the second is two-thirds of the string length from that same bridge and therefore closer to the tail of the piano than to the keys. In other words, once the player has located the node for the first overtone at the midpoint of the string, nodes for every higher overtone can be located closer to the player seated or standing at the keyboard than the midpoint of the string. To dampen the fundamental and sound any particular harmonic, the pianist should touch the appropriate node with the flesh at the very tip of a finger. The player should use the smallest area of contact between the flesh and the string as possible so as to allow the harmonic to sound freely. For the strings in the top octave of the piano, even the lowest overtone is difficult to produce. Because the resonating string length is so short and the node proportionally so tiny for these highest-register strings, it is difficult if not impossible not to dampen the harmonic from sounding at all. Even the very tip of the fingers is too broad to be in contact with only the node.

In the notes to the score of his *Gnomic Variations*, George Crumb recommends removing contact with the fingertip that is touching the node as soon as the harmonic is sounded to allow the harmonic to resonate more fully, and this is indeed very good advice. Using a light touch with the fingertip only at the node and then removing the stopping finger the instant the string is set into motion results in a fuller harmonic. As Crumb puts it, "For a more beautiful resonance, the finger touching the nodal point should come off the string *immediately* after the key is struck."[3]

It is also possible to stop a string at a node using some material placed at the node of the string rather than a fingertip. Most such devices I have used take a moment to situate, and another moment to remove, and between those two actions the fundamental (or any different harmonic beyond the one produced with that particular node stopped) are completely unavailable. Mostly rather than being described as techniques for playing harmonics, these are preparations that, in addition to producing a color change to the string's output, also result in a harmonic speaking from a particular string or set of unisons.

OTHER HARMONIC TECHNIQUES

In addition to playing one overtone at a time, a pianist can play two, three, or even four harmonics at once. This is easiest using adjacent strings. George Crumb

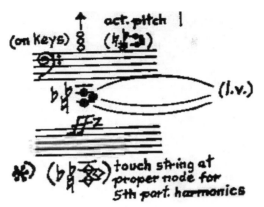

Figure 6.4. Harmonic cluster, George Crumb,
Vox Balaenae
Copyright © 1971 by C. F. Peters Corporation. Used by
  permission.

takes advantage of this in his 1971 trio *Vox Balaenae* by asking the pianist to play
octave harmonics in three-note chromatic clusters (see figure 6.4).

For three-note and four-note harmonics, the notes must be in close intervals,
so Crumb's three-note chromatic clusters are quite easy to play. For two-note
harmonic constructions, a larger interval between the two notes is also possible,
so long as there is no brace interrupting the span (and with an outer limit set by
the particular pianist's finger length). I think, for most pianists, a minor seventh
and perhaps even a larger span should be practical. Pianists with longer fingers
may be able to touch two nodes on strings an octave or even a minor ninth apart.

For three-note constructions, all qualities of triads work (at least in close spacing and root position; see figure 6.5). The string spacing allows this from the bass

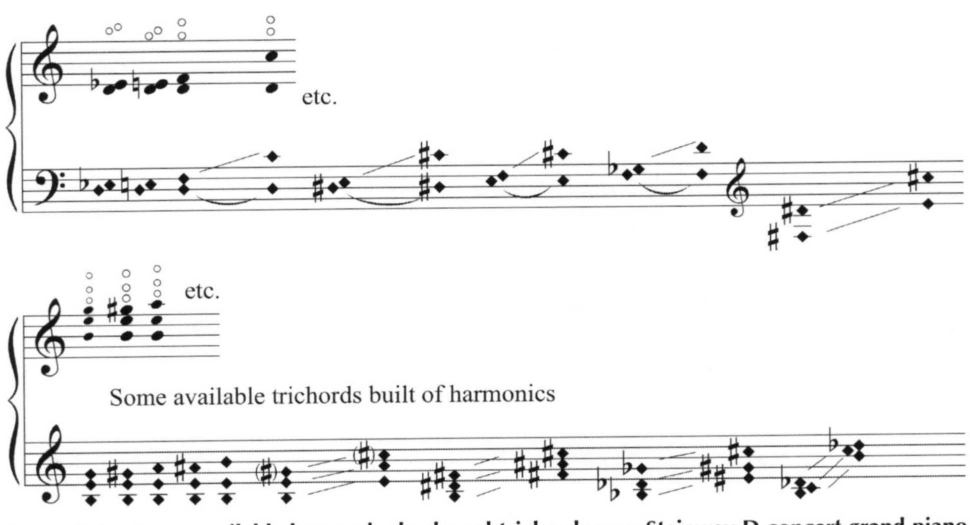

Some available harmonic dyads

etc.

etc.

Some available trichords built of harmonics

Figure 6.5. Some available harmonic dyads and trichords on a Steinway D concert grand piano

through high-middle register, but the overstrung bass strings block the needed access for some of the tenor register. Harmonics for very short strings at the very top of the piano's compass are mostly very difficult to sound if not impossible, and for several notes just below (starting at about D6), the dampers block access.

All of the two-, three-, and four-note chords described so far are played assuming that these are formed on different strings (or different unison sets of strings) but using the nodes on these various strings corresponding to the same division of the string. I have shown above a major triad, and it is easiest to finger the three constituent notes of this triad by touching, for instance, the second partial node on each of the three strings (or string unison sets). Using these corresponding nodes has the added benefit that the harmonics produced by the same proportion of string on strings of similar length near to each other in register produce a dynamically balanced set of harmonics—the dyad or trichord is balanced. It is possible at least to finger different (noncorresponding) nodes on strings close to each other, say the fifth partial harmonic on the C1 strings and the fourth partial harmonic on the E1 strings. These both produce as a harmonic the pitch E in the same octave, but the fifth partial is fourteen cents flatter than the corresponding equal-tempered note, and the fourth partial harmonic is in tune with the equal-tempered note.

A composer could exploit approaching different nodes to find larger intervals available in different places in the overtone series on nearby strings (unison sets). In doing so, a pianist could sound intervals between those two notes larger than the octave or so graspable when touching the corresponding nodes, but I think the partials that are significantly different in their tuning from their nearest equal-tempered neighbors open up even more striking possibilities. One could write a microtonal trill or tremolo. Sounding the fourth partial of B♭1 produces B♭3, and sounding the seventh partial of C1 also produces B♭3. However, while the fourth partial B♭ is in tune with the B♭ as played on the key, the seventh partial B♭ is thirty-one cents flat! Touching both of these (noncorresponding) nodes and then playing the two corresponding keys in quick alternation produces a microtonal tremolo (see figure 6.6).[4]

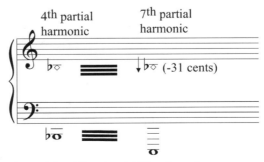

Figure 6.6. Microtonal trill or tremolo

A pianist can easily produce a glissando of natural harmonics by repeatedly sounding the string with one hand (by striking the key or plucking or striking the string with a yarn mallet or by some other means) and lightly sliding a fingertip of the other hand along the length of the string. Especially along the lower bass strings, almost every position along the string serves as a node for a harmonic that speaks well, so with each change of the fingertip's position on the string, another harmonic sounds. If the player continues this across a significant portion of the string, various overtones reappear, so this "glissando" is not a long steady ascent or descent.

Harmonics don't have to be sounded by playing on the keys. It is also possible to play harmonics pizzicato or with other means of setting the strings into motion. While one hand touches the node, the pianist can set the string into motion by plucking the string with fingers, fingernails, or various plectra; by striking the string (with a mallet or any other striking device); by bowing the string with a tongue depressor bow (see chapter 8); by bowing with monofilament; or by using an EBow. Plucking a harmonic close to the tuning-pin end of the string (sul ponticello) is particularly effective. When plucking a string in order to sound a harmonic, the point of contact of the plectrum needs to be narrow so that the harmonic speaks. Using the flesh of the finger for plucking may not allow the harmonic to ring freely (your mileage may vary depending on the fleshiness of your own finger). For the same reason, a thin but not-too-flexible guitar pick may also prove more effective than a broader, softer pick material. A muted harmonic (which can be played using a set-in-place mute or with an assistant muting the string or touching the node for the harmonic) is a subtle effect, providing a darker, "woodier"-sounding harmonic than an unmuted one. And, yes, even a muted pizzicato harmonic is possible—even without an assistant. The pianist can touch the node with a fingertip of one hand and with the other hand mute the end of the string lightly with the fleshy side of the first joint of the thumb and pluck with the index finger.

NOTATING HARMONICS

Through the years, different composers have chosen different solutions for how to notate piano harmonics. Kurt Stone in his book on notation suggests using an ordinary note for the key that should be struck (or for the string or strings on which the harmonic will be located, if the harmonic is sounded in some other way than by striking the key); in other words, the fundamental gets an ordinary note. Above that note, Stone recommends showing the resultant pitch as a small, stemless notehead within parentheses and then placing a small circle above that note (a common symbol meaning "harmonic" in string writing).

I believe this notation works well and suggest that placing the resultant note in a separate staff from the one used to indicate the string (and possibly the key) on which this harmonic is located helps to clarify.

Beyond this notation, some composers add a bit of text that locates the produced note within the overtone series of the fundamental, saying, for example, "fifth partial." This extra information is not necessary but helps to ensure that the performer understands which overtone of which fundamental the composer really wants. For overtones that are noticeably distant from their nearest equal-tempered neighbor, I also recommend indicating with an accidental or other symbol that this note is approximately a quarter-tone flat or whatever the case may be (alternately, the composer can specify in text near the notated harmonic "forty-one cents flat"; see figure 6.7).

Figure 6.7.   Notation for harmonics

Composer Johan Svensson, working closely with pianist Jonas Olsson, has devised a notation that goes a step further, using diamond-shaped noteheads to indicate the keys to be played, showing the resultant pitches on staves above the fingered notes and, between, indicating both the fractional proportion of the string and the particular node to be fingered on the string. In an email from the composer on June 15, 2017, Svensson explained that he and Olsson have opted to add this information to show the pianist in the score which nodal point to use because this tells the pianist something about hand position inside the piano, which is useful information when the composer asks for many different harmonics to be played in quick succession, as in Svensson's *Study for Piano*, no. 2 (see figure 6.8). The fraction gives the proportional division of the string, and the number below it gives the node to be used, numbered from the tuning-pin end of the string. A notation of *5/1* divides the string into five equal segments (the fifth partial harmonic) and indicates playing this harmonic at the first nodal point from the end of the string; the *2* below the *5/1* indicates using the second finger. The *9/2* given for the first note of the example indicates the ninth partial harmonic played at its second

Figure 6.8. Harmonics and multiple nodal positions, Johan Svensson, *Study for Piano*, no. 2, m. 1

nodal point. This nodal point is essentially halfway between the *4/1* division and *5/1* division of the string, so very close in placement to the fifth partial harmonic to be played next.[5] Svensson's étude capitalizes on the proximity of so many different notes available as harmonics by using a narrow band of strings. The moves from one node to another here mostly traverse very small distances, so the pianist has a home hand position for phrases. Note the tempo: this short study demonstrates just how quickly a player can sound harmonics.

SELECTING PARTIALS

Harmonics are available on the strings for most of the compass of the piano. The strings for the topmost register of the instrument are so short that even the octave harmonic does not ring in a full way for the top octave. On a well-maintained 7'3" piano, I can produce the octave harmonic on every note up to C6. For the next few notes, the dampers cover the midpoint of the strings, and above those, the strings are just too short to produce even the octave harmonic reliably. The third partial is also very prominent and should be available on the strings through the D5 fundamental (though, again, some strings in the tenor register are covered, in this case by the overstrung bass strings).

The Sauter Omega 220 piano provides painted curves on the soundboard, indicating the placement of the most prominent harmonic partials (see figure 6.9). These painted curves are color-coded, with a black line indicating the placement for an octave above the fundamental (the second partial), a red line indicating a twelfth above the fundamental (the third partial), and a light blue line indicating placement for two octaves above the fundamental (the fourth partial). The pianist playing one of these Sauter pianos can look through the strings to the soundboard markings and see where the nodes are.

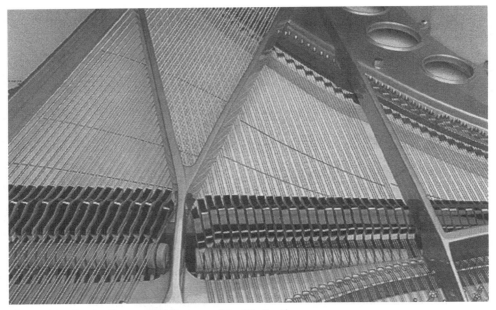

Figure 6.9. Sauter Omega 220 "extra register" indications

Some of the overtones are so prominent that their nodal placement is more forgiving, and their nodes seem "big." Especially on the fat, long bass strings, it is easy to play the second partial by touching within an inch or so of the midpoint of the string. This overtone rings so easily that it overwhelms the much higher partials (which would activate much tinier lengths of string) whose nodes are very close to it. A similar phenomenon can be witnessed with bowed string instruments, in which the octave harmonic above the fundamental may be activated by a very hasty slide of the left hand to the second partial node and then immediately away. There is a good amount of virtuoso string writing that takes advantage of how easily the second partial rings and how little time a finger of the left hand needs to touch this node to enable the bow's movement to sound it.

The most practical, and in some ways the most useful, partials are mostly clustered low in the overtone series. Certainly, on the lowest bass strings, it is very easy to produce most of the overtones through the eleventh partial. I have had some difficulty getting the sixth partial to speak, but all of the others in that part of the series ring easily. I am especially fond of the fifth partial (two octaves and a major third above the fundamental), the seventh partial (two octaves and a minor seventh above the fundamental), and the eleventh partial (three octaves and a diminished fifth above the fundamental), as these three partials are among those that are palpably distant from their nearest equal-tempered equivalent. By playing these overtones, suddenly a piano, tuned as usual in equal temperament, can produce microtones—notes that produce beats with their near neighbors played directly on the keys as ordinary.

Testing on a Sauter Omega 220 and using the lowest C on the instrument as the fundamental, I have been able to play partials 1 through 20 (with some difficulty in producing partials 6 and 16), as well as a few of the even higher partials (including 22, 24, and 29). Not all of these very high partials are easy to produce reliably, and if the pianist is using a fingertip to touch the node on the string to produce the harmonic, the thickness of that particular fingertip may determine whether a particular harmonic sounds freely or not.

OTHER WAYS TO SOUND HARMONICS

Up to this point, I have only detailed sounding harmonics by touching a node with the fingertip of one hand while sounding the note by depressing the corresponding key as usual. Nodes can be touched with simple preparations, and harmonics can be sounded in many other ways!

First, another way to secure the string at a node (in addition to touching the node with a fingertip) is to insert an object between the strings at a node. Cap pencil erasers work well for this purpose (see figure 6.10). Cut a slit across opposite edges of the base of the eraser, and snap the eraser onto the middle string of a three-string

Figure 6.10.   Cap erasers placed at nodal points on strings covered by overstrung bass strings

unison set so that the outer edges of the eraser press against strings 1 and 3 of the set; then slide the eraser along the strings into position at a nodal point for a prominent harmonic. If you then activate the strings by striking the key, the mass of the eraser modifies the sound of the note and produces changed timbre and pitch. However, if you touch the head of the eraser with a fingertip and strike the key while touching it, instead of the "prepared piano" sound, you can simply hear the proper harmonic for that nodal point. Preparing the string in this way means that you lose access to that note's fundamental, but it also means that it is possible to play harmonics even on strings that are mostly covered by the bass strings. Simply insert the eraser into the appropriate strings, and then, on most instruments, you should be able to squeeze a finger between the covering bass strings well enough to touch the eraser and sound the harmonic. If the eraser is too tall and once in position it touches the overstrung bass strings, then remove it, clip off part of the eraser top with scissors, and return it to position. So far, I have not uncovered a piece that requires this sort of preparation in order to produce harmonics.

It is certainly also possible to sound harmonics in ways other than striking the keys with one hand while touching nodes with the other. On the wound strings, harmonics can also be activated by a quick scrape on the string windings (most effective on the longer strings of the instrument's lowest register; see figure 6.11). If the pianist first raises the dampers with the pedal to allow the strings to vibrate freely, it is quite easy to sound harmonics by plucking the string (with fingertips, fingernails, or a guitar pick or other plectrum; see figure 6.12). A pianist can also touch a node with a finger of one hand and strike the string with a mallet in the other hand. Basically, the only limitations are the number of hands needed for a particular technique and the audibility limits set by the overall string length, the vibrating string length, and how well the par-

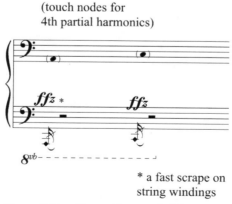

(touch nodes for
4th partial harmonics)

* a fast scrape on
string windings

Figure 6.11. Harmonic sounded by scrape on the string winding

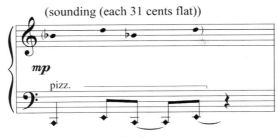

(sounding (each 31 cents flat))

l.h.: touch nodes for
7th partial harmonics

r.h.: pluck C and E strings
with fingertip

Figure 6.12. Pizzicato harmonics

ticular technique itself speaks. The EBow is particularly effective at bringing out particular harmonics, and the player can slide an EBow along a string or unison set and pause over different nodes, bringing out different harmonics and smoothly morphing from one to another.

7

The Piano Is a Big Box, and the
Pianist Is a Noise-Making Animal

HITTING THE INSTRUMENT AND
VARIOUS OTHER PERCUSSIVE SOUNDS

Striking a Single String

The piano is a specialized type of percussion instrument. As such, it takes no great leap to consider striking the strings with objects other than the piano's hammers. With smaller beaters, it is possible to strike a single string or unison set. If the player is armed with a beater in each hand, it is possible to play the piano like it's a cimbalom. Beaters intended for cimbalom or for hammered dulcimer work well for this. Cimbalom beaters (often called hammers), in particular, are available with a variety of striking surface materials, from plain wood to wood wrapped with string to calfskin. Any of these can be used to play on the strings of the piano. Cristofori's most significant change from the harpsichords he was then currently building to his piano was that, rather than plucking the strings as in the harpsichord, the piano struck the strings with hammers. The hammerheads for Cristofori's instruments are parchment rolls faced with a thin strip of leather. They are small and not particularly robust, but they are hammers used to strike the strings, and striking the strings with other implements is an easy way to uncover additional timbres.

It is also possible to strike individual strings with small plastic, rubber, or yarn mallets; chopsticks; teaspoons; metal knitting needles; and wooden dowels, and each of these materials produces a slightly different timbre. Mark Engler had the idea that a guitar's strings could be struck with a hammer-like beater to get a hammered-dulcimer-like sound from it and created the Engle hammer. This small beater with wooden handle and a polymer head also works well for striking individual strings and unison sets on the piano.

109

Striking Multiple Strings Simultaneously

If the musical passage does not require hitting individual notes but rather asks the player to strike multiple notes at a time, then many other beater choices present themselves. Larger percussion mallets and beaters, such as timpani mallets or bass drum mallets, can be used for a single strike to a range of strings or for multiple attacks in a row—a "roll" on the strings of the piano. Single hits to a range of strings or rolls can also be performed with the hands; a hit with a flat hand—palm and fingers—can be very effective, especially to a set of strings in the bass register while the damper pedal is depressed. Such a hit sets lots of strings in motion with the direct contact from the hand and also rings the rest of the piano's strings sympathetically. Barney Childs's ensemble work *Jack's New Bag* has the pianist hit the strings with a plastic flyswatter.

Several composers have taken advantage of balls to sound the strings. C. Curtis-Smith's *Rhapsodies*, which makes extensive use of bowed strings, also has the performer sound the strings by rolling a golf ball on them. For his 1972–1973 work *A Song of the Degrees* for two pianos and percussion, Curtis-Smith devised another way to play on the strings with a golf ball; he specifies extending a length of tubing of slightly larger diameter than the ball just above a set of unison strings and dropping the golf ball through the tubing to guide it in bouncing on the strings. Priscilla McLean's 1975–1977 work *Invisible Chariots* uses tennis balls on the strings to sound them. In Harry Somers's 1968 theater work *Improvisation*, performers bounce both tennis balls and ping-pong balls on the strings of a piano. Alcides Lanza's 1971 work *plectros III* for piano and tape makes several uses of the synthetic rubber Wham-O Super Ball, asking the performer to bounce the ball on the strings, to rub a Super Ball on the bass strings, and to make moaning sounds by rubbing the piano's lid with Super Ball mallets (Lanza was one of the first musicians to create mallets with Super Balls for their heads).

If the strings are first muted by leaving the dampers in place (not engaging the damper pedal) and then further dampened by placing a heavy object on the bass strings, such as an old-fashioned phone book, a palm hit to the bass range of strings covered by the heavy object produces a dull thud, somewhat like a concert bass drum hit when its head is muted.

Striking the Piano, Other Inside Surfaces

There are, of course, other places inside the piano to tap or hit. On many pianos, hitting the structural braces produces a dark, woody sound. Depressing the damper pedal and then hitting these braces on many instruments produces a clearly pitched tone, a different one for each brace, and the piano's strings will vibrate in sympathy with this. A louder sound can be coaxed from the braces by hitting them with a yarn mallet.

Flat spots on the plate can also be hit with the knuckles or soft mallets. Take care of the finish on the braces and the plate—you should not use hard mallets on these surfaces if you do not wish to damage them.

The soundboard is built to amplify sound and transfer that energy into moving a lot of air to get the sound to the listener's ears, so tapping or hitting the soundboard can produce a full percussive sound. Grand pianos give the pianist access to the soundboard through various sound holes scattered around the surface of the plate where it is not needed for attaching hitch pins, braces, and other components (see figure 7.1).

Figure 7.1.   Grand piano plate with eight sound holes

In addition, the plate for most models of grand piano either starts just to the left of the lowest bass string or has a large gap in the plate between the lowest bass string and the inner rim of the piano (see figure 7.2). Either way, therefore, on most grand pianos, the pianist has access to a large section of the soundboard to the left of the lowest bass string. For knuckle raps or soft mallet hits to the soundboard, hitting within this space likely works better than trying to hit the soundboard through one of the much smaller sound holes.[1]

Several composers have asked for percussive playing involving the tuning pins. Sofia Gubaidulina asks for a glissando across the tuning pins with a bamboo stick in her *Piano Sonata* (see figure 7.3). Helmut Lachenmann asks for a similar glissando across the tuning pins with chopsticks in *Guero*. *Guero* also asks the pianist to grip the end of an individual tuning pin and pluck it. More recently Mu-Xuan Lin asks for a similar glissando on the tuning pins but with a credit card in her *Pale Fire* (2015), calling the technique *peg guiro* in reference to Lachenmann's use of the technique (see figure 7.4).

Figure 7.2.   Grand piano, large gap in the plate near the lowest bass string

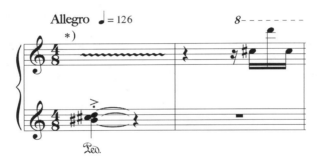

*) Glissando on piano pegs with bamboo stick.

Figure 7.3.   Glissando on the tuning pins with a bamboo stick, Gubaidulina, *Piano Sonata* (1965)

Replicated by author.

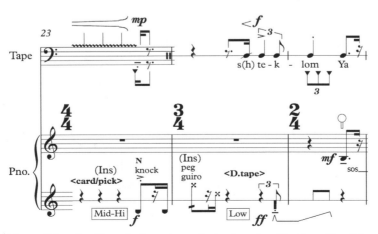

Figure 7.4.   Credit card glissando on the tuning pins, Mu-Xuan Lin, *Pale Fire*, mm. 23–25

Striking the Piano, Outside Surfaces

The outside of the piano, being mostly wood, can also be used as a percussion instrument. In addition to playing on and hitting the key surfaces (covered in chapter 4), there are lots of other places to hit. For almost all of these exterior piano surfaces, composers should restrict themselves to hitting with their fingers and hands or perhaps soft mallets, lest they risk marring the finish of the instrument. Medium to hard mallets or any harder beaters will almost assuredly damage the finish and quite possibly the wood underneath it.

Slamming the fallboard against the cabinet behind it can produce a very big sound—if you engage the damper pedal first, this fallboard slam sets the piano's strings to vibrating, adding all of that resonance to the percussive sound of the slam itself. This became a popular gesture in piano compositions and in improvisations involving the piano in the 1970s and may have become a modernist cliché at this point.

Other surfaces that can easily be hit (at least with the fingertips, knuckles, or an open-handed slap) include the music desk, the key blocks and cheeks placed on either side of the keyboard, the fallboard (on its underside when open, on its top when covering the keys), the sides of the instrument, the top or underside of the lid, the key slip in front of the keys, the underside of the key bed, and (though not part of the piano itself) the bench and its various parts.

Other Friction Sounds

Friction sounds like those covered in chapter 4 are not limited to the strings. A Super Ball mallet dragged on practically any of the piano's furniture surfaces makes some sound (though it may also leave residue on the surface). Aaron Holloway-Nahum's *Remember Me?* (2015) for two pianos and two toy pianos asks for Super Ball mallet drags across the fallboard and the piano bench (neither is a particularly resonant surface, but both produce some sound).

Though it is a delicate sound, rubbing paper on various surfaces of the piano can produce a white noise effect. Stephen Scott's *Aurora Ficta (False Dawn)* (2008), written for his Bowed Piano Ensemble (one piano, multiple performers), has several of the performers "bowing" the structural braces on the plate by running long strips of paper underneath them. My trio *errours, faults, sinnes, folies* asks the pianist to slide paper against paper on the shelf to either side of the music rack, providing a gentle bed of noise.

There are also several pieces that call for the pianist to play percussion instruments on or near the piano while also playing on the piano. The next section, "pianist as noisemaker," covers many of those.

Several composers have explored bouncing balls on the strings to sound them. They also have asked the pianist first to place a ball or balls on the strings and set the strings in motion by playing on the keys; the vibrating strings set the balls into motion, and the rebounds restrike the strings. If the balls are used to strike the string, then they belong here in the percussion section. If they are used passively—rested on the strings and left to vibrate as the strings are set into motion in other ways (such as by playing on the keys), then they more properly belong in chapter 9 as examples of surface preparations.

PIANIST AS NOISEMAKER

The second section of this chapter covers techniques that involve the player making percussive sounds "near" the instrument (such as vocal percussive sounds, clapping, and stomping) and using the instrument as a resonator for other things, as well as additional tasks for the performer (whistling, singing, moaning, speaking, train sounds, popping balloons, playing harmonica). For example, Crumb's *Makrokosmos*, book 1, in the fifth piece of the set "The Phantom Gondolier," asks the pianist to moan, hum, and sing. In the tenth piece of Crumb's *Makrokosmos*, book 2, he requires the pianist to whistle in several ways, including ordinary whistling, with molto vibrato ("quasi Theremin"), and senza vibrato.

Asking the pianist to whistle and make various vocal sounds is not a new thing. Pianist and composer Thomas "Blind Tom" Wiggins's piano solo depiction of the Civil War Battle of Bull Run, *The Battle of Manassas*, has the pianist whistle and make "chugging" vocal sounds, both in imitation of a train (see figure 7.5). More recently Crumb's *Vox Balaenae* (1972) and Shockley's *Hoc florentes arbor* (2016; see figure 7.6), each a chamber work including flute, employ the pianist's whistling as a way of approaching the flute's sound.

Aaron Holloway-Nahum's *Remember Me?* for two performers playing two pianos and two toy pianos has the performers do some setup before the performance, attaching balloons to the underside of one of the pianos. Then, during the performance, one pianist lies on the floor, extending partially underneath the piano, and pops the balloons.

Figure 7.5.   Whistling and vocal "train" sounds, Wiggins, *The Battle of Manassas*, page 9, fourth system.

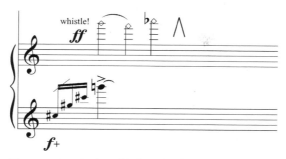

Figure 7.6. Pianist whistles, Shockley, *Hoc florentes arbor* (2016), page 4, first system (unmeasured).

Speaking Pianist

The piano recitation, or melodrama, was a genre explored by many composers, especially many in the nineteenth century, including Franz Schubert, Robert Schumann, Franz Liszt, and Richard Strauss. Strauss, for example, composed his *Enoch Arden* in 1897 on a text by Tennyson for the actor Ernst von Possart. Liszt composed a handful of melodramas, including *Lenore* (1857–1858) and *Der Traurige Mönch* (1860). Though these melodramas were all conceived to be performed by a pianist (usually the composer) and a separate person delivering the text (often a professional actor), it is a very small step from these nineteenth-century piano recitations to composers asking the pianist to serve as reciter. George Crumb, for example, asks the pianist to speak a text dramatically within "The Phantom Gondolier" piece from his *Makrokosmos*, volume 1, and within just a few measures also has the pianist hum, sing, and half-sing.

Pianist and composer Frederic Rzewski, a frequent performer of his own music, has several works that ask for speech and other vocal sounds from the pianist. His *De Profundis* (1992) specifies, in addition to speech, rhythmically notated breathing, grunts, and—yes—singing from the pianist (see figure 7.7). It also asks that the pianist wear an attached microphone and hit various parts of her own body,

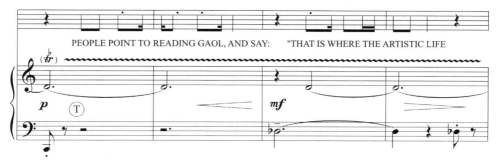

Figure 7.7. Speaking pianist, Frederic Rzewski, *De Profundis*, mm. 33–36
Replicated by author.

adding human body percussion to the many sounds produced on the piano in that piece. Rzewski, in *De Profundis*, in the mammoth *The Road*, and in several other works, also sets the precedent for piano works that ask the pianist to speak a text as part of an overtly political work. Adam Tendler's *HATE SPEECH* (2013) has the pianist speak texts taken from a Montana politician's bigoted post concerning the death of Matthew Shepherd.

Composers have devised various solutions for how to notate a spoken text for the pianist to perform, displaying differing levels of specificity. In some scores, the composer simply places the text on the score, with a few words about the mood and style of delivery. Other scores divide the text into small chunks and places those over or within specific measures, showing roughly how the text should align with the piano's notes. Humperdinck's melodrama *Die Königskinder* (1897), which was composed for a separate pianist and actors, gives a very detailed setting of the recitation part, specifying the "inflections, pitch, and accentuation that actors are to employ."[2] Edward Kravitt argues that Humperdinck's complete musical notation of a reciter's part was probably an influence on Schoenberg's monodrama *Pierrot Lunaire* for reciter and chamber ensemble that appeared about fifteen years later, but both of these works employ reciters separate from the pianist.

A short passage from "The Phantom Gondolier" in *Makrokosmos* illustrates a pianist-reciter moment in which the composer gives a lot of detail for the spoken part (see figure 7.8). My *I feel open to . . .* with a text taken from a long list poem by Denise Duhamel and scored for violin, piano, and drum set asks all three players to speak texts and varies between showing that a text can be spoken to any natural rhythm within the space of a measure, sometimes with a

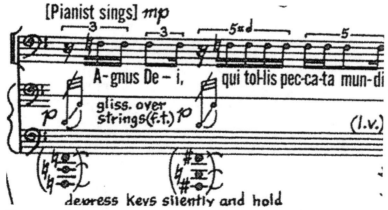

Figure 7.8. Pianist as reciter, George Crumb, "The Phantom Gondolier" from *Makrokosmos*, vol. 1

Copyright © 1973 by C. F. Peters Corporation. Used by permission.

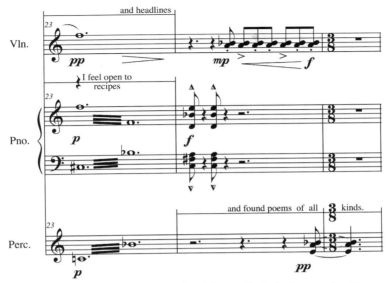

Figure 7.9. Speaking pianist, both with specified rhythms and with entrance specified but rhythms free, Alan Shockley, *I feel open to . . .*

specific entrance, and showing that a text should be delivered with a specified rhythm (see figure 7.9).

Interestingly enough, composer Brian Ferneyhough, who is known for the extreme amount of detail in his scores, gives very few details on the speaking part of his work for speaking pianist *Opus Contra Naturam* (see figure 7.10). This work marries intense control with freedom, displaying the composer's usual level of detail for its rhythms and the timbre of the notes played on the keyboard but leaving the pedaling to the performer to determine ad libitum and only suggesting coordination of the speaking part with the keyboard rhythms by placing the text within and across measures.

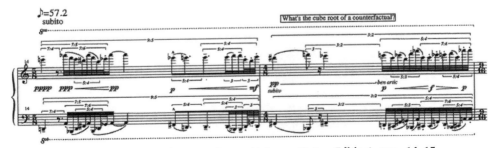

Figure 7.10.   Brian Ferneyhough, *Opus Contra Naturam* (Peters Edition), mm. 14–15

Copyright © 2000 by Henrichsen Edition, Peters Edition Ltd. Used by permission of C. F. Peters Corporation.

Singing Pianist

A pianist who also sings is commonplace in popular music, with such songwriter-pianists as Ray Charles, Little Richard (Richard Wayne Penniman), Aretha Franklin, Jerry Lee Lewis, Stevie Wonder, Ronnie Milsap, Carole King, Elton John, Billy Joel, John Legend, Tori Amos, Alicia Keys, and Norah Jones frequently singing and playing the piano simultaneously. Likewise, in jazz, there have been many pianist-singers, including Nat King Cole, Nina Simone, Shirley Horn, and Diana Krall, to list just a representative few.

In like fashion, there are also several pop music pianists who sometimes play harmonica while also playing piano. Billy Joel, for one, frequently dons a harmonica holder, enabling him to play the piano as usual with both hands while simultaneously playing a melody or tonic-dominant chords on the harmonica or both. Other than a few composers asking a pianist to sing for a brief passage, I have not uncovered a lot of "classical" repertoire that calls for singing pianists.

Piano Plus Other Keyboard Instruments

To ask the pianist to double on some other keyboard instrument is almost to be expected. There are dozens of pieces that ask the pianist to play either separately for separate sections of the work or to play simultaneously with one hand each on the piano and another keyboard instrument, such as piano and melodica, piano and synthesizer or electronic keyboard, and piano and toy piano. (Several examples of this last combination can be found in appendix A in the repertoire section devoted to works including toy piano.)

Because his music often adds microtones to the equal-tempered gamut, composer Mathew Rosenblum has several chamber works that ask the pianist to double on an electronic keyboard mimicking a piano in timbre. This keyboard is then given the microtones, and Rosenblum divides the part between the hands, enabling the pianist to cover all the usual equal-tempered notes and some additional microtones without retuning the piano. Rosenblum's *Circadian Rhythms* (1989) for cello, percussion, and two keyboards (one player), for example, asks the keyboardist to play an ordinary acoustic piano tuned normally and a digital sampling keyboard with seven pitches altered: He asks that C♯, D♯, F♯, and G♯ each be tuned thirty-seven cents sharper than their usual equal-tempered tuning and B♭, C, and F be tuned fifty-one cents flatter than usual. The part gives each keyboard its own grand staff, and the player rests the keyboard on top of the piano, so that she can play both simultaneously. Synthesizer and sampling technology has advanced enough in the past several years that electronic devices can mimic somewhat convincingly individual piano notes (though still most of this mimicry fails to convince for passages or lines where the resonance of the entire acoustic instrument would be missed).

Piano Plus Percussion

Early in his career, rock-and-roll pianist Jerry Lee Lewis performed some gigs playing piano with his right hand and simultaneously playing drums with his left.[3] Despite the piano being a percussion instrument itself, the combination of piano and percussion played by a single player has not become a standard combination.

Pianist Danny Holt has single-handedly worked to change that, commissioning several composers to write this combination for him and also commissioning works for piano and percussion for one player in combination with a second instrumentalist playing viola ("trios for two"). Holt started performing piano-percussion works in 2003 with Jascha Narveson's *Etude Brutus?* and, beginning in 2009, has incorporated several other piano-percussion pieces into his live performances. Holt has worked out some strategies for instrumental placement and modified some of his equipment and given information about these combinations to composers, encouraging them to think of these combinations as a foundation on which they can build. These include an extended linkage system for the pedal mechanism of a kick drum, one that allows him to extended the kick drum's pedal to be very close to the piano's pedals. For several works, he has constructed foam and cardboard bumpers to allow him to place a glockenspiel on top of the treble-register structural braces of a grand piano, so that he has access to the glockenspiel with one hand while continuing to play the piano with the other.

Figure 7.11. Pianist/percussionist Danny Holt's piano with percussion setup

Composers often treat percussionists as utility players and, in addition to asking them to strike drums and mallet instruments, ask them to play whistles and other wind instruments, toy instruments of various kinds, and just about anything else that can produce sound. Once the floodgates have been opened to a pianist doubling on percussion instruments, then it's a quick step to asking the pianist to cover various utility instruments as well. Peter Maxwell Davies's 1969 work *Vesalii Icones* for dancer, solo cello, and instrumental ensemble asks the pianist to play a klaxon, a whistle, four lengths of bamboo, and an out-of-tune autoharp and to make sounds by scraping an ordinary knife on a plate.

Pianist/Dancer

My Spirit Is Dancing by Kah Hoe Yii turns the pianist not only into a percussionist but also a bit of a dancer. The work asks the pianist to wear jingles on each wrist and around each ankle. The wrist percussion is activated by the slightest gesture at the keys, so the on-the-keys, trill-laden writing gains an accompanying bed of jingling and rattling sounds. Some gestures begin at the keyboard and extend to the pianist shaking an arm in the air away from the piano to continue the jingling sounds. The piece also has the pianist stomp and jump adding staccato jingles from the ankle percussion.

Pianist-composer Eleonor Sandresky has now written several works for herself, labeling herself a "choreographic pianist." Sandresky's works, like Yii's *My Spirit Is Dancing*, specify movements for the pianist to do while also playing on the keys of the piano. Yii does say that his piece was inspired by Balinese dance, but whereas almost all of the dance movements within *My Spirit Is Dancing* produce—and are intended to produce—sounds, Sandresky's choreographic movements add, not sound, but mostly a theatrical layer to the performance.

Piano in the Landscape, Piano as Spectacle

The piano is an icon of Western culture and of classical music. Like all such icons, it draws artists to it both to honor this position and to attack it, therefore symbolically questioning the status of the culture and societal class it represents. Though John Cage's *4'33"* is scored for any instrument or instruments, the shock caused by the premiere performance by David Tudor at the piano ensured that this radical work would always be associated with the piano. Cage's score parses four minutes and thirty-three seconds (or any other segment of time) into three tacet sections—the performer does not play her instrument at all for the duration of the piece.

Composer La Monte Young turns the piano into a prop or a character in a theatrical work in his 1960 work *Piano Piece for David Tudor #1*, instructing the performer to feed and water the piano or to leave it to eat on its own, as if it were a farm animal. The piece is over, the score explains, "after the piano has been fed" and "after the piano eats or decides" not to.[4]

Young's *Piano Piece for Terry Riley #1* from the same volume of experimental works again involves a performer and a piano and no piano playing. In this work, the performer pushes the instrument "up to a wall" and then continues "pushing in the same direction regardless of new obstacles and continue[s] to push . . . whether the piano is stopped against an obstacle or moving." The piece ends once the performer is "too exhausted to push any longer."[5]

In 1973, pianist Yosuke Yamashita played a burning piano for a short film. In 2008, he again played a burning piano for five hundred spectators. Dutch composer Gilius van Bergerijk has written a series of works for piano and obstacles, including one for amplified piano with a missing leg, a mattress, and a car jack.[6]

Annea Lockwood has composed a series of works she calls "Piano Transplants." These include her *Piano Garden* (1968), which involves half-burying a piano, planting fast-growing trees and plants around it, and leaving it to be engulfed by the plant life. Her *Piano Drowning 1* (1972) and *Southern Exposure* (1982, realized 2005) both involve situating a piano very close to a body of water and watching as it is, over weeks and months, gradually engulfed. Her *Piano Burning* (1968) has the performer set an upright piano on fire and play it as long as she can. The instructions for all of the pieces in the series state, "All pianos used should already be beyond repair."

8

Bowing

There are many string instruments on which the player bows the strings in order to sound them. There are a few instruments on which it is typical to bow the strings as well as to make those strings sound in other ways. Much of what endows the piano with its characteristic sound and what differentiates its sound from that of its precursor, the harpsichord, is the fact that, on the piano, the strings are struck by hammers rather than plucked. But the metal strings of the piano can also be bowed, though the techniques for doing so may be unfamiliar to most pianists. As bowing the piano may avoid completely using the action of the instrument, the sound of the bowed piano does not sound very much like a piano at all and can therefore open up a whole new world of sounds available from the instrument.

In 1972, pianist-composer C. Curtis-Smith developed a technique for bowing the piano strings. He went on to write several works that involve the pianist bowing the strings. For these, Curtis-Smith took long strands of monofilament, applied rosin to them, and looped these strands around various strings of the instrument. Then, over the course of a piece, the pianist plays bowed notes along with notes actuated by ordinary keystrokes. Curtis-Smith's *Rhapsodies* (1972) is the first of several of his works to incorporate bowed piano notes. Bowing the piano's strings contributes significantly to the palette of piano sounds, as, using a bow, the pianist can play a smooth crescendo and a smooth decrescendo of a single bowed note.

Rhapsodies includes six very full pages of details on the construction of bows, for their placement within the instrument, and for their use in performance. The instructions call for bows made of four-pound and six-pound monofilament fishing line, and Curtis-Smith explains that the four-pound line works the best. *Rhapsodies* asks for bows varying in length from twenty-five inches to sixty-six inches, with individual bows composed of from fourteen to sixty strands of monofilament. *Rhapsodies* exhibits the composer's great care in preparation and not inconsiderable trial and error leading to his finished practice of bowing, as demonstrated by the included diagrams and text explaining how to construct each bow, how to thread each among the strings, where to place each end of the bow to facilitate a smooth performance of the work, and a suggested color-coding for grips at the ends of the bows to aid the performer. Curtis-Smith even specifies the brand of rosin, saying the player should use "*Hills Rosin* (any other brand gets sticky in warm weather)."[1]

In addition to lower test line, Curtis-Smith also recommends cheaper fishing line, as, he explains, it tends to have a rougher surface, which makes for a better bow surface. For bowing several closely placed strings, a thicker bow (one composed of more strands) works better than a thinner bow. If a bow is only used for two pitches, then the player can use a bow with fewer strands. To bring out higher overtones; for large intervals (close to an octave or larger); or for long, unbroken crescendo and descrescendi, Curtis-Smith recommends a longer bow.[2] Curtis-Smith also recommends beginning each bow stroke with a slack bow; "as the bow is brought into motion, the *speed* must first be increased, *then and only then* may the pressure or tension be *gradually* increased."[3] Bows that need to be drawn by a single hand must, according to Curtis-Smith, be very thick (composed of many strands of monofilament).

In 1976, composer Stephen Scott heard pianist David Burge performing a piece by Curtis-Smith that included bowed notes (it was *Rhapsodies*). Witnessing this technique inspired Scott.[4] He asked Curtis-Smith how he constructed his bows. Scott reasoned that navigating quickly from string set to string set in the piano is challenging because there are so many different strings and they are spread across a large span, so it would be easier to divide this task among multiple players. A year after hearing Curtis-Smith's bowed piano in concert, Scott founded a bowed-piano ensemble at Colorado College. Works for the ensemble are usually performed by ten to twelve players stationed around a single piano.

MONOFILAMENT BOWS

To bow the strings of the piano, one must first create and rosin a bow. The piano's string placement as well as the strings' proximity to the soundboard preclude using a violin or other preexisting bow. Ordinary fishing line, with rosin applied to it, works very well, and a "bow" comprised of several rosined strands of monofilament works well (see figure 8.1). First, loop the rosined fishing line bunch underneath a piano string (or underneath a set of unison strings). When a player pulls the ends of the fishing line, applying friction between it and the string or strings while the dampers are lifted, she produces a long, "bowed" note.

Lengths of rosined fishing line form the primary bows for Stephen Scott's Bowed Piano Ensemble (see figure 8.2), still centered in Colorado Springs but now independent of Colorado College. For many works, each of the ensemble's

Figure 8.1. Monofilament bow

players is responsible for bowing one or more notes on the piano, so lines are divided across the ensemble. To gain better access to the strings, the Bowed Piano Ensemble typically removes the lid of the instrument. They label pitches on small tabs placed on the ends of each fishing-line bow.

Figure 8.2.   The Bowed Piano Ensemble
Courtesy ATLAS Institute, CU Boulder

Figure 8.3. Steinway Model D set up with monofilament bows for a bowed piano ensemble performance
Courtesy ATLAS Institute, CU Boulder

BOWED HARMONICS

In addition to sounding the fundamental of the string using a bow, it is possible to bring out various overtones on the strings using bows. David Burge, the dedicatee of Curtis-Smith's *Rhapsodies*, details Curtis-Smith's use of bowed harmonics in the final movement of *Rhapsodies*, explaining that, by looping a few very thick (multistrand) bows around some of the lowest bass strings of the piano, the player can "with careful manipulation of the speed and pressure exerted by the bow at different points on the string" sound a "nearly unbelievable number of discrete partials . . . ranging from the fundamental pitch of the string to somewhere above the 32nd partial five octaves higher."[5]

POPSICLE-STICK BOWS

Scott has devised other types of bows that produce different sorts of attack and sustain characteristics, for instance, making short sforzando-attack bows by affixing horsehair to the surface of wooden popsicle sticks. Once rosined, this horsehair surface becomes a short bow that can produce a very short note when dragged across a piano string. If one affixes bow hair to both sides of the popsicle stick, it is even possible to bow two adjacent strings at the same time, which means it is possible to bow a harmonic minor second with one bow by placing the popsicle-stick bow between two sets of unisons and angling the bow to press against strings from two different unison sets at the same time. Scott refers to the monofilament loops as "soft bows," and soft bows are better suited for long notes that speak somewhat slowly. "Rigid bows," such as those made from horsehair and popsicle sticks, produce shorter notes and can produce staccato and accented attacks. Scott has fashioned other "rigid bows" by affixing horsehair to tongue depressors or nail files.[6] Players can also use these short rigid bows for playing a steady tremolo of repeated notes.

ADDITIONAL BOWS AND BOW STANDS

Another bow material that Scott has used more recently is a small piece of plexi-glass. The surface of the plexiglass needs to be made rough by sanding with sandpaper, and then it can be pulled across the surface of the string to "bow" it. (This technique could just as easily be classified as a friction sound played on the strings, but I include it here with bowing.)

In his 2005 work *Gaeta* for two pianos and two percussion, composer Drew Baker calls for a method of exciting the piano's strings that involves the second-ary transfer of friction. For this technique, the player takes a two-foot length of cassette tape, ties one end to a piano string, and holds the tape taut with one hand. Using moistened fingertips, the player grips the tape between her thumb and fore-finger and slides the gripped fingers along the taut tape. This rubbing action along the tape transfers to the string and sounds it. *Gaeta* also calls for this method of bowing with the tape attached to a bass string and close to the bridge pin, to pro-duce a high-pitched squeak. Because this tied cassette tape technique is a little bit like the "bowed" timpani technique, in which vibrations from the bowed untram-meled end of a ruler with its other end extended onto the head of a drum transfer from the ruler to the drumhead, I include it here as another bowing technique. It could just as easily be classified as another friction technique.

For his chamber work *Quadrivial* (1997), composer Michel van der Aa devised a bow station and specifies looping small lengths of bow hair around a few piano strings and tying the ends to elastic looped over a boom mic stand that has been extended over the piano (see figure 8.4). This is a great way to set up several bowed notes for a single player to play. All of the bows are in place beforehand, and looping the elastic over the mic stand keeps all the bows within easy reach and easily differentiated from one another by the player.

Figure 8.4.   Mic stand bow station for Michel van der Aa's *Quadrivial*
Photo by Michel van der Aa; used by permission.

Outside of a few of C. Curtis-Smith's works and the repertoire of the Bowed Piano Ensemble, the technique of bowing the piano's strings has not yet been widely exploited. Because the monofilament bows can be positioned ahead of time and their ends draped on racks, extended over the sides of the piano, or affixed to the plate with magnets, they can be kept mostly out of the way of the pianist, the strings, and the action and allow all of the instrument's note to ring as normal. This means that with careful placement, it is possible for a composer to include a few bowed notes within a solo piano work that uses other nontraditional techniques or otherwise has the performer sounding the remainder from the keys. Constructing monofilament bows is cheap and easy, using them does not risk damaging the instrument, and the sound of a bowed piano string is strikingly different from other sounds of the instrument. I expect more composers will exploit these, and more pianists will add these to their improvisation toolbox.

9

Preparations

Though composers in the past have tried out several different names for the practice, placing materials directly onto the strings of the piano or attaching items to the strings is generally now called preparing the piano.

This chapter covers all of the now-standard preparations to the strings, and a few preparations to other parts of the piano (the keys, the hammers, the pedals). There are a few preparations that can potentially harm the instrument. Some art works require that an instrument be sacrificed. However, I will make it clear when I am aware of any dangers a particular preparation or technique may pose for the instrument. It is undeniable the theatrical impact the destruction of a violin in Peter Maxwell Davies's *Eight Songs for a Mad King* has or the direct brutal nature of shattering a violin in Nam June Paik's *One* or of Jimi Hendrix lighting his Stratocaster on fire in his live performance of "Wild Thing" at the 1967 Monterey Pop Festival. However, for most concert performances in most venues, the performer has a responsibility not to damage the instrument, and the performer does not need the added stress of worrying that some upcoming passage may permanently damage a more-than-$100,000 instrument that belongs to someone else.

PREPARATIONS BECOME STOPS BECOME PREPARATIONS

There is a long history of pianists experimenting with placing materials on the strings of the instrument. In the earliest days of the piano, pianists did experiment with changing the sound of the instrument by placing materials on the strings. Piano makers, likewise, experimented with endowing their instruments with ways of offering other colors. Some early fortepianos had as many as six pedals, several of which triggered placing different materials against the strings or between the hammers and the strings to modify the sound color of the instrument. Eventually, piano makers abandoned most of these, settling on two standard pedals and eventually—at least for most grands and most higher-grade uprights—adding a third standard pedal, all three of which affect tone color. As it currently stands, only a small percentage of upright pianos are equipped with a third pedal that lowers a felt strip between the hammers and the strings, called a muffler rail or practice rail. This is a bit like one of the pedal-operated stops present on some early fortepianos—the moderator or celeste stop. This mechanism lowers a wedge-shaped piece of cloth or leather between the hammers and strings—the lower the pedal is depressed, the thicker the graduated material placed between hammers and strings and the more muted the sound.[1]

Another early fortepiano pedal found on some instruments is the bassoon stop. This lowers a paper roll (sometimes covered in silk) onto the strings, so that, as the strings are set into motion by the hammers, the strings vibrate and buzz against the roll.

Though most of these early timbre-changing stops have been abandoned by piano makers, to some extent, one might view many preparations as motivated by the same desire to coax a larger color palette from the piano. Several preparations use the same materials and produce a similar effect to the ones produced by the pedal or hand stops that some early pianos exhibit.

As several common preparations trace to some of those eighteenth-century stops and further back to the experimentation that led to the stops themselves, it's possible to view modern piano preparations as a sort of cyclical return of timbral experimentation. First, there were early piano performers and piano makers experimenting with placing foreign objects on top of the strings of the piano or between the hammers and the strings, threading or wedging objects into the strings, or clipping or otherwise attaching objects to the strings, all to enable the instrument to produce additional timbres; then there were makers constructing mechanisms and stops to allow pianists to enjoy these timbral changes conveniently by marrying the preparation to a hand stop or a pedal control. But, piano makers failed to adopt these extra controls in a wide way, and these soon disappeared from the instrument, only to be revived in the modern era by pianists and composers experimenting and resuscitating many of these timbral modifications once again as preparations.

JOHN CAGE AND THE PREPARED PIANO

Composer John Cage's name is inextricably linked with this concept of the prepared piano. There is a now-famous story that Cage was writing music for a dance recital, but in the venue for the performance, there was a small stage with no wings and no pit. The hall had a piano but no room for percussion instruments. Cage says that, at the time, he wrote either percussion music or twelve-tone music when writing for pitched instruments. For the dance, he began writing a twelve-tone piano piece but was dissatisfied and began experimenting with transforming the piano into an instrument that would make more percussive sounds. Kyle Gann, in describing Cage's first experiments with preparing the piano says, "It was a virtual percussion orchestra at his fingertips. He liked the sound. He had invented what he would later call the prepared piano. Quickly, he wrote a work for the dance called *Bacchanale*."[2] Cage himself credited the origins of his piano experimentation to his teacher Henry Cowell. Cowell had called his techniques for playing the piano directly on the strings "string piano." In 1972, in writing the foreword to Richard Bunger's *The Well-Prepared Piano*, Cage makes it clear how important working with Cowell was to his own experiments with the piano, specifically mentioning assisting Cowell by depressing the damper pedal for *The Banshee*. Cage was to use Cowell's term *string piano* for a few of his own early pieces that experimented with the piano but later coined the term *prepared piano* as his preferred label.

An exhaustive detailing of every possible preparation is beyond the scope of this (or possibly any) book. Because there are so many, and for ease of discussion, I group together preparations in a few different classes. Several authors before me in writing about piano techniques and preparations have chosen different ways of classifying these. The "messiness" of preparations for the piano defies a tidy categorization. In a few following places, the text acknowledges this messiness, but grouping several techniques together and discussing them as related to one another contributes to an understanding of these techniques, and that justifies this effort, despite the many exceptions, the techniques, and preparations that seem to belong in more than one category or the ones that blur the distinctions between categories.

CLASSES OF PREPARATIONS

- *Surface Preparations*: These involve resting something on the surface of the strings or placing something between the hammers and the strings (without attaching the item to the hammers), so that the item touches the surface of the strings when the performer engages the hammers.
- *String Preparations*: These, like the surface preparations, also involve the strings but involve inserting materials between the strings, clipping or otherwise affixing items to the strings, or threading items through multiple strings.

These first two classes of preparation are the ones typically meant when someone discusses the prepared piano. But, there are other preparations that I feel are different enough from these to deserve classifying them separately:

- *Hammer Preparations*: These involve attaching something to the hammer. Probably the most familiar of these is the so-called tack piano. This class also includes preparations that involve wrapping the hammers to change the striking surface.
- *Double (Triple and Other) Preparations*: These are mostly self-explanatory; it is possible to apply more than one preparation to a single "note," such as applying both a surface preparation and a string preparation.
- *Una Corda String Preparations*: These involve the use of the una corda pedal in some way to engage or disengage a preparation.
- *Key Preparations*: There are a few ways of preparing or attaching items to the keys or key surface.
- *Pedal Preparations*: There are a few ways of attaching an object to the pedal or pedal mechanism, either to lock the pedal in place or to add a new sound to the action of pedaling.

ON PREPARATIONS, STRING MATERIALS

One thing to consider when working inside the piano, either when playing on the strings or when adding foreign objects to the strings, is that there are many delicate parts on the interior of the piano, and many even very sturdy components work together in a delicate balance for the normal action of the instrument. If the composer or performer wishes to cause no damage to the instrument, then she should proceed with great care.

Most preparations involve adding foreign objects in some way to the strings. All modern pianos use strings of two different kinds with very different exterior materials. Practically all pianos constructed over the last century use flat, nickel-steel strings for the mid- and upper register of the instrument, and most instruments use these strings for all of the triple-unison notes. Modern pianos use a different sort of string for the bass and tenor registers. If these lower-pitch strings consisted of the same material as the strings for the upper register, they would need to be longer and much thicker, and the steel would be too stiff to ring in a like manner to the upper strings. Instead, the strings for the lower register of the instrument have a core of similar material to the upper-register strings that is wrapped with a lighter material; for practically all modern pianos, this outer material is copper. Some bass strings may have a single layer of this outer wrap; others may have two. These wrapped strings, especially the lowest bass strings that have only a single string per note, are significantly thicker than the upper-register strings. The exterior copper winding is also much softer than steel; these wound strings are easily tarnished and much easier to nick or otherwise damage than the upper-register "flat" strings.

For example, a steel bolt may be carefully wedged between two upper-register strings without any real risk of damaging the strings, whereas that same bolt might very easily score, scrape, or otherwise damage the bass strings. Generally, when looking at playing on the strings or preparing the strings using metal implements, harder metals can be used for the flat steel strings of the middle- and upper-register notes, whereas, if possible, substitutes for steel should be used on bass and tenor strings. Fortunately, in many cases, brass and other soft metals can be substituted with very similar effect as harder metals for use on these wound strings.

STRINGS AND THEIR DISTRIBUTION

The distribution of strings by number of unisons per key changes over the compass of the piano, with the lowest bass notes having only one string per key, the tenor register using two unisons per key, and all the notes from the middle register of the piano to the top note of the instrument using three unisons per key. The exact notes where these changes take place vary across different makes and models. You can find the technical specifications of these unison distributions for many concert and semiconcert grand pianos in appendix C. Because many preparations involve wedging an object between unisons or clipping or attaching items to a single string, some objects attach more easily, whereas others can only be threaded among a group of three strings oriented very close to each other.

Modern grand pianos are overstrung, with the bass strings running diagonally from the tuning pins to the bridge and crossing over some of the middle-register strings.[3] Grand pianos use two bridges, with a curved bridge used for all of the strings from the middle register to the top (the long bridge), and with the bass register strings run diagonally over some of the middle-register strings and affixed to a separate bass bridge. For all of the large overstrung grand piano models detailed in appendix C, all of the wound strings are attached to the bass bridge, and all of the flat steel strings are attached to the long bridge; three of the smaller instruments detailed in appendix C carry a few wound strings on the long bridge: the Steinway Model A and the Yamaha C1 each have a few copper-wound triple unisons attached to the long bridge, and the Steinway Model M has two copper-wound double unisons attached to the long bridge.

Over the full compass of every piano, string lengths change incrementally from the lowest note to the highest on each instrument, with the longest string used for the lowest note of each instrument and the very shortest strings (in triple unison) used for the highest note on each instrument. For a concert grand piano, the range of string lengths is significant, from a 79¼-inch-long string for A0 on a Steinway Model D and three unisons each only about 2 inches long for C8 at the top of the same instrument.

Another distinction that shows up on all modern pianos is that, as the strings for the highest notes on the instrument are so short, their sustain is also very brief. Because of this, there are no dampers for the topmost strings on the instrument, leaving on most instruments about an octave and a half of notes with no dampers.

SURFACE PREPARATIONS

Richard Bunger in *The Well-Prepared Piano* refers to preparations involving resting an item on top of the strings as "surface preparations," a useful term. These are among the easiest preparations to install and remove, and with most surface preparations, there is very little risk of damaging the strings of the instrument by the actions of installing or removing the preparation. According to Cage, once he had the thought that he might be able to change the sound of the piano by preparing the strings in some way, the very first thing he tried was placing a pie plate on top of the strings.[4] As Cage discovered, the pie plate did change the sounds of some of the piano's notes, but the plate was so light that the strings' vibrations very quickly moved the plate, returning many notes to their ordinary state. Let's look at some of the most common surface preparations in addition to the pie plate.

Paper

A sheet of paper placed on top of strings in the midrange or lower dulls the sound of those notes a bit and adds a slight buzz to the beginning of the sound of each prepared note (see figure 9.1). The resultant sound is gently buzzy. In the upper register, the strings are so short that there is not enough room to place a piece of letter-sized paper on the strings. For this register, a strip of paper modifies the sound some but not to the extent of a sheet of paper in the lower registers. This preparation produces a similar sound to the bassoon stop and probably led to its creation.

Figure 9.1. Surface preparation, paper on the strings

Cardstock or Poster Board

A large sheet of cardstock or poster board on the strings rattles for a shorter time than paper for each note but imparts a little more percussive accent to each note's onset. The longer string lengths, again, make this preparation more effective in the low and midrange than in the upper register.

Glass Rod

Composer George Crumb in his trio *Vox Balaenae* calls for placing a solid glass rod on the strings (see figure 9.2). This makes for a bigger timbral change than paper or cardstock, especially at high dynamic levels; playing forcefully on the keys causes the glass rod to bounce significantly from the top of the strings and to hit the strings on its rebounds. This surface preparation coaxes a jangling, metallic sound from the instrument.[5]

Figure 9.2.   Surface preparation, glass rod on the strings

Hardwood Dowel

Placing a heavier hardwood dowel on top of the strings produces a sound very similar to the glass rod. Smaller diameter or softwood dowels, because of their lightness, are not particularly effective—without more weight, these preparations bounce around too much, too quickly, and too unpredictably, leaving notes clear of their preparations.

Brass Rod

A length of brass produces a similar effect to the glass rod. A thin bar of brass (square in its cross-section) stays in place better than an actual round rod.

Pencil

Ken Ueno in his solo piano work *Volcano* calls for placing an ordinary wood pencil on top of the strings in the top octave of the piano, calling this a "*balzando*" (leaping, bouncing) effect (see figure 9.3). The lightness of the pencil means that, as a surface preparation on lower strings, it would bounce quite violently, and with forte playing, it likely would bounce quickly away from its intended register strings. The very short strings of the piano's top octave do not move the pencil as high into the air, and the strings in this register are of such short compass that the capo d'astro on one side and the bridge on the other help to keep the pencil in place—it is also hemmed in on the sides on almost every instrument by a brace to the left and the brace forming the treble edge of the plate on the right.

Figure 9.3.   Surface preparation, pencil on the strings

Chain

Crumb calls for a very light chain to be placed on the strings in his *Makrokosmos*, book 1.[6] I have also experimented with different gauges and lengths of chain as surface preparations. Smaller-gauge chain, such as what Crumb calls for, produce a bright and jangling harpsichord-like sound. Larger-gauge chain can be more cumbersome to deal with—it is harder to get the chain into place so that it consistently modifies the sound of all the notes in the range that the composer has specified (see figure 9.4). However, the sound is even more percussive and bright at its onset than with the small-gauge chain. I refer to this effect as "chain piano" and have used it in a few works.

It is also possible to produce a striking effect with larger-gauge chain that is much less effective with very light chains; the player can release the dampers and drop the chain onto the strings, producing a cluster wherever the chain lands; the chain can then remain in place (or mostly so) to modify the notes with the prepared sound. Note that a large-gauge, hard metal chain should not be dropped onto the wound strings. If dropped onto the steel strings, the player should take care as well; drop from only three or four inches above the strings, and be sure not to drop the chain onto any of the metal braces or onto the plate.

Figure 9.4.   Surface preparation, heavy-gauge chain on the strings

Balls

Pianists can bounce balls on the strings to sound the strings (this is discussed in chapter 7 as a kind of percussive playing), but balls of various sorts can also be used passively as a surface preparation: placing the balls (e.g., several ping-pong balls; see figure 9.5) on top of the strings and then setting the strings into motion in some other way (such as simply playing on the keys *ordinario*) sets the balls to vibrating against the strings, much as a strip of paper placed on the strings vibrates; the balls create a gentle buzzing sound. Voler Bertelmann (a.k.a., Haschka) uses this in works including *Mount Hood* from his 2015 album *Foreign Objects.*[7] Roger Zare's *dark and stormy night* for piano with ping-pong balls and obbligato page turner (2006) also uses this preparation, with the work starting with the pianist strumming the bass strings, on which six balls have been placed. Zare explains that there is a theatrical aspect to the use of the ping-pong balls, as the vibrating strings can send the balls flying into the air. The page-turner assists throughout the piece by placing balls on top of the strings, removing them, and replacing them as necessitated by the violent vibrating of the balls by the piano's strings.

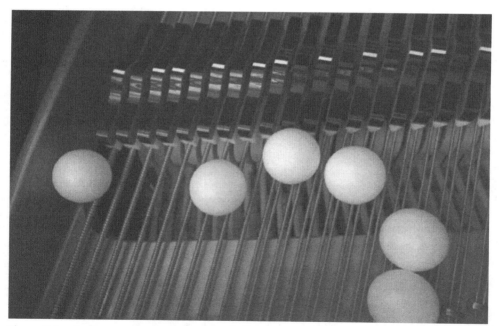

Figure 9.5.   Surface preparation, ping-pong balls on the strings

Aluminum Foil

Placed on the surface of the strings, a sheet of aluminum foil adds a gentle buzzing to the piano's sound (see figure 9.6). This buzzing is lighter in sound than the buzz of paper on the strings, and it sustains longer (a few seconds for middle-range strings).

Figure 9.6. Surface preparation, aluminum foil on the strings

Small Metal Condiment Bowls with Paper Clips

Small metal condiment bowls with paper clips make a small sound when the hammer strikes the strings and then set up a secondary buzzing of the paper clips as they vibrate within the bowls (see figure 9.7).

Figure 9.7. Surface preparation, paper clips in a small metal condiment bowl on the strings

It is relatively easy to fashion a preparation from masking tape in combination with dimes or other small, light pieces of metal that can take advantage of the flexibility of the masking tape to bounce the dime against the vibrating strings. Richard Bunger calls this a "sitar stop" and suggests affixing the end of each strip of tape to an agraffe, with the dime resting on the strings. This preparation is sort of a "cousin" to the mandolin rail, a stop found on some antique (and a few modern) instruments.[8] The mandolin rail extends leather tabs with metal buttons on them, which intervene between the hammers and the strings; the hammers strike the leather, and the metal buttons become the new striking surface on the strings. This "sitar stop" extends similarly flexible tabs (the strips of masking tape) and places metal against the strings. It differs most markedly by placing the metal not in the path of the hammers but elsewhere on the surface of the strings, where it can buzz against them.

Composers and performers have experimented with many other surface preparations, including a metal ruler, resting a railroad spike on top of small strip of aluminum foil,[9] hacksaw blades, and small candy dispenser rattles (Tic Tac boxes), among many others. Several composers have called for small percussion instruments to be placed on top of the piano's strings. Matthias Bamert's 1972 *Introduction and Tarentella* for flute, percussion, and piano has the player lay a tambourine on top of the strings and then strike the head of the tambourine with a mallet. Carson Kievman's *The Temporary and Tentative Extended Piano* (1977, revised 1992) asks the player to place five to fourteen finger cymbals with the straps removed on the piano's strings. Lukas Foss's *Ni bruit ni vitesse* (1972) has the player drop and rest metal prayer bowls on the strings. Others have called for small cymbals, bells, and crotales, among other metal percussion instruments to be placed on the strings.

ACTIVE SURFACE PREPARATIONS

All of the preceding surface preparations could be classified as passive—the item used for preparing the string is positioned and left to modify the timbre of the vibrating string or to vibrate against the strings. There are some other surface preparations whose use is more dynamic. These might be labeled as active surface preparations. An example of an active surface preparation already covered in a preceding chapter is muting with the fingers or hand; for these, the pianist presses against the string while sounding the string in some way (through playing on the key, pizzicato, or in some other way). The pressure of the "mute" and its position may even be changed dynamically as the pianist sounds notes. There are some other active surface preparations that composers have used.

CHISEL PIANO, GLASS TUMBLER SLIDES, AND OTHER SLIDE TECHNIQUES

Players can use various hard, flat (flat-edged) objects to stop one of the unison sets of steel strings on the piano and thereby access notes higher than the fundamental on those strings. This is a little like slide technique on a guitar—the player presses the slide on the string and then excites the string in some way, sounding a note on the effectively shortened length of sounding string that is stopped by the slide.

George Crumb calls for a version of this technique in his chamber work *Ancient Voices of Children* by asking the pianist to press the blade of a ⅝-inch chisel on a unison set, to pluck the string, and then to slide the chisel to produce a melody of different notes. For this work, Crumb specifies that the player should use the strings for F4, and the slide melody that the player produces by stopping the strings with the chisel use pitches C♯5 and higher.

Pressing a steel chisel against the steel strings violates the general principle that the materials used on the strings should be softer than the strings. Years ago, when Crumb coached a student trio I was playing in for our upcoming performance of his *Vox Balaenae*, which also uses this "chisel piano" technique, Crumb suggested having the piano technician or someone in the repair shop on campus soften the temper of a chisel for our use. Tempered steel is steel that has first been hardened, then heated to an exactly calculated temperature and quenched so that it has the proper balance of hardness and flexibility. Tempered steel can be reheated (again, to a calculated temperature) and then cooled to make the metal more brittle. The idea for the chisel with softened temper was to weaken the steel enough that, when pressed against steel strings, the chisel and not the strings would be the first to chip or otherwise give way.

Over the years, I have used my "weakened" ⅝-inch chisel for a handful of different performances, and I have also loaned it to students for use in performances of *Vox Balaenae*. So far, I have never harmed any strings using it. However, using the ⅝-inch metal chisel, even with the metal softened, still raises concerns—it remains a tool fashioned of very hard metal and a very sharp implement. Without taking great care, a player could very easily accidentally damage herself or the instrument with its blade. I have found that brass bars with a milled hard edge work just as well as the chisel and are not only much less dangerous to wield but also considerably softer than steel and so are much safer to use on the steel strings of the piano. A machine shop could fashion a brass block to given specifications. An inexpensive solution for these brass pieces is to buy a brass setup gauge. These come in small sets of different sizes, and a whole set costs less than a single ⅝-inch chisel and includes rectangular bars of different sizes so that the player can try out different options and choose the one that works the best for the performance.

Composers have used other hard materials as slides to stop the steel strings and then slide against them to access other notes. Pressing the hard edge of a glass tumbler against the strings works well and may help the pianist to generate a note from the lengths of the strings on either side of the glass. Pressing the glass against the strings makes it possible to produce notes from either side of the glass on the same strings and create a smooth glissando of one note down while the other note slides up at the same time.

Guitar slides of various hard materials (glass bottlenecks, brass Dobro guitar slides) also work well for this same slide technique on the strings of the piano. Composer C. Curtis-Smith in his *Rhapsodies* has the pianist invert a small wine bottle and place the neck between two sets of triple unisons, then press and slide the bottle along one of these unison sets. This, like the earlier glass tumbler slide produces two pitches, and moving the bottle along the length of the strings produces glissandi in contrary motion of the two notes.

Another type of technique that might fit in the category of an "active" surface preparation would be any playing method that asks the player to hold an object against the strings to allow the string vibrations to bounce against the object once the string is set in motion in some way. Crumb, in one section of *Vox Balaenae*, asks the pianist to pluck the string for a low B repeatedly. After each pizzicato, the pianist then must loosely hold a paper clip that has been bent into a hammer shape against the string. The string's motion initiated by the plucking vibrates against the paper clip hammer and quietly buzzes the low B, providing a drone for the rest of the trio to a play over. In performances of my *break the levee* for piano and percussion quartet, I have used a plastic calculator within a sliding hard plastic case as a combination mute and rattle—pressed against the strings while they were set into motion from the keys, the calculator and case buzz very briefly against the strings at each new note's onset, lending a muted electric-guitar-like sound to notes around E3.

PLACEMENT OF PREPARATIONS

Because it is to John Cage that we attribute at the least the flowering of the prepared piano, if not its "invention," we have Cage to thank for some of the practices for specifying those preparations. Fortunately, Cage provides a good amount of detail in several of his scores for prepared piano. For example, Cage's 1942 work *Totem Ancestor* includes two pages, in four columns, of information on just the preparations (see figure 9.8). The first column gives the note on a staff, which indicates the string or strings to be prepared; the second column lists the preparation material, specifying what should be wedged into the strings of that note;

Tone	Material	Strings (left to right)	Distance from Damper (inches) (approximate)
 𝄞	SCREW or BOLT	2 - 3	2
 𝄞	SCREW or BOLT	2 - 3	2
 𝄞	SCREW or BOLT	2 - 3	2
 𝄞	SCREW with nuts (free to rattle)	2 - 3	2
 𝄞	SCREW or BOLT	2 - 3	2

Figure 9.8. John Cage, *Totem Ancestor*, "Table of Preparations"

Copyright © 1960 by Henmar Press, Inc. Used by permission of C. F. Peters Corporation. All Rights Reserved.

"SCREW with nuts (free to rattle)," for instance. The third column lists between which strings of the unisons to place the material (between strings 2 and 3, for instance) or, if something is to be threaded through the unisons, which strings it should be over and which ones under. The final column gives the distance beyond the dampers to place the material.

Cage's score gives a lot of detail, but it also leaves some unanswered questions. Neither the table of preparations nor the rest of the score indicate the character or the pitch of the resultant sound for the preparations. This score does not give (indeed none of Cage's prepared piano scores give) any information for what model of piano the composer intends to be prepared. The position of items used for preparing the piano strings has a large bearing on the resultant sound. Cage's tables give approximate distance from the dampers, but this placement lands on a different position depending on the scale length of the particular instrument. Even limiting the possible piano models to concert grand or semi-concert grand pianos, there is a wide variance of piano scales possible. Even within one maker's pianos, there are different models with very different scale lengths. If I place the very same materials (a particular size of wood screw, for instance), approximately two inches beyond the dampers on a Steinway B, that distance indication places the wood screw in a very different place within the string's length on a Steinway C or Steinway D because of the differences in their individual scale lengths. Following

Cage's specifications actually produces very different sounds on these different instruments (not to mention on many of the smaller grand pianos that Steinway also makes, as well as the many other models of pianos produced by any other maker). For the first years when Cage was experimenting with preparing pianos, he was doing the preparations himself and performing on the instruments himself, so he knew what sound he was looking for with each preparation and which instrument he was using. By the time lots of other pianists were performing these pieces, the composer had gotten very interested in involving indeterminacy in his composing. In Cage's foreword to Bunger's *The Well-Prepared Piano*, Cage notes of his prepared piano works that "as the music left my home and went from piano to piano and from pianist to pianist, it became clear that not only are two pianists essentially different from one another, but two pianos are not the same either." He also writes of being led "to the enjoyment of things as they come, as they happen."[9] Nevertheless, Cage became aware of the fact that his score specifications were not enough to ensure consistent sounds from his preparations across different models of piano. Cage relates that, in the late 1940s, a pianist asked him to come hear him play Cage's *The Perilous Night*, and Cage was dismayed, writing, "His preparation of the piano was so poor that I wished at the time that I had never written the music."[10]

Pianist Philipp Vandré navigates these problems by matching his instrument to Cage's. Vandré recorded Cage's *Sonatas and Interludes* for a 1994 album, which, according to the liner notes, is the first recording of the piece issued that captured a performance on the model of piano on which Cage composed the piece, a Steinway Model O baby grand.[11]

For specifics of positioning, Cage's score is missing one of two bits of information, either of which would help the performer to place the material in such a way that it would produce a similar effect each time it is used. The score either needs to add on which model piano it should be played, or it needs to give instead of or in addition to the approximate measurement in relation to the dampers the ratio in relation to the overall length of the string (two-fifths of the string length, for instance).

Christian Wolff in his *For Prepared Piano* (1952) mostly follows Cage's model. Wolff does not specify the piano model or give the measurement in proportion of the string, but he does add one more bit of specifics about the results expected from the preparation: He lists the altered pitch that should be produced by the correctly placed preparation. For example, for a preparation to be added to the three strings of F♯4, Wolff's score instructs the pianist to add a "[s]trip of jar rubber interlaced under strings 1 & 3, over 2 about 2 . . . [inches] from dampers."[12] The score then says that this preparation should sound F♮4, lowering the pitch of these strings by a half step. This added information about the resultant sound assists in positioning the strip of rubber properly—the pianist starts with the threaded rubber at about two inches beyond the dampers and then adjusts it as needed by the particular string scale of the instrument being prepared to bring out the correct lower pitch.

MEASUREMENTS TO WORK ON ALL MODELS OF PIANO

I suggest, for composers who wish to give specifications that performers can apply universally, that, rather than giving a measurement in relation to the dampers, she instead give locations as proportions of the string. Bunger calls this method "both more versatile and more exacting, but also considerably more cumbersome to implement."[13] Rather than giving placement in inches or centimeters, the score specifies materials placement in fractions of the string length, such as one-quarter of the string or two-fifths of the string. Theoretically, placement of a preparation material at any of the nodes marking the same proportion of the string (such as one-seventh, two-sevenths, three-sevenths, four-sevenths, and so forth) produces the same sound, but there are many other variables, including where on the string the hammer strikes, the differences in location over the soundboard between different placements, and differences in their proximity or overlap from overstrung bass strings (or if the preparation is on one of the bass strings, then differences in location above the lower tenor-register strings).[14] Because of these other variables, in practice, placement at different nodes marking the division of the string into the same proportions can sound noticeably different.

Bunger's own music gives the measurements in the "universal approach" his book advocates; his *Two Pieces for Prepared Piano* (1977), for instance, uses nine types of string preparations, calling for nineteen different prepared notes. For thirteen of the nineteen prepared notes, Bunger's score gives instructions at which proportion of the strings to place the foreign object, saying "at the one-third node" for a plastic credit card threaded through the strings, for instance. For four of the remaining notes, the work uses a felt strip for muting and specifies merely "behind dampers" for its placement, as exact placement is not crucial to the preparing material's effect—no matter which size piano, the felt strip mutes the tone in a similar fashion if wedged between the strings behind the dampers. For two high notes, the preparation used is a bit of vinyl tubing, slit so that it caps string 2 and wedges between strings 1 and 2 and strings 2 and 3. For this preparation, the score, rather than giving a measurement for placement, specifies its placement should be at the "point of Max. Resonance."[15] Bunger's score adds another couple of useful details to the table of preparations for this score: The score displays a line drawing of each preparation in place between the strings represented in cross-section. This makes for an easy score to read and releases the performing pianist from much of the responsibilities of deciphering what the materials are and how to transfer their proper placement to different models of piano.

STRING PREPARATIONS

Some small items can be loosely attached to the bass strings and can add a rattling sound once the string is set into motion, thereby shaking the item against the string. Composer Sharon Hesse uses the small plastic closures that come on grocery store loaves of bread for this purpose (see figure 9.9). These produce a very light rattle. Similar rattles can be looped around single strings or unison groups, including circular paper clips and large safety pins. Substituting a heavier material for the paper clips, pins, or plastic can produce a more prominent—though usually shorter-lived—rattle. One step heavier is a small length of light metal wire; a 1½-inch length of a wire coat hanger is easy to bend into shape for this purpose; a nail bent into a loop also provides a similar weight. For an even heavier rattle, which produces louder rattles but has a greatly reduced duration for the rattling because the weight dampens the string faster, I have made rattles from small lengths of mild steel. However, again, the copper windings of the bass strings are more delicate than steel, so I recommend using brass materials rather than steel

Figure 9.9.   String preparation, plastic bread clips on bass strings

for heavier rattling loops, as using a much softer metal ensures that your rattles do not nick the copper windings. These various metal rings, as well as the paper clips and safety pins, can be looped onto strings in all registers of the instrument. There are subtle differences between the sounds of these different materials.

The Well-Prepared Piano identifies five patterns for placing objects between the strings; of these, two describe patterns of threading through sets of triple unisons: the "peak" and the "weave." Bunger's peak pattern runs the preparation material under strings 1 and 3 and over string 2 of a triple unison set. Conversely, the weave pattern takes the preparation material over strings 1 and 3 and under string 2 of a triple set.[16] There are many materials that can be threaded through the strings in one of these two patterns, including strips of paper or cardboard, playing cards, plastic credit cards, short lengths of lamp cord, mason-jar-lid rubber gaskets, lengths of window insulation, strips of felt, and ordinary plastic straws (see figure 9.10).

Such flexible items work well for threading through the strings. Thin items, even those that are not flexible, also work well. A coin threaded into any of the triple unisons can produce a sound much like a small, pitched gong (see figure 9.11).

Figure 9.10. String preparation, straws in strings

Figure 9.11.   String preparation, coins threaded into strings

The coin stops the string (which, theoretically, shortens the string lengths that are vibrating) but also adds to the mass of the vibrating strings, so the gong-like sound is at least a little lower than the unprepared strings. Smaller coins work well. It is best not to try to thread the coin too close to either end of the vibrating string, and you should take caution threading even a small coin into very short strings. In an article in *Contemporary Keyboard* (and later reprinted as part of the second edition of *The Well-Prepared Piano*), Richard Bunger cautions that inflexible items should only be threaded near the center of the strings and only in the middle register, saying specifically of the thinnest of American coins, the dime (only 1.35 millimeters thick), should never be used above C5 and "should never be placed within five inches of either end of the sounding portion of any string."[17] Depending on the spacing between unison groups, when threading a wider coin in a triple-unison group, it is possible to add a rattle to the gong-like sound produced by the coin by positioning the edge of the coin to touch or over-lap very slightly the outside string of the adjacent unison group. If slightly more of the coin overlaps this other string, then it is possible for it to lower the pitch of that string as well, producing a microtone from one string of that group, leaving the other two strings of the group to sound normally, and producing some sort of augmented unison between them.

Screws, Bolts

Larger screws and bolts change the pitch more significantly than smaller ones (see figure 9.12). Using longer bolts and adding a couple of nuts threaded tightly all the way onto the bolts adds even more mass. Screws and bolts come in many different designs, diameters, lengths, and materials, and these distinctions can make differences in the sound when used as string preparations. Cage uses various sorts of screws and bolts in several of his prepared piano works. More recently, Anna Thorvaldsdóttir's 2013 piece *Trajectories* for piano and electronics uses screws as its only preparation materials—asking that the pianist insert screws between two of the three unisons for twenty-five different notes (and leaving the particular size and material for the screws up to the performer).

To insert screws or bolts, follow the usual steps: depress the damper pedal to release the dampers, then gently move the strings apart using a plastic knife, a popsicle stick, or a wood or rubber wedge, and place the screw or bolt in place, and then remove the tool. Any metal harder than brass can easily damage the windings of the copper-wound bass strings, so, if possible, restrict use of screws and bolts to the steel strings and choose a softer substitute for the screw or bolt

Figure 9.12. String preparation, screws and bolts in the strings

for the bass strings (a wood dowel, for instance). If that, again, is not possible, wrapping the windings with yarn or twine before inserting a screw or bolt into the bass strings provides some protection to the strings but may also noticeably alter the sound. A slightly different sound may be preferable to damaging the strings.

Bolts with Washer and Nut

Jingling, rattling sounds can easily be added to the sound of placing a bolt between the strings of a set of unisons; simply add a washer or even multiple metal washers onto the bolt, with a nut to keep it loosely in place.

Golf Tees

Golf tees inserted between unison strings produce a light gong sound. Wedging one golf tee between one pair of a triple set of unisons adds mass to that pair and lowers their pitch. It does not affect the pitch of the third string of the unison set, so striking the key for this unison set once prepared produces more than one pitch.

Pencils

Composer Kui Dong's *Earth, Water, Wood, Metal, and Fire* (2001) has the pianist place ordinary wood pencils between the steel strings of several middle- and upper-register notes for the "Water" movement of the work. These, like golf tees, produce a gong-like sound.

Richard Bunger devised a more elaborate but related preparation—wedging a small wooden dowel vertically between two unisons, thereby dampening the strings to some extent, then screwing a wood screw into the top end of this dowel, with a few metal washers threaded into the screw, to add a rattling sound to each note as well.

If the object is placed between the strings in such a way as to dangle closely to the soundboard, then it's possible that, once the strings are set into motion, the object will strike the soundboard. *The Well-Prepared Piano* cautions against such preparations, as the object used for the string preparation could damage the soundboard (or at least the finish of the soundboard). But, this is a way to add a percussive tap at the beginning of each new key strike to the sound already produced by the object wedged in the strings. I suggest that special care must be taken if an object wedged in the strings will also be striking the soundboard. Cage uses this configuration in works, with a string preparation that extends to strike the soundboard. He specifies protection for the soundboard, asking the pianist to rest a small piece of cardboard on the soundboard between it and the wedged item. This still allows the wedged item, say a long golf tee, to add a percussive strike to the note onset, but it will strike the cardboard (which protects the soundboard).

DIRECTLY ATTACHED OBJECTS

There are many small implements that can easily be attached directly to the strings.

Poster Putty

As mentioned in chapter 5, make a ball of a pinch of poster putty (Blu-Tack), and press it onto the string or set of unison strings. A tiny amount does not affect the sound, so poster putty can be used as a way to mark harmonic nodes on strings to assist the player in quickly locating the node for a particular partial. A larger amount of poster putty mutes the sound. The resultant sound is dull but differs (and is more resonant) than muting the strings with the fingertips.

Masking Tape

Masking tape can be run parallel to a bass string and then pressed lightly along the length of the string. If you select tape that is wide enough, the edge of the tape brushes lightly against the neighboring string. This produces a gentle rattling sound as the taped string vibrates.

Strips of masking tape can also be run perpendicular across several strings at once. In Carl Schimmel's *The Blatherskite's Comeuppance* (2004) for wind ensemble, the pianist is instructed to place masking tape across the strings from above G6 to the top note to achieve a "plinky" sound.

Clothes Pins and Clips

Wooden clothespins, alligator clips, and plastic hair clips can all be clipped directly to the strings. In addition, one-half of a wooden clothespin makes a useful wedge that can be placed between two unisons (best used between two strings of a triple-unison set). A similar wedge can be fashioned from a section of bamboo for a slightly different sound.

Large Italian Metal Clips

Large metal clips have two rounded channels outlined within the jaws of the clip, similar to the ones found on standard wooden clothespins, and can be clipped directly to single-unison bass strings (see figure 9.13). These channels perfectly clasp the bass strings and create a wonderfully resonant, moderately deep, bell-like sound. And, best of all, if you mark the string position for placement beforehand, these can be attached or removed in the middle of a piece in a couple of seconds.

Figure 9.13.   String preparation, large Italian metal clips

Cap Pencil Eraser

An old-fashioned cap pencil eraser works as a simple attachment to any triple-unison note. Use a knife to cut a slit across the middle of the bottom of the eraser, and then snap this slit over the second string of the three unisons. The two halves of the eraser press against the outer two strings, so all three strings are stopped with a single eraser. This produces a round, muted sound.

Honey Dipper

A wood honey dipper, with the large end wedged between two of the single-unison bass strings, can be gently flicked or tapped on the handle to produce a complex, metallic resonant sound (see figure 9.14). The spacing of the middle of bass strings can vary greatly from piano model to model, so the honey dipper may not work as a preparation on every piano or wedged between particular strings on a piano.

Figure 9.14. String preparation, honey dipper

ONE NOTE, MULTIPLE PREPARATIONS

The three-string unisons lend themselves to multiple preparations. You can wedge a flat eraser between strings 1 and 2 of a triple set of unisons at one position and then a bolt between strings 2 and 3 at a different position. It is even possible to add further preparations; with this example, the composer or performer could add an additional surface preparation, so in addition to the wedged eraser and bolt, she could rest a sheet of cardstock on top of a range of strings including this prepared note. Bunger refers to such instances of multiple preparations on the same set of unisons as "hybrid preparations." I prefer the label "double preparation" (or "triple preparation," and so forth). There are many possible combinations beyond the scope of this text, and I encourage musicians to experiment with these.

Many preparations are dynamic—they respond quite differently when setting the string or strings in motion at a low dynamic level or at forte or fortissimo. In this way, some notes of a prepared piano may behave in some ways analogously to, say, some multiphonics on a clarinet or other wind instrument, in which some multiphonics sound two notes at a low dynamic and project a much more complex sonority, with three or four or more sounding notes at a louder dynamic.

UNA CORDA PREPARATIONS

Part of a piano's standard una corda pedal mechanism can easily be repurposed to make available two different timbres from a single set of unisons and played by a single key. The una corda pedal once depressed slides the keys and action a few millimeters to the right. On an unadulterated instrument, this has the effect of moving the hammers so that they strike strings 2 and 3 but do not strike string 1 of a set of unisons. For many objects attached to the strings, if one takes care that that preparation is only attached to string 1, when the player plays without the una corda, we can hear the timbre produced by the preparation, and once the player engages the una corda pedal and the hammer hits only strings 2 and 3, the timbre of the note should be very close to that of an ordinary note free of preparations.

Pianist and composer Michael Harrison has devised a very specialized piano that at its heart takes advantage of the una corda mechanism. Harrison worked with piano technicians Rick Wheeler and Don Person to modify a grand piano in order to give him access to more pitches from the ordinary piano keyboard. The instrument, which Harrison calls the "harmonic piano," has the middle string from each set of triple unisons removed and the hammers filed to reduce the strike surface of each hammer. The modified hammers hit only string 1 of each unison set; when the player engages the una corda mechanism, moving the hammers to the right, the narrowed strike area of each hammer hits only string 3 of each unison set. This modification enables Harrison to tune the left unisons to one tuning scheme and the right unisons to another, and in conjunction with the una corda pedal, the pianist can then access two differently tuned notes from each key on the piano (except in the bass register, where there is only one unison per key). Harrison's piano has an additional rail with mutes attached to it positioned in the gap left by the removed string 2 from the unison sets. This rail is tied to the una corda mechanism, so that, when the una corda is not engaged, it mutes string 3 of each unison set and, when the una corda is engaged, it mutes string 1. Harrison often tunes one set of unisons to five-limit just intonation and the other set to seven-limit just intonation, giving him access to many additional notes while playing the ordinary, unmodified keyboard. Even discounting the changes in the sound of the instrument caused by tuning it in just intonation, Harrison's harmonic piano sounds considerably different from other modern grand pianos: Harrison has configured the instrument so that only a single string at a time sounds when the pianist plays on the keys and created a piano with permanently installed una corda preparations.

DAMPER PREPARATION

As I have thus far only uncovered one work that prepares a damper and uses the mechanism of the damper pedal, I have not assigned a separate category to this preparation but instead mention it here because it depends on the damper mechanism (if not the actual damper pedal). Carson Kievman's 1992 work *The Temporary and Tentative Extended Piano* asks for hand bells to be hung above the dampers of two notes on the instrument and then has a cap nut affixed to the dampers of those two notes using double-sided tape. Depressing the keys for these two notes raises the dampers and strikes the hand bells with the cap nut. As the dampers are delicate, I advise against mounting anything to them. If, however, you decide to prepare the damper head in this way, I suggest placing the bells in such a way that the damper head with its cap nut only lightly strikes the bell surface, and I caution against using double-sided tape; the player could substitute a small loop of painter's tape.

HAMMER PREPARATIONS

Hammer preparations are founded on the idea that the materials of the surface striking the strings contribute much to the piano's characteristic sound. Many of the preparations I classify as hammer preparations involve modifying the hammers of the instrument. Because modern pianos have hammers covered with wool felt, a not particularly sturdy material, most ways of modifying the hammer striking surface are irreversible. Many hammer preparations damage a piano's hammer and necessitate replacing the hammer felt or replacing the entire hammer itself to restore the piano its usual sound. Repairing or replacing all of the hammers of a piano is an expensive and labor-intensive job. Fortunately, in most cases of such destructive hammer preparations, there are substitute preparations available that do not damage the instrument.

The tack piano is easily the most well-known hammer preparation. To prepare the hammers, press an ordinary tack into the wool at the striking surface of the hammer. I have played a tack piano a few times and have to admit that the sound is very appealing. But wait before doing this! The problem with this preparation is that it in all likelihood will permanently damage the hammers, so you should not stick tacks into the hammers of any instrument that you don't personally own and, even then, not into one that you do not ever want to be a tack piano permanently.

The tack piano can be found in many pieces. Lou Harrison's *Concerto in Slendro* calls for two tack pianos tuned in just intonation. His Symphony No. 2 (*Elegaic*) calls for tack piano, as do a few of his songs and chamber pieces. Count Basie and Joe Zawinul each recorded tack piano performances, and in the pop world, there are tack pianos included in recordings by such varied artists as the Beach Boys, Elvis Costello, Rolling Stones, Cheap Trick, Captain and Tennille, Fleetwood Mac, Ben Folds, Coldplay, and the Doors, as well as movie soundtracks by Jon Brion and the musical *Avenue Q*. Glenn Gould even commissioned a tack piano from Steinway (he called it a "harpsipiano"), and he used it in some performances of Bach.

The sound of the tacks actually in some ways mimics the sound of a very old piano. As a piano ages, the felt in the hammers hardens and compacts. This can make for a very hard striking surface, which produces a harsh, hard sound. If the old piano has also been allowed to get woefully out of tune, that, combined with the hardened hammers, gives it that "honky-tonk" piano sound. The tacks (plus detuning unisons) is a way of mimicking that old, neglected piano sound. Abbey Road Studios in London has a piano dedicated to the tack piano sound but without using tacks—they have a Steinway upright with lacquered hammers, so that the felt has been permanently hardened. Lacquering hammers is similarly permanent to inserting tacks into the hammers—to return that piano to being capable of producing a more usual piano sound would most likely require replacing all of the hammers. However, the lacquer-hardened hammers do have one advantage over using actual tacks—the lacquer has no chance of flying off and damaging other parts of the piano, whereas tacks can come off in performance.

Another method for producing the tack piano sound without using tacks is the mandolin rail. This is an attachment to the inside of an upright piano that allows you to lower a felt "curtain" between the hammers and the strings. The bottom of the felt is separated into strips, and metal tabs (like tack heads) are crimped onto the bottoms of these tabs. The hammers hit the strips, and the metal hits the strings. There don't seem to be any current pianos produced with the mandolin-rail option, but mandolin rails or the parts necessary to make your own mandolin rail are available. Installing the rail is fairly simple, and unlike inserting tacks into the hammers, the tabs do not instantly irreparably damage the hammers. I classify a mandolin rail as a type of surface preparation rather than a hammer preparation, as the rail does not attach to or modify the hammers at all.

I wanted the ability to have this tack piano sound on any piano without creating and installing a mandolin rail and certainly without permanently damaging the hammers. After spending a few days thinking about how to get this sound, I awoke one morning with a solution—and with it a whole new "family" of preparations!

HAMMER-WRAP PREPARATIONS

As far as I know, the following preparations are all new—so new that either no one at all has written a piece using the preparation, or in cases where I have managed to write a short study using the preparation, that study is the only piece that takes advantage of this particular preparation.

I call all of these hammer-wrap preparations because, though the following preparations can result in very different timbral effects, the method of preparing the instrument follows in each case almost exactly the same procedure. The basic idea at the foundation of these (as well as all other hammer preparations) is to change the piano's sound by changing the material that contacts the string. Hammers on modern pianos have a wood core and layers of wool felt wrapping. This wool is what is in contact with the strings when the key sends the hammer to strike the strings. The tack piano effect is so striking because this preparation to the hammers substitutes contact from the metal tack heads for the usual felt of the hammer: The metal (of the tack heads) strikes the strings.

The wrap materials need to be very light so that they do not add a lot of weight to the hammers and thereby change the feel and slow the speed of the instrument. All of my hammer-wrap preparations (so far) use a small length of aluminum foil to cover the hammer. Aluminum foil works well because it is very thin and light, and it is also very easy to crumple and attach to the hammer and later to uncrumple and remove. Hammer-wrap preparations are also very inexpensive, so it is possible to experiment with dozens of different strike materials for a very low outlay of money, and this also, I think, encourages much more experimentation in this category of preparations.

To wrap each hammer, you need a long enough piece of foil that it is a little more than twice the length of the hammerhead so it extends to the wooden back of the hammer (near where the hammer attaches to the hammer shank), and there is a little extra to crumple and wrap around both the wool and wood of the hammer. This means approximately a five-inch length of foil. For width, the wrap requires at least an inch to ensure that the full striking surface of the hammer is covered, and you may even want a piece that is three or four inches wide and therefore basically covers the whole hammer. This extra length adds negligible weight but ensures that the hammer wrap won't slip off the hammer midperformance. Nevertheless, the more foil used, the more there is that needs to be compressed against the hammer so that the foil does not rub against the adjacent hammers.

There are lots of different materials that can be glued to the wrap to form the new contact surface of the wrapped hammer. Because this idea arose out of my seeking a substitute for the tack piano effect, one that wouldn't damage the hammers, the first materials I sought were those that would provide this sound. Fortunately, this was easy. I found some small metal buttons to glue in place, and then I found metal self-stick circles that were even easier to affix. I found sheets of these self-stick pieces at various big box stores, and smaller craft stores may have them as well. I was able to buy enough pieces to prepare an entire piano for not much more than the price of a box of tacks.

The following is a list of some other materials you can affix to the aluminum foil, with brief descriptions of the resultant effect.

HAMMER-WRAP SURFACES

- *Aluminum Wrap Alone* (without any additional materials attached to the foil)
- *Metal Buttons or Self-Stick "Tack Heads"*: These produce the tack piano sound. It's a metallic, bright sound without the subtlety and fine control that the piano's regular hammer surface produces, but it produces the tack piano effect without damaging the instrument and without permanently modifying the instrument to install a mandolin rail.
- *Rubber*: I've tried a few different rubber items but so far had good results from both small, flat pencil erasers and small lengths of rubber insulation (see figure 9.15). For the insulation, acquire a long piece from your local hardware store, and cut into inch lengths; then glue these to the aluminum foil pieces ready for wrapping.

Figure 9.15. Hammer-wrap preparation, rubber

- *Wood*: I've found that very small, very thin (and usually brightly painted) squares of wood are available at craft stores in small boxes of several dozen pieces. These work really well—they're light, about the size of a dime, and easy to glue to the aluminum foil wrapping. The sound is similar to the metal-button or tack-head sound. (I do wonder if a softer, less-smooth wood surface might produce a more different sound.)

   I also tried breaking toothpicks into small lengths (with a length about the width of the face of one of the hammers) and then gluing several of these short lengths across the hammer (on the aluminum foil wrap, of course). The toothpick lengths run perpendicular to the strings, and if you were very careful with positioning, you might be able to get away with only using a single toothpick length per hammer, but I found it easier to glue three to five lengths to be sure that the striking surface was covered than to glue only a single length and have to spend a lot of time fine-tuning its position.

- *Leather*: Many early pianos featured doeskin- or leather-wrapped hammers, so I thought that, if there were a way of adding a leather surface to the hammers of a modern piano (with all of its concomitant advances to the action), we might have a perfect blend of old sounds and new control. I've tried a few different thicknesses of leather but so far produce the best results with small lengths of very thin, pliant leather glued to the aluminum foil wrapping, providing a round, dark sound.

- *Plastic wrap*: Not wanting to be so enamored of my aluminum foil wrap idea that I closed my mind to other possibilities, I have also tried plastic wrap. You can wrap the hammerhead in a small length of plastic wrap rather than aluminum foil; it shares many of the qualities of the foil. It is thin and light, and it can attach to the hammer and to itself without the need for an adhesive. Other striking surfaces can be created by gluing other materials onto the plastic-wrap-covered hammer just as those with the aluminum foil wrap.

At this writing I have only been exploring hammer-wrap preparations for a few weeks, so I expect to find—or for others to find—different formulae for some of these and to find many other wrapping materials and techniques than what I have devised so far (see figure 9.16).

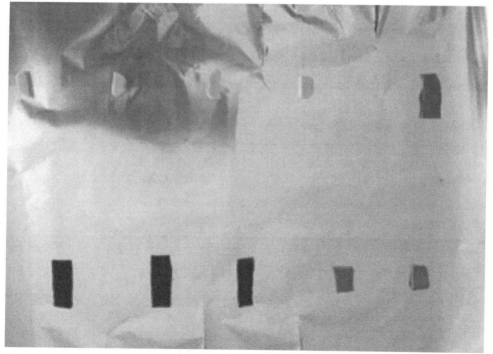

Figure 9.16. Hammer-wrap preparations: leather strips and flat erasers glued onto aluminum foil, ready to wrap onto hammers.

KEY PREPARATIONS

One preparation that may be applied directly to the keys is piano tuner's mutes used to wedge individual keys in place. Wedging select keys in place in their "at rest" position is a way of enabling the pianist to perform an ordinary on-the-keys glissando yet to sound, rather than all of the naturals or all of the chromatic notes, some subset of those notes. (See the discussion of harp glissando in chapter 3.) Wedging the keys in place takes time, so this preparation may entail a lot of effort for a limited musical use.

Another way of preparing the keys is to rest items on the key tops or to attach items to the key tops:

- *Small weights*: Small weights can be rested on individual key tops to allow those notes to ring freely (see figure 9.17). The pianist can strike the key first and then, while holding it down, add the weight or depress the key silently and add the weight, which produces a similar effect to depressing that key silently and catching its damper with the sostenuto pedal. William Duckworth's 1977–1978 cycle for piano *The Time Curve Preludes* includes this technique as a way of accumulating drones through the individual pieces. Duckworth's

Figure 9.17.   Key preparation, weights on key tops

score explains that the pianist should assemble seven key weights "by taping together four piano key weights" for each of the seven keys.[18] The score indicates that the keys should be depressed silently and then held in place with the lead weights before the pianist begins each prelude. Each prelude of the twenty-four has its own specific drone notes, with one prelude using a single drone note (prelude 12, the last piece in the first book of preludes, uses a single F drone) and another prelude making use of all seven weights (prelude 4 of the first book has seven drone notes). Composer Neely Bruce, the pianist for the premiere of *The Time Curve Preludes*, has experimented further using stacks of key leads to weigh down keys in this fashion. Bruce suggests assembling each key weight from five key leads (adding one additional lead to Duckworth's suggested four to hold the key down more securely) stacked together and taped as a bundle with masking tape. Bruce has used these in a few compositions and improvisations and dubbed them "Duckworth weights."[19]

- *Small Jingle Bells*: Small jingle bells can be taped to the key tops so that, when the player depresses a key, it shakes the jingle. (So far I don't know of any works that call for such a preparation.)
- *Very Small Shakers*: Small shakers can also be rested on the key tops to add their sound to ordinary on-the-keys playing. Small plastic candy dispensers, such as those used for Tic Tacs, are narrow enough to rest on individual white keys at the end of the exposed key at the fallboard (see figure 9.18). Forceful

Figure 9.18. Key preparation, Tic Tac shakers on keytops

key returns shake the candy dispenser and add a subtle rattle to the note's ordinary onset. The candy dispenser can be taped with masking tape to the key top, or placed on a white key between two black keys on any D, G, or A key (the taller black keys secure the shaker in place). Alternately, these can be rested horizontally across pairs of black keys to access the same effect.

- *Drumstick or Dowel*: A drumstick or wood dowel can be rested on top of the black keys at the fallboard. The return from depressing one of the black keys lightly taps the wood.
- *Electronic Key-Top Triggers*: There are also electronic control surfaces that can be attached to the key surfaces. These do not in themselves add sounds to the pianist's key strikes but instead offer the player controls of external electronic devices from the surface of the keys without asking the player to play some other external keyboard controller. (See the discussion of McPherson's TouchKeys overlays in chapter 2.)

PEDAL PREPARATIONS

String preparations that are activated by the una corda pedal are covered earlier in the una corda preparations section. So far I have not uncovered many composers experimenting with pedal preparations. For pedal preparations, I have limited discussion here to devices added in some way to the pedals themselves, not to the strings and engaged in some way by the use of the pedals. A very basic pedal preparation is to apply a weight to a pedal to keep it engaged. A brick or other heavy item can be leaned on the damper pedal, for instance, to keep all the dampers released from the strings for an entire work (see figure 9.19). Cowell in the score for *The Banshee* calls for an assistant to depress and hold the damper pedal down throughout the work. Weighting the pedal serves the same purpose and removes the need for an assistant. Another way of producing this effect is to wedge the pedal in its down position. To do so, press the pedal down, and place a small compressed wool or rubber wedge in the gap produced on the back of the pedal lyre when the pedal is depressed. Theoretically, small jingles or some other small sound producers could be tied or taped to one of the pedals in order to be rattled or rung each time the player depresses the pedal (see figure 9.20).

Figure 9.19. Pedal preparation, wool wedge in damper pedal mechanism

Figure 9.20. Pedal preparation, jingle tied to una corda pedal

NOTATION FOR PREPARATIONS

In most instances, when the piano is prepared and those prepared notes are sounded from the keys, the notation typically does not reflect the differences in timbre. For most of Cage's works for prepared piano, if the table of preparations were to be removed from the score, the score's appearance would suggest a simple, often modal line played *ordinario* on the keys. If the prepared notes should be sounded in other ways (e.g., pizzicato), then the score can use the notation for that sounding technique.

I believe this is clear, but especially in instances in which the work only requires a few preparations or in which the prepared notes clearly form a different voice or voices within the texture, the composer may want to build a separation of this voice into the score. An easy way to do this is to use different notehead shapes for different choirs of sounds. For a piece with a single prepared bass string with a wooden clothespin on it to produce a wooden "thunk" and three middle-register strings with threaded coins on them to produce gong-like sounds, in addition to a table of preparations with explanations and a legend, the score could use square noteheads for the single bass note and noteheads with circles around them for the three prepared middle-register notes.

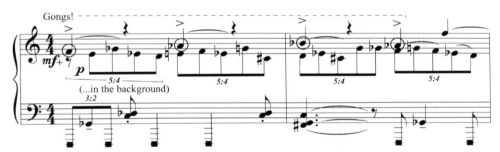

Figure 9.21. Notation for limited prepared notes

The Toy Piano

Though the toy piano is a separate, distinct instrument from the piano, there are many contemporary pianists who augment their performances by playing toy pianos both simultaneously with the piano and separately from it. The toy piano to some extent is becoming part of the standard touring kit for many pianists, and there are even a few pianists who travel performing solely on the toy piano. Because of this popularity, a little background, general performance information, and notes on extended techniques and preparations for the toy piano serve as a supplement here.

HISTORY

Most sources date the first appearance of the toy piano to some time in the nineteenth century. The toy piano was used as a way of introducing small children to the keys of the piano in a small size that was on the scale of other toys. Some early forms of the instrument used small glass bars as the resonating material, and these were struck by small wooden mallets or hammers triggered by keys.

Albert Schoenhut, born to a toymaking family in Germany, began making toy pianos as a young man, and in 1866, a representative for the Philadelphia department store Wannamaker's heard about Schoenhut's work with toy pianos and brought the seventeen-year-old to Philadelphia to repair the glass bars in the German-made toy pianos that the department store was importing, which were getting damaged in transit.[1] At some point, Schoenhut, in the instruments he was constructing himself, began replacing the delicate glass with metal bars, creating a much more durable and portable instrument. Schoenhut considered the pianos he was making as true instruments and included music with them to encourage children to make music with his toy pianos. In 1872, he founded the Schoenhut Piano Company to manufacture toy pianos.[2]

From the 1950s through the 1970s, the two main makers of toy pianos were the American competitors Schoenhut and Jaymar, and in the late 1970s, Jaymar acquired Schoenhut. After some financial difficulties, a new Schoenhut Piano Company emerged in 1996 and is now the most familiar marque in the toy piano world (see figure 10.1). From 1939 until a fire destroyed their factory in 1970, Michelsonne Paris manufactured toy pianos created by Victor Michel (see figure 10.2). Michelsonne toy pianos are difficult to find, especially outside Europe, but are very much prized for their unique, delicate sound. The tone is quite different from Schoenhut or Jaymar toy pianos or their many Chinese copies—the fundamental is much more prominent on Michelsonne instruments, and the overall sound is much more delicate.

Figure 10.1.   Thirty-seven-key Schoenhut toy piano

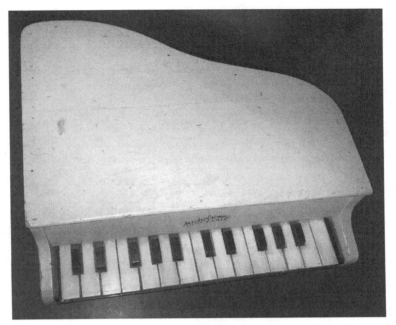

Figure 10.2. Twenty-five-key Michelsonne toy piano

MATERIALS

Most toy pianos today use plastic keys with a greatly simplified action in comparison to a piano's. The keys set into motion small wooden or plastic hammers, which then strike metal rods. There are still some toy pianos that use small, flat metal bars (resembling small glockenspiel bars) instead of the rods, but these are much less common here in the twenty-first century. Models that resemble grand pianos as well as tabletop models and both low and tall uprights are all common. Toy pianos do not have any sort of pedal mechanism, and there are no dampers.[3] The sound from the resonating rods or bars has a similar envelope to that of the piano—the loudest and most harmonically rich sound is at the onset, and there is a very quick tapering of all that sound soon after, with a tiny amount of sustain of mostly the lowest few partials beyond that.

RANGE

Unlike the piano's long-standard eighty-eight keys, toy pianos come in many different configurations. Some instruments are diatonic notes only and may have as few as eight keys (some of these "white-key only" instruments have the black keys represented in some way—either with black rectangles painted at the tail ends of the white keys or with stationary black keys arranged within the keyboard but unconnected to any mechanism for sounding). Among the chromatic

Figure 10.3. Sounding ranges for typical twenty-five-, thirty-, thirty-seven-, and forty-nine-key toy pianos

instruments, different toy piano models present a variety of the number of keys and their distribution, with most instruments having at least an octave and a half span and some having as many as forty-nine keys (see figure 10.3). Instruments with more than thirty-seven keys are much less common than smaller ones (see figure 10.4). Some composers and pianists have begun to consider a thirty-key model running from a low C to a high F as the standard instrument that most players have access to. The thirty-seven-key models usually add a lower fifth to that range, running from a low F up three full octaves to a high F. Schoenhut currently makes chromatic models with eighteen, twenty-five, thirty, and thirty-seven keys in many different colors, finishes, and furniture styles. Michelsonne Paris made chromatic models with thirteen, sixteen, twenty, twenty-five, thirty, thirty-seven, and forty-nine keys.

Figure 10.4. Forty-nine-key Jaymar toy piano

Composers should be safe in scoring for a thirty-key instrument, and at least in North America, there are plenty of used and inexpensive Jaymar and Schoenhut instruments available, as well as affordable new instruments by Schoenhut, so that providing an instrument to a player for a performance shouldn't be that difficult to do. There are very few pianists who travel with their own concert grand piano, but many players carry with them a thirty-key (or even thirty-seven-key) toy piano. Famed toy pianist Margaret Leng Tan, for instance, has a travel case for her Schoenhut so that she can carry it more easily onto a plane for touring.

So far, notation is almost but not completely standardized for the toy piano. Many composers score for the toy piano as an octave-transposing instrument, notating the part down an octave from sounding pitch. The notation thereby mostly does not require ledger lines and allows the player to identify middle C (as notated, not sounding) on the instrument in about the middle of the keyboard, just as it is on a standard piano. One notable exception to this practice is the HOCKET piano duo. They prefer for composers to notate at pitch for the instrument because their repertoire includes a lot of works that use both standard pianos and toy pianos. In this way, the notation acknowledges the sonic placement of the toy piano's notes in the same location in pitch space as the piano's notes (rather than displaced by an octave on the toy piano). Thomas Kotcheff of HOCKET says that, if notated at sounding pitch, the F3 to F6 "standard" toy piano range is the same as that for the melodica and shares the same bottom note as the piano accordion, so notating at pitch is a way of unifying the notation across these three keyboard instruments. Another advantage to notating the toy piano at pitch is that the toy piano is a "high" instrument, so it is a little strange to see notes well into the bass clef for it. As Kotcheff puts it, the "toy piano is a treble instrument with a treble range and reading notes in bass clef is extremely counterintuitive."[4] Nevertheless, most toy piano scores transpose an octave lower than sounding.

DYNAMICS AND ARTICULATIONS

With its more primitive action and its hard plastic (or, in some older instruments, wooden) hammers, the toy piano has a much more restricted dynamic range than a piano. Fine distinctions between *ppp* and *pp* or between *ff* and *fff* are beyond the capabilities of most, if not all, of these instruments. Composer David Smooke, a huge advocate for the toy piano, suggests that, without amplification, the true dynamic range is perhaps as narrow as only mezzo-piano to mezzo-forte.[5] A composer can treat the toy piano a bit more like the harpsichord than the piano and add more doublings and more new note attacks to give the effect of a higher dynamic and reduce the number of new note onsets and doublings for a very low dynamic. Notes on the toy piano have very short sustain (with the notes in the upper register of the instrument having considerably shorter sustain). On most instruments, the toy piano's sustain is perhaps most comparable to the sustain of notes in the top octave of a standard piano, and with its comparably tiny case and resonating surfaces, even the most resonant bass notes of a forty-nine-key toy piano sustain, at the most, like a high-tenor note on a piano; the drop-off of sound after the rich percussive note onset on the toy piano is just too drastic to leave much sound to sustain for long.

Dense chords and clusters are very effective on the toy piano and exploit the fact that the sound is all packed into the onset of a new key attack. Just as many fine gradations of dynamics may be impossible for a player to convey, there are fewer articulations that prove effective on the instrument, as well. Staccato or slurred phrases are reasonable details for a player, as are heavy accents, but further gradations of articulation are likely to prove impossible for a performer to campaign for successfully.

THE ACTION

Most modern toy piano models share a similar action design: A plastic key pivots on a thin balance rail that works in the manner of the balance rail and the balance pin of a piano. There is no action rail or separate action assembly. Instead, the tail of the key has a plastic hammer that swings on an axle from an at-rest position against the tail of the key itself toward the sounding rod when the head of the key is depressed (see figure 10.5). A combination of the ricochet of the hammer off the rod and the force of gravity returns the hammer to its at-rest position. There is no heel cushion for the hammer shank to rest on. There are no adjustable parts and no padding. The keys exert very little control over the hammer's motion; they merely launch the hammer in a straight line in the direction of the sounding rod. Because there are no bridles or any repetition parts to assist with the hammer's return, on many instruments, the return can be somewhat sluggish.

On a new or well-maintained vintage instrument, the mostly plastic action can be quite fast, though the primitive single escapement action does not handle repetitions particularly quickly. The extreme lightness of the action and the shallow key dip combined can also prove a detriment to speed, as the player doesn't find the resistance she expects from a piano's keys and may miscalculate exactly when in the keystroke to reverse direction to restrike. Repeating a single note steadily and very quickly is challenging, but a player can more easily play a trill or tremolo alternating notes or even alternating chords at a very fast rate.

On most toy pianos, the action is quite noisy. Unlike the padded elegance of the modern grand piano's action, most toy piano actions use no soft materials at all—no leather, no wool felt, no paper. Part of the characteristic sound of the instrument

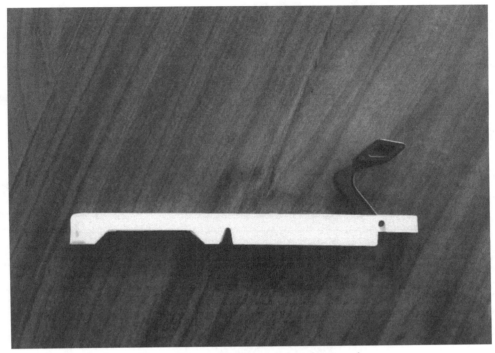

Figure 10.5. The key and hammer assembly from a Schoenhut toy piano

is the sharp, percussive clack of the hard plastic hammer hitting the metal resonating rod. Added to this is the additional clack of the plastic hammer's return to its at-rest position against the plastic tail of the key. Whereas the hammer return of a well-regulated modern piano can be almost silent, with the hammer shank coming back to rest against a rail thickly padded with soft wool, hard plastic meeting hard plastic marks the key return of a toy piano's hammer. In this way, the toy piano's key release can sound somewhat reminiscent of a harpsichord, with the sound of the harpsichord's plectrum touching the string as the jack returns to its at-rest position when the key is released.

With a little work, the clacking at key release on a toy piano can be reduced a bit. Because this additional operating noise is caused by the hard plastic of the back of the hammer hitting the hard plastic of the tail of the key, padding either of these surfaces in some way may reduce the plastic-on-plastic sound. On my forty-nine-key Jaymar instrument, I have set small strips of wool felt in the mortise of the key tail so that the back of the hammer hits this felt instead of the plastic, and this has reduced the sound some while not slowing the action in any appreciable way. I can imagine that placing a very small piece of rubber either on the back of the hammer or on the tail of the key might have a similar effect, but care would need to be taken that the weight of the hammer wasn't increased in such a way as to slow its motion or detrimentally affect the feel of the action. On a couple of Michelsonne instruments and on one German copy of a Michelsonne toy piano, I have seen just this sort of padding—each of these toy pianos had a small foam strip affixed to the tail of each key, cushioning and thereby quieting the hammer returns.

THE PHYSICAL CHALLENGES OF THE TOY PIANO

As toy pianos were originally designed as starter pianos for young children, the actual instrument can be physically awkward for an adult to play. Different pianists face this challenge in different ways. Pianists Thomas Kotcheff and Sarah Gibson (HOCKET duo) carry boxes with them and place their upright Schoenhut toy pianos on top of these, raising the keyboard height to a comfortable level. Some "grand" models feature detachable legs, and once the legs are detached, the body of the instrument can be placed flat atop a desk or a small table or even on top of a grand piano's music desk, providing other solutions. Some performers sit on the toddler-height bench that comes with many toy piano models and embrace this low posture. Margaret Leng Tan sits on a miniature bench while resting one knee on the floor. Finally, some players sit cross-legged on the floor and reach up to the toy piano's keyboard. This posture addresses the physical placement of the keyboard.

Another physical distinction facing the pianist when playing the toy piano: the size of the keys. Most contemporary Schoenhut models have keys the same width as a piano's keys, as the maker markets these as pedagogical instruments that help a child to transition to a full-size piano. The Schoenhut Model 3798 has naturals approximately $^{15}/_{16}$-inch wide, the same width of most full-size pianos' keys, but this is not a width held standard on different models or makes of toy piano. Some of the Michelsonne toy pianos I've measured have slightly narrower keys, with $^{7}/_{8}$-inch-wide naturals.

The much shorter key length on toy pianos can have a significant effect on performance. Short keys mean that the player has much less territory to use for finger crossing and simply to navigate fitting chords under the hand or to transition from one hand position to another. Xenia Pestova, a frequent performer of the toy piano who has commissioned several works for toy piano and toy piano with electronics, addresses the variability of key sizes for toy pianos, warning the performer, "[I]t is therefore vitally important for the performer to practice on the instrument they intend to use in concert to avoid unpleasant surprises."[6]

REPERTOIRE FOR TOY PIANO

John Cage's *Suite for Toy Piano* (1948) is often cited as the starting point for repertoire specific to the instrument, music not simply adapted from standard piano

Figure 10.6. Example from Cage's *Suite for Toy Piano*
Copyright © 1960 by Henmar Press, Inc. Used by permission of C. F. Peters Corporation. All Rights Reserved.

literature (see figure 10.6). In 1996 artist-composer Trimpin devised a work he called *klavier nonette* for installation in a gallery in Seattle. He retrofitted nine toy pianos with MIDI-controlled player mechanisms and added a master control that worked like a jukebox—gallery goers could select which piece they'd like to hear and insert a quarter, and the computer would send MIDI information to the nine toy pianos stationed throughout the gallery space. For this work, Trimpin issued a call for scores and chose several works by different composers, placing those works alongside a few piano works arranged for the piece.

There is now a good body of solo music for toy piano, and there are also works for toy piano in combination with other toy instruments, works for toy piano and electronics, and works for piano with toy piano. French musician Pascal Ayerbe has created albums of music played at least primarily on toy instruments, often featuring performances on a Michelsonne toy piano as a part of the large toy instrumentarium. Pianist Margaret Leng Tan, who worked with John Cage in preparing his *Suite for Toy Piano* for performance, has become a specialist in toy piano performance and has released multiple albums of works for toy piano. She also has commissioned many works for toy piano or for toy piano in combination with other toy instruments.

The toy piano is experiencing a boom right now, with festivals of toy pianos on both coasts of the United States in 2016, as well as many concerts focused on music for the instrument. More and more composers are beginning to experiment with the instrument, and more and more pianists are adding works for toy piano to their concert performances.

In addition to Margaret Leng Tan, many other pianists have gravitated to the toy piano, including Phyllis Chen, Xenia Pestova, Nadia Shpachenko-Gottesman, Mark Robson, the HOCKET duo, Isabel Ettenauer, Shiau-uen Ding, Adam Marks, and Pascal Meyer. Several contemporary composers have also been drawn to the instrument, among them Karlheinz Essl, Phyllis Chen, David Smooke, and myself.

In 2001, partially influenced by the University of California, San Diego's, Geisel Library–hosted annual Toy Piano Festival, the U.S. Library of Congress designated a unique call number and subject heading for toy piano scores—separate from piano scores.

TUNING

Intonation for toy pianos can be problematic. Vintage instruments have often strayed at least a little from A-440 Hz, and often the intonation across a single instrument is also off to some extent. The overtones are so prominent in the sound of the instrument that, even when a toy piano is in tune, the clash from the discrepancies between the just intonation of some very strong overtones and the equal-tempered tuning of the fundamentals from other keys is present. Many composers and performers see this as part of the charm of the sound. However, the fundamentals themselves can at least be tuned.

To lower the pitch of one of the sounding rods, the free end of the rod may be wrapped with a small length of fine copper wire.[7] Wire wrapping does change the timbre of the note very slightly, but some players willingly trade changed timbre for a few notes for a more in-tune instrument that can be played better alongside a piano and other instruments in an ensemble.

Raising the pitch is a more delicate operation because, unlike wire wrapping the rods, it's a permanent modification. To raise the pitch, the rod length needs to be shortened. This can be done by filing by hand or by grinding off a small amount of the free end of the rod using a rotary tool, such as a Dremel tool, or even a bench grinder. If you're attempting this operation, grind only a very small amount off the rod at a time, as, once the rod is shortened too much, the only way to lower the pitch is to wrap the rod with wire (and change the timbre of the note, as mentioned earlier).

These modifications to change tuning could also be used to open up tunings for the instrument, retuning several notes on a toy piano to make an alternate tuning or various microtones available on it.

CLUSTERS

There are at least a few techniques for the piano (some of which still get classified as extended) that can easily be transferred to the toy piano, though the effect on the instrument may be quite different. A very simple transfer is clusters in all their many varieties. Diatonic and chromatic clusters can be fingered for specific notes or played with the fists, palms, or (on very large toy pianos) even the forearms. The clusters can be rolled up or down (or both simultaneously) and played at all available dynamic levels. On most toy pianos, quite large clusters are easily possible with the palms (on some instruments of smaller compass, two hands are even enough to play a full-compass cluster). There is something quite joyous about toy piano clusters, and lots of composers have taken advantage of these.

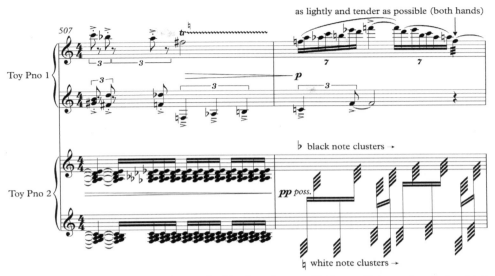

Figure 10.7.   Alternating black-key and white-key clusters, Holloway-Nahum, *Remember Me?*, **p. 61, mm. 507–8**

Composer Aaron Holloway-Nahum's *Remember Me?*—a giant work for two pianos and two toy pianos—has the players migrate from both playing on pianos at the opening to both playing on toy pianos later in the work. It includes several interesting techniques for both piano and toy piano, including many different cluster passages for the toy piano. Figure 10.7, for example, is a passage alternating black-key and white-key clusters. Thomas Kotcheff's *death, hocket, and roll* (2014) for two toy pianos has lots of rhythmic clusters, often played locked together by two performers on two toy pianos (see figure 10.8).

Figure 10.8.   Rhythmic unison clusters, Kotcheff, *death, hocket, and roll*, **m. 50**

GLISSANDO

On-the-keys glissando also transfers well from the piano to the toy piano. Holloway-Nahum's *Remember Me?* makes use of glissandi, sometimes mixed with clusters (see figure 10.9).

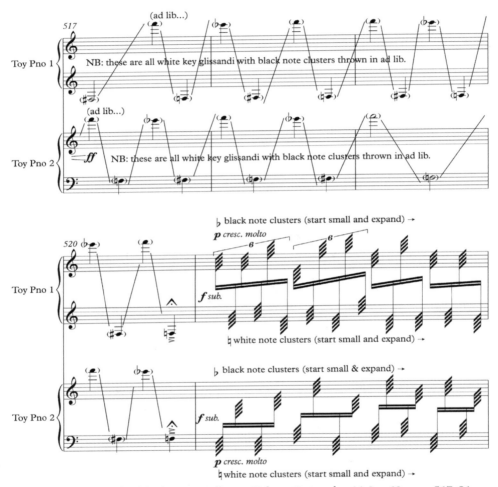

Figure 10.9.   Glissandi with clusters, Holloway-Nahum, *Remember Me?* p. 63, mm. 517–21

UNDERPRESSURE

The guiro effect, or underpressure on-the-keys playing (used by Lachenmann in his 1969 work for solo piano *Guero*), also transfers nicely to the toy piano. This glissando on the key tops without depressing the keys far enough to allow the hammers to strike makes a lovely full-clacking sound on the toy piano and can be executed on the sharps or naturals alone, or on both simultaneously—and even in contrary motion. Because piano makers pride themselves on silencing as much of the sounds of the action as possible, and because a carefully regulated piano keyboard leaves very little play in the key action that does not get transferred as energy directed at striking the strings, the toy piano's comparatively loose and noisy action actually generates much more sound for the guiro effect on the piano. Aaron Holloway-Nahum's *Remember Me?* uses underpressure glissando (actually using the term *underpressure*) and asks the players to "caress" the keys.

Samara Rice's *OnomataPiano* (2016) for two toy pianos has the players drag their hands across the keys without sounding pitches as one of many percussive and theatrical motions within her piece (see figure 10.10). Rice's piece also has taps and slaps to the body of the piano and taps with the fingertips to the ledge right in front of the keys—all very effective transfers to the toy piano.

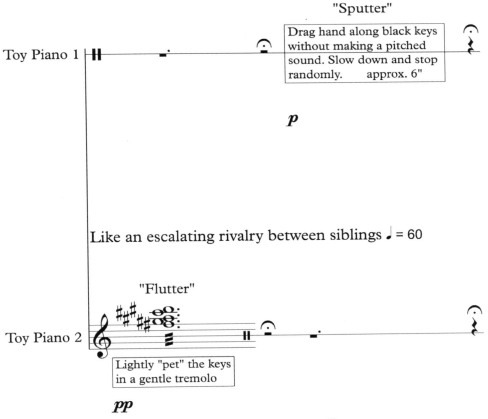

Figure 10.10. Underpressure glissando, Samara Rice, *OnomataPiano*

OTHER TECHNIQUES FOR THE TOY PIANO

So far, only a few composers have explored inside-the-instrument techniques on the toy piano. Nevertheless, there are several techniques that are easily available on most instruments. For most of these, the player needs access to the sounding rods. For many upright instruments, removing the top of the instrument and a single front panel reveals the sounding rods. Toy pianos with a grand piano design sometimes allow the lid to be raised and propped just like on a full-size grand piano, and on some instruments, this may reveal the sounding rods. Others either have a fixed lid that or include an additional thin board underneath the lid that must be removed. Gaining access to the sounding rods makes available many additional techniques.

MUTING

If the particular model of toy piano allows access to the tone rods, then it is easy to mute them. The easiest muting technique is simply to grab the very end of a rod with the fingertips of one hand while striking the keys as usual with the other. This produces a dull clunk instead of the normal resonant note. Varying the position of the muting fingers while continuing to strike the key produces this dull clunk with a varying pitch and so provides a method for playing microtones and even a muted glissando on the toy piano.

PLUCKING AND GLIDES ON THE TONE RODS

The player can pluck the resonating bars or strike them with the fingertips and fingernails. These both produce a very delicate sound, but this can be effective with amplification. The player can also pluck the rods using various plectra—heavy guitar picks and standard golf tees each serve this purpose effectively. Toy piano player and composer David Smooke has done a lot of work—much of it live improvisation—using these techniques.

PERCUSSION

The player can also strike the rods with various beaters. Because the toy piano has no dampers, the rods are always free to vibrate. The spacing between the sounding rods is quite tight, so larger beaters will necessarily strike multiple notes at once. Metal knitting needles; pencils; chopsticks; and small, hard plastic mallets bring out different timbres from the instrument; and there are many other beaters that also work effectively with the toy piano's metal rods.

The instrument also lends itself to being played on other surfaces with mallets and other strikers. Hitting the case sides or top either separately or in conjunction with sounding notes *ordinario* can be quite effective. On some instruments, hitting the soundboard produces a nice, dry percussive sound. On some instruments, dragging a Super Ball mallet along the soundboard or the cabinet's flat surfaces produces a little friction skip sound (a short moan).

BOWING

Bowing the tone rods is a very nice sound. The toy piano's tone rods can be bowed using an EBow or rosined fishing line. To provide a little more control, tie the ends of the fishing line bunches to some spools to use as handles. These make it a little more cumbersome to move the bow from one tone row to another (which you might be able to do faster if you were just using loops of fishing line without handles), but the handles make it easier to get a solid consistent sound from the rod.

Bowed toy piano notes are distinctive from most of the other sounds the instrument provides—they're long sounds without a sharp, percussive onset of the sound. An effective combination is to use electronic modification to drop the sound a couple of octaves and add some delay, along with a few bowed notes to provide the background for the short, high-pitched, percussive sounds we associate with the instrument.

FULL-COMPASS DEAD-STROKE

Through manipulating the instrument's position to take advantage of gravity, it is possible to produce a dead-stroke on the toy piano—a note in which the hammer strikes the tone rod and then remains at rest against the rod, immediately dampening the note.[8] Because most toy pianos are quite light, it is possible to produce a "global" or full-compass dead-stroke—a simultaneous dead-stroke of every hammer on the instrument. It's easiest to manage this on an upright model toy piano, one in which the tone bars are vertically suspended (perpendicular to the keys). For such an instrument, the player needs only to lift and tilt the piano backward. This movement tilts all of the hammers toward the tone rods, and gravity keeps the hammers at rest against them until the player tilts the instrument back toward its normal at-rest position. Especially on larger-compass instruments, this move makes a loud and satisfying "kerchunk" sound. I've seen this technique used in a couple of theatrically oriented, partially improvisatory toy piano works. For lack of a better name for it, I call it a full-compass dead-stroke.

PREPARATIONS

The toy piano lends itself to experimentation. Many experiments we might hesitate to try out on a piano for fear of damaging such an expensive instrument the toy piano allows us the freedom to try. There are a few simple preparations that are easy to do on the toy piano. You can "prepare" individual tone rods with a pinch of poster putty (Blu-Tack) and mute a few or all of the rods. Muting on the toy piano is perhaps not as drastic a timbral change as it is on the piano, but it still opens up an additional sound. Muting with the fingers slows down performance, but it also gives the player a lot of control over the level of muting and allows for a gradual transition from a completely damped, pitchless sound to a full *ordinario* sound. Another preparation is to attach alligator clips to the rods (see figure 10.11). These go on and come off really quickly, and the sound is, to my ear, a bit like prepared piano with screws wedged into the strings.

I first tried out hammer-wrap preparations on the toy piano before transferring these to the piano (see chapter 9). I've discovered that you can prepare the instrument by attaching softer materials to the hammers, changing the striking surface and thereby changing the timbre produced. Attaching a small slice of a rubber eraser to the hammer face produces a sweeter, more delicate sound.

Figure 10.11.   Tone rod preparation, alligator clips

Appendix A

Repertoire

The number of recent and contemporary composers and pianists expanding the resources of the piano precludes an exhaustive assemblage of works here. In some cases, a composer is represented by a single work, while other relevant works do not appear. A few composers are represented by several works. The following list of scores give, I hope, a healthy starting point for pianists looking for repertoire that takes advantage of extensions to classical technique and expansions of the possibilities of the piano through physical and electronic augmentation. For each listing I give, wherever possible, the date of composition rather than of publication. And, most listings include a brief listing of some of the special techniques or preparations involved.

FOR SOLO PIANO

Adler, Samuel. "Bells and Harps." From *Gradus*, book 3. 1979. [muting, harmonics]

Anderson, T. J. *Watermelon*. 1971. [silently fingered notes, black- and white-key glissandi]

Baker, Drew. *Stress Position*. 2008. [amplification; extreme hand position requires the pianist to play with both arms extended for entire piece; part of the piece must be performed in darkness—theatrical aspects]

Bartók, Béla. "Harmonics," from *Mikrokosmos*, vol. 4. 1926–1939. [silently depressed keys]

Behrman, David. *Ricercar*. 1961. [prepared piano]

Berger, Arthur. *Five Pieces for Piano*. 1969. [two prepared notes (rubber mute, metal screws), hand muting]

Berio, Luciano. *erdenklavier*. 1969. [keys held for continued resonance, rhythmic notation for damper pedal]

————. *Sequenza IV.* 1965–1966, 1993. [silently resonating notes, fingered clusters]

Bettison, Oscar. *An Inventory of Remnants.* 2009. [piano/toy piano/glockenspiel/melodica/percussion (one player)]

Beyer, Johanna. *Clusters (or, New York Waltzes).* 1936. [clusters]

————. *Suite for Piano.* 1939. [double-forearm clusters, fist and open-hand clusters, glissando cluster over all eighty-eight keys]

Boone, Benjamin. *Inside Antics.* 2007. [pianist uses plates, coffee cups, and eating utensils on the strings and drinking glasses as slides on the strings]

Boulez, Pierre. *Sonata No. 3.* 1955–1957, 1963, 1967, 1977. [half una corda]

Bresnick, Martin. *Ishi's Song.* 2012. [pianist sings, also sostenuto pedal effects]

Brown, Earle. *Four Systems.* 1954. [graphic score, score suggests that one way of interpreting thick bars is as clusters]

Bunger, Richard. *Two Pieces for Prepared Piano.* 1977. [various string preparations including clothespin wedges, screws, vinyl tubing, credit card, coins, erasers]

Byron, Don. *7 Etudes for Piano.* 2008. [singing pianist]

Cage, John. *Music of Changes.* 1951. [pizzicato, beaters on strings, silently depressed notes, also proportional notation]

————. *The Perilous Night.* 1943–1944. [various preparations]

————. *Sonatas and Interludes.* 1946–1948. [various preparations]

————. *Two Pastorales.* 1960. [prepared piano]

————. *Water Walk.* 1959 [piano and many noisemakers, one performer; plays strings with mechanical fish, strum glissandi]

Cassidy, Aaron. *Ten monophonic miniatures for solo pianist.* 2003. [amplified piano; playing keys with backs of fingers, knuckles, and fingernails; different kinds of muting; pizzicato]

Castro Larrea, Abel. *Lengua Animal.* 2014. [scrapes on strings, glissandi, harmonics]

Childs, Barney. *37 Songs.* 1973. [prepared piano]

Ciach, Brian. *Piano Sonata No. 4.* "The Great Scream." 2014. [pizzicato, clusters, glissandi along string length while sounding with key, palm slaps to bass strings]

Cope, David. *Parallax.* 1976. [hitting bass strings with metal edge of a ruler]

Cowell, Henry. *Aeolian Harp.* 1923. [strummed strings, "autoharp" strumming]

————. *Antinomy.* 1914. [forearm cluster tremolo]

————. *The Banshee.* 1925. [strummed strings, string sweep]

————. *Sinister Resonance.* 1930. [stopping low-bass string with heavy pressure, then sounding with key]

————. *Tides of Manaunaun.* 1917. [various types of cluster, including rolled forearm clusters and clusters with melody notes at the top of the cluster]

————. *Tiger.* 1928. [hand and forearm clusters, silently depressed notes]

Crumb, George. *Eine Kleine Mitternachtmusik (A Little Midnight Music).* 2002. [silently depressed kets, strummed notes, harmonics with fingernail scrape, mallet hits to braces, pizzicato, pianist whispers/speaks]

————. *Gnomic Variations.* 1981. [pizzicato, glissandi on strings, muted notes, harmonics, silently depressed notes caught with sostenuto]

———. *Makrokosmos*, book 1. 1972. [autoharp effect, pizzicato with ft and fn, harmonics, others]

———. *Makrokosmos*, book 2. 1973. [harmonics, pizzicato, whistling, singing]

Curran, Alvin. *Inner Cities 1–14*. 1993–2010. [various vocalizings, growls, shrieks, etc.]

Curtis-Smith, Curtis. *Rhapsodies*. 1978. [bowed piano, small wine bottle used as slide, golf ball on strings, pizzicato, others]

Dench, Chris. *E-330 plays*. 1991, 2003. [extensive use of pedals, including tre corde outer voices quickly alternating with una corda inner voices, half-pedaling, slow pedal release, sostenuto pedal use]

———. *Piano Sonata*. 2015. [detailed pedal indications, tempo changes indicated with acceleration/deceleration, lines above staff, fingered clusters]

———. *tiento de medio registro alto*. 1978, 2003. [fingered cluster, with particular fingerings suggested—including four notes to be played with two fingers]

Deyoe, Nicholas. *Fantasia III*. 2005.

———. *NCTRN*. 2014. [prepared notes, clusters]

Duckworth, William. *The Time Curve Preludes*. 1978–1979. [weights on key tops]

Edgerton, Michael Edward. *Noise is interrupting my practice: Silence is when my reaction is quiet. Silence is my protest against the way things are*. 2014. [piano and amplification]

Eggert, Moritz. *Hämmerklavier XII*. 2002 [prepared piano, kazoo, and harmonica one player]

Ferneyhough, Brian. *Lemma-Icon-Epigram*. 1981. [silently depressed notes, extreme dynamics, very detailed pedal indications]

———. *Opus Contra Naturam*. 2000. ["shadow play for speaking pianist," score includes spoken part]

Fox, Christopher. *At the edge of time*. 2007. [prepared piano]

Friar, Sean. *Chrysalis*. 2016. [piano/percussion, one player]

Fuhler, Cor. *Love Is Statistic Static* for piano, radio, and optional couch. 2015. [magnets, homemade electrical devices, large vibrators, EBow, other]

Garcia-De Castro, Federico. *Rendering*. 2014. [glissandi on strings, harmonics, single-note repetitions using all five fingers]

Ge, Gan-ru. *Gu Yue (Ancient Music)*. 1985. [prepared piano, harmonics]

Gosfield, Annie. *Brooklyn, Oct. 5, 1941*. 1997. [play on the keys using baseball balls and catcher's mitt, uses balls on the strings]

Greene, Arthur. *Seven Wild Mushrooms and a Waltz*. 1976. [prepared piano]

Griswold, Erik. *Danny Boy adrift in the rising tide*. 2016. [singing/speaking pianist]

———. *Three Latin Rhythms*. 2002. [prepared piano]

———. *Two Sichuan Folk Songs*. 2002. [prepared piano: rubber and elastic strips, bolts]

Gubaidulina, Sofia. *Sonata*. 1965. [glissandi with bamboo stick on tuning pins]

Hakim, Talib Rasul. *Sound-Gone*. 1967. [strike strings with hands, pizzicato, drinking glass on strings, other]

Harrison, Jonathan. *Land of the Rose*. 1992. [modified piano with retuned unisons and una corda used to toggle between two notes on each key]

Hostetler, Randy. *8.* 1986. [clusters with elbows, fists, backs of hands, underpressure glissandi; pianist also tosses, plays clusters on the keys, underpressure glissandi, and on the strings with a billiard ball (8 ball)]

Hovhaness, Alan. *Fantasy for Piano.* 1952. [hard rubber mallets and timpani mallets, rolls on bass strings]

Ivanova, Vera. *6 Fugitive Memories.* 2015. [play strings with beater]

Ives, Charles. *Piano Sonata No. 2: "Concord, Mass., 1840–1860."* 1947. [clusters; cluster board]

Johnson, Robert Sherlaw. *AF.* 1997. [mallet rolls on bass strings, harmonics, muted notes, exploits difference in tuning between overtones and string fundamentals]

Kagel, Mauricio. *MM51 "Ein Stück Filmmusik für Klavier."* 1976. [with metronome]

Kievman, Carson. *The Temporary and Tentative Extended Piano.* 1977, rev. 1992. [pianist sings, plays Indian cowbells, prepared dampers used to strike hand bells, finger cymbals placed on strings, theatrical elements]

Krieger, Ulrich. *Oberfläche.* 2013. [piano/percussion, one player]

Kurtág, György. *Játékok (Games)*, in eight volumes, for solo, four hands, and two pianos. 1973–2010. [extremes of dynamics *pppppppp* (8) to *ffffffff* (8), silently depressed notes]

Lachenmann, Helmut. *Guero.* 1969, rev. 1988. [guiro technique on the key tops, glissandi along tuning pegs and on strings beyond bridge, uses partially graphic notation]

———. *Serynade.* 1997, 1998, rev. 2000. [clusters, silently depressed keys, extended pedal usage]

Lockwood, Annea. *RCSC.* 2001. [pizzicato, strumming, fingertip muting, scrape on strings with metal lug nut]

———. *Red Mesa.* 1989, rev. 1993. [pizzicato, strumming, glissandi on strings with wood of mallet and with coin, harmonics, mallet hits to braces, etc.]

Lunetta, Stanley. *Piano Music.* 1967. [rapid tremolo clusters]

The New Percussion Quartet. *Be Prepared!* Mid-1970s. [a pianist begins playing an allegro by Mozart, while the group slowly appears on stage and begins inserting preparations into the instrument]

Palestine, Charlemagne. *From Etudes to Cataclysms.* 2005. [set of pieces for Doppio Borgato—double grand piano with thirty-seven-note pedalboard along with eighty-eight-key keyboard]

Payne, Maggi. *Holding Pattern.* 2001. [three EBows on strings]

Poleukhina, Marina. *for thing.* 2013. [for two music boxes using the piano as a resonator, choreographed movements on the piano]

Rykova, Elena. *101% mind uploading.* [prepared piano with neodymium magnets and EBow, three performers, piano with percussion]

Rzewski, Frederic. *De Profundis.* 1992. [rhythmically notated breathing, grunts, speech, singing; percussive sounds on cabinet of instrument—on top of lid, underside of keyboard, etc., supplemented with "Harpo horn"; also percussive sounds on body of pianist]

———. *Four North American Ballades.* 1978–1979. [clusters]

———. *The People United Will Never Be Defeated!* 1979. [glissandi with palms, sforzato chords with quick catching of resonance with pedal, fallboard slam, pianist whistles]

————. *The Road*. 1995–2003. [strumming, preparations, scratching parts of the piano, speaking, humming, singing, squeeze toys, whistles, razor; extended duration (about ten hours)]

Scelsi, Giacinto. *Aitsi for amplified piano*. 1974. [clusters, individual note releases, amplification/distortion optionally controlled by pianist]

Schankler, Isaac. *Alien Warp Etude*. 2012. [microtonal piano]

Schoenberg, Adam. *Picture Etudes*. 2013. [pluck strings with guitar pick, optional kick drum and gong]

Schoenberg, Arnold. *Drei Klavierstücke*, op. 11. 1909, rev. 1924. [silently depressed notes. Note: though Schoenberg revised these pieces in 1924, the silently depressed notes are present in the first publication in 1910.]

Sciarrino, Salvatore. *Due notturni crudeli*. 2001. [very detailed pedal markings, three staves throughout]

————. *Notturno No. 4*. 1998. [silently depressed notes, extensive sostenuto indications/ use of resonance]

Scott, Stephen. *Arcs*. 1980. [one piano but requires ensemble of players, bowed piano strings using monofilament line and short bows constructed of horsehair and popsicle sticks, pizzicato using guitar picks]

————. *Music One for Bowed Strings*. 1977. [one piano but requires ensemble of players, bowed piano strings using monofilament line and short bows constructed of horsehair and popsicle sticks]

Sdraulig, Charlie. *Collector*. 2014–2015. [a catalog of movements to be played (mostly without sound) on the surface of the keys and body of piano]

Seelig, Sarah. *Tingsha*. 2010. [piano/tam-tam/glockenspiel/percussion (one player)]

Shockley, Alan. *black narcissus*. 1996. [for pianist and Bösendorfer 290 SE reproducing piano; notes muted with palms, larger-than-human-hands clusters, autoharp of large chords voiced silently by player mechanism, glass windchimes, pianist walks away from playing instrument, etc.]

————. *Nothing hidden that will not be revealed*. 2007. [autoharp, pizzicato, harmonics, percussive tapping to piano cabinet, chain on strings ("chain piano"), dropping chain on strings for percussive cluster, masking tape on bass string, sforzando scrape on string windings]

————. *wndhm (1785)*. 2005. [pizzicato, muted notes, pizzicato while muted, sul ponticello pizzicato]

Silvestrov, Valentin. *Sonata no. 2*. 1975. [slow/timed releases of damper pedal; half and one-third damper pedal]

————. *Triada*. 1962. [half and one-third damper pedal, slow/timed releases of damper pedal]

Smooke, David. *Requests*. 2003. [rhythmic taps to wood of instrument while also playing on the keys]

Southworth, Christine. *Sharktooth Frenzy*. 2014. [piano/snare drum/bass drum, one player]

Srinivasan, Asha. *Mercurial Reveries*. 2014. [pizzicato, muting, silently depressed notes/ sostenuto effects]

Steen-Andersen, Simon. *Pretty Sound (up and down)*. 1976. [cluster board for all eighty-eight keys, contact microphones]

Stockhausen, Karlheinz. *Klavierstück VII*. 1955. [silently depressed notes and sostenuto held notes sounded by accented single notes]

———. *Klavierstück X*. 1961. [clusters, cluster glissandi, pianist to play with fingerless gloves]

———. *Klavierstück XII*. 1983. [pianist hums, sings, speaks, glissandi on strings, pizzicato]

———. *Klavierstück XVI*. 1995. [for piano, synthesizer, or both together; synthesizer part precisely notated, with piano part "extracted" from it by the player]

———. *Luzifers Traum, oder, Klavierstück XIII*. 1982. [mallets, rubbing strings with rubber ball, steel balls on the strings]

Szalonek, Witold. *Mutanza*. 1968. [mallets]

Tholl, Andrew. *hitting things won't solve your problems (but it might make you feel better)*. 2009. [piano/percussion, one player]

Thorvaldsdóttir, Anna. *Scape*. 2011. [aluminum thimble, EBow, prepared strings (screws)]

Ueno, Ken. *Volcano*. 2011. [pencil as surface preparation; rhythmic, accented damper pedaling and pedal releases]

Ustvolskaya, Galina. *Piano Sonata No. 6* [clusters of all sizes]

Vierk, Lois V. *To Stare Astonished at the Sea*. 1994. [scrapes on windings of bass strings, various glissandi using guitar picks]

White, Barbara. *Reliquary*. 2001. [pizzicato]

Wiggens, Thomas "Blind Tom." *The Battle of Manassas*. 1861. [clusters, whistling, vocal sounds]

Wolff, Christian. *For piano with preparations*. 1957. [prepared piano]

———. *For Prepared Piano*. 1951. [prepared piano]

———. *Suite I for Prepared Piano*. 1954. [prepared piano]

Xenakis, Iannis. *Mists*. 1980. [extensive indications for no pedal, half, and full pedal: 0/1, 1/2, 1/1]

Yates, Peter. *Epitaphs and Youngsters*. 2015. [for speaking pianist and slide show]

Yii, Kah Hoe. *My Spirit Is Dancing*. 2010. [jingles on wrists and ankles, pianist must dance to some extent, finger muted notes]

Young, La Monte. *The Well-Tuned Piano*. 1964–1973, 1981–. [unique just intonation tuning]

Zare, Roger. *Dark and Stormy Night*. 2006. [ping-pong balls on the strings, page turner assists.]

Zorn, John. *Carny*. 1989. [clusters, playing key with nose]

FOR PREPARED OR EXTENDED PIANO WITH ELECTRONICS

Behrman, David. *Wave Train*. 1966. [piano resonances and feedback]

Bloland, Per. *Elsewhere Is a Negative Mirror*, part 1. 2005. [piano with electromagnetically controlled resonance)

Coulombe, Renee T. *Sympathetic Resonance*. 2014–2015. [solo prepared piano and electronics]

Dobrian, Christopher. *Distance Duo*. 2001. [disklavier and interactive computer improviser]

———. *JazzBot*. 2005. [disklavier and computer-controlled robotic percussion instruments]

Hall, Nathan. *Tame Your Man*. 2012. [piano, electronics, and bondage artist; clusters with chest; theatrical elements; pianist is restrained in various ways through course of piece]

Harvey, Jonathan. *Homage to Cage, . . . Chopin (und Ligeti ist auch dabei)*. 1998. [prepared piano and CD]

Hayes, Lauren Sarah. *Kontroll*. 2010. [prepared piano, electronics, and self-playing snare drum]

Herriott, Jeff. *Velvet Sink*. 2001. [prepared piano and live electronics]

Johnson, Tom. *Triple Threat*. 1979. [speaking pianist, tape (pianist speaks, records, and plays back recording during performance)]

Jordanova, Victoria. *Piano Sonata*. 1996. [amplified "aged" piano and interactive electronics]

Lee, HyeKyung. *Opposed Directions*. 1997. [disklavier and live electronics]

Ligeti, Lukas. *Delta Space*. 2002. [disklavier and live electronics]

Lin, Mu-Xuan. *Pale Fire*. 2015. [piano and tape, plucked key lips, credit card glissandi on tuning pegs, other]

Lippe, Cort. *Music for Piano and Computer*. 1996. [piano and computer]

Lucier, Alvin. *Music for Piano with Slow Sweep Pure Wave Oscillators*. 1992. [piano and tape with computer-generated sounds]

———. *Nothing Is Real*. 1990. [piano, amplified teapot, recorder, miniature sound system, piano lid used as resonator]

Maxfield, Richard. *Piano Concert*. 1961. [piano and tape; no single note played traditionally on the keyboard; includes toy gyroscope on strings, rubber tire segment as mute, squeegee, small chains rubbed on underside of braces]

Miller, Alexander Elliott. *88 MPH*. 2015. [magnetic resonator piano]

Mumma, Gordon. *Gambreled Tapestry*. 2007. [piano with internal live electronics]

Neuwirth, Olga. *Kloing!* 2008. [computer-controlled piano, pianist, and film]

Nichols, John, III. *The Pillar*. 2013. [amplified prepared disklavier and electroacoustic sounds]

Risset, Jean-Claude. *Duet for One Pianist*. 1989. [disklavier]

Schankler, Isaac. *Man on Wiire*. 2010. [piano and live electronics]

Stroppa, Marco. *Traiettoria*. 1989. [piano and computer-generated tape]

Thorvaldsdóttir, Anna. *Trajectories*. 2013. [prepared piano and electronics; single screws between two of the three strings for twenty-five notes]

Wilson, Olly. *Piano Piece*. 1969. [prepared piano and stereo tape]

FOR PIANO, FOUR HANDS, OR FOR MULTIPLE PIANOS

Bettison, Oscar. *Liminal*. 2009. [six pianos and audience percussion; includes a few notes prepared with coins in strings, harmonics]

Beyer, Johanna. *Movement for Two Pianos*. 1936. [fingered clusters]

Braxton, Anthony. *Composition No. 95*. 1980. [both pianists also play melodica and zither]

Brown, Earle. *25 Pages*. 1953. [one to twenty-five pianists]

———. *Corroboree for 3 (or 2) pianos*. 1970. [clusters]

Cage, John. *A Book of Music*. 1960. [two prepared pianos]

———. *Three Dances*. 1977. [two prepared pianos]

Crumb, George. *Celestial Mechanics, Cosmic Dances for Amplified Piano, Four Hands (Makrokosmos, book 4)*. 1979. [four hands, one amplified piano]

———. *Music for a Summer Evening (Makrokosmos, book 3)*. 1974. [two pianos and percussion, two players]

———. *Otherworldly Resonances*. 2005. [two amplified pianos]

———. *Zeitgeist (Tableaux Vivants)*. 1987. [two amplified pianos]

Curtis-Smith, C. *A Song of the Degrees*. 1972. [two pianos and percussion; golf ball bounced through tube against the strings]

Feldman, Morton. 1972. [five pianos; one pianist doubles on celesta; pianists hum]

Foss, Lukas. *Ni bruit ni vitesse*. 1972. [two players, one on keys, one on strings of instrument; Japanese bowls dropped on strings]

Griswold, Erik. *Runaway Variations*. 2016. [piano duo, also playing gongs, snare, and bass drum]

Harley, Briana. *Hella Hyped: The Reigning Piano*. 2016. [two pianos; cluster by lying down on keys; soft mallet hits to metal brace; cluster with forehead; clapping, glissandi on strings with guitar pick; theatrical directions to sit and stand while playing; full-compass cluster "as best you can"]

Hartke, Stephen. *Sonata for Piano Four-Hands*. 2014.

Johnston, Ben. *Knocking Piece for Piano Interior*. 1967. [two performers, one piano; percussive hits to interior surfaces]

Mattingly, Dylan. *Dreams and False Alarms*. 2009. [two pianos, one tuned down a quarter tone]

Rzewksi, Frederic. *Winnsboro Cotton Mill Blues*. 2006. [two pianos; clusters]

Schankler, Isaac. *Because Patterns*. 2015.

Schoenberg, Adam. *Bounce*. 2013. [two pianos; a few fingered clusters, optional kick drum played by pianist]

Shockley, Alan. *bristlecone and pitch*. 2014. [two pianos; strummed strings, cardstock on strings, pianist asked to clap and stomp while playing on keys, silently depressed notes/ sostenuto pedal effects]

Shockley, Alan. *No. 267 [affinities]*. 2018. [two pianos; pizzicato, harmonics, autoharp technique, monofilament bows]

FOR PIANO IN COMBINATION WITH OTHER INSTRUMENTS

Baker, Claude. *Tableaux Funebres*. 2003. [string quartet and piano; hand muting; scrape on metal string windings; harmonics; palm strike to bass strings; rhythmic f.t. taps to soundboard; tremolo on strings with fingers of both hands]

Baker, Drew. *Gaeta*. 2005. [two pianos and water percussion; slate slid on strings, "bow" strings with loops from cassette tapes; harmonics with nodes fingered by pianists and sounded by percussionists]

Bedford, David. *Music for Albion Moonlight*. [flute, clarinet, violin, cello, melodica, piano; clusters (with palms and cluster bar), pizzicato, key weights, muting, taps to wood, other]

Besharse, Kari. *Music Box*. c. 2015. [piano and guitar: scrapes to strings, muting, other]

Bloland, Per. *Of Dust and Sand*. 2010. [alto saxophone, prepared piano, electronics]

Cage, John. *Concerto for Prepared Piano and Chamber Orchestra*. 1950, 1951. [prepared piano, including bolts and screws with metal washers, other]

———. *Credo in US*. 1942. [percussion quartet including piano and radio or tape]

———. *The Wonderful Widow of 18 Springs*. 1961. [soprano and piano; pianist taps the cabinet with fingertips and knuckles (no *ordinario* playing at all)]

Cendo, Raphaël. *Furia*. 2009, 2010. [cello and piano]

———. *Rokh I*. 2011, 2012. [flute, piano, violin, cello; piano preparations]

———. *Tract*. 2007. [clarinet, trombone, harp, piano, violin, viola, cello; harp string wrapped around bass strings of piano]

Crumb, George. *Vox Balaenae*. [amplified piano, flute, and cello; includes autoharp technique, harmonics, pizzicato allowing string to vibrate against "hammer" made from paper clip, stopping, and glissandi on strings using chisel, glass rod on strings]

Czernowin, Chaya. *Sahaf (Drift)*. 2008. [saxophone (or clarinet), electric guitar, piano, and percussion; weighted block on strings, smooth transition from ordinario to muted sound, roll fingers and hands lightly over surface of keys, coin scrape on strings]

Deyoe, Nicholas. *Ashley, Christopher, Andy*. 2014. [violoncello, piano, percussion; pianist and percussionist each have an assistant; for piano, an assistant mutes strings with towels and hands and plays one note]

———. *Immer wieder*. 2015. [soprano, clarinet, trombone, violoncello, piano; harmonics, muted notes]

Doolittle, Emily. *Our Pieces about Water*. 2000. [flute, clarinet, bassoon, horn, trombone, piano, cello, double bass; tambourine laid on strings of piano]

Eggert, Moritz. *The Son of the Daughter of Dracula against the Incredible Frankenstein Monster (From Outer Space)*. 2004. [two theremins, two percussion, violin, cello, piano; forearm clusters, pizzicato, hit the strings, glissandi on strings]

Friar, Sean. *Etude for English Horn and Prepared Piano*. 2012, rev. 2014. [a few prepared notes]

Fure, Ashley. *Soma*. 2012. [piccolo, bass clarinet, cello, two percussion, piano; harmonic screeches with scrape of roll of duct tape on strings and with scrape of spine of CD jewel case on strings; glass tile on strings, glissandi on strings with card in various ways]

Garland, Peter. *The Three Strange Angels*. 1972–1973. [piano, bass drum, and bullroarer; full-compass white-key clusters with cluster board]

Griswold, Erik. *A Wolfe in the Mangroves*. 2007. [prepared piano and percussion quartet]

Gubaidulina, Sofia. *Der Seiltänzer (Dancer on a Tightrope)*. 1997. [violin and piano; glass tumbler on strings of piano]

Hannay, Roger. *Fantôme*. [piano, clarinet, viola; glissandi on strings, tapping with mallets and fingers on the metal plate, braces, and soundboard, clave on strings]

Hartke, Stephen. *Meanwhile*. 2007 [flute, clarinet, viola, cello, and piano]

———. *Netsuke*. 2011. [violin and piano]

Harvey, Jonathan. *Flight-Elegy*. 1983–1989. [piano, violin; Strums on strings, fingernails on strings, slow damper release "howl"]

Iannotta, Clara. *Troglodyte Angels Clank By*. 2015. [flute, clarinet, horn, trumpet, two percussion, piano, harp, string quintet; vibrato, cylindrical magnets, monofilament bows, circular paper clips, tape, marbles, guitar pick]

Kagel, Mauricio. *Trio in Drei Sätzen*. 1988. [violin, cello, and piano]

Lee, Ingrid. *Nomentum*. 2010 [piano/percussion (one player) and viola]

Mayuzumi, Toshiro. *Pieces for Prepared Piano and Strings*. 1958.

Mumma, Gordon. *Medium Size Mograph*. 1963. [any number of pianos and pianists, live electronics, and tape; clusters, harmonics, pizzicato, sounds not involving the strings, other]

Pan, Xingzimin. *Kaidan*. 2013. [flute and piano; glissandi, pizzicato, stroke strings with fingers, fingertips, and palms; stroke strings with folded piece of cardboard; clusters; palm hits to strings]

Pärt, Arvo. *Tabula Rasa*. 1977. [two violins, string orchestra and prepared piano; bolts in strings for twenty-five notes]

Prins, Stefan. *Fremdkörper #2*. 2010. [soprano saxophone, electric guitar, percussion, piano, live electronics; play on the strings with hairbrushes, place on the strings a smooth stone, an aluminum pizza plate, strum with cards, one prepared note; also uses two additional staves for all inside-piano playing]

Rakowski, David. *Gli Uccelli di Bogliasco*. [two pianos and flute; pizzicato]

Riley, Terry. *The Bowed Rosary*. 1988. [bowed piano ensemble (one piano, multiple players) and synthesizers]

———. *Flexible Mind*. 2005. [prepared piano and voice]

Roy, Élise. *Coalescing (Flutescape III)*. 2013. [flute, piano and electronics; pick scrape on strings, palm hit to strings, bowed strings, harmonics, muted notes, pizzicato followed by rattled bounce of implement on strings, pianist hums, sings, audibly swallows, produces vocal fry]

Saariaho, Kaija. *Cendres*. 1998. [alto flute, cello, piano; pizzicato]

Scott, Stephen. *Pacific Crossroads*. 2008. [bowed piano, multiple players, and orchestra]

Shockley, Alan. *Hoc florentes arbor*.[flute and piano; harmonics, pizzicato, glass tumbler slide on strings, pianist whistles]

Smooke, David. *Hurricane Charm*. 2009. [two pianos and two percussionists; includes third partial harmonics, muted notes, right hand of pf 1 plays toy piano]

Stockhausen, Karlheinz. *Mantra*. 1970. [two pianists and live electronics, both pianists also play crotales and woodblocks, electronics]

———. *Refrain*. 1959. [piano, celesta, vibraphone; pianist also plays three woodblocks, vocalizes; all instruments amplified]

Tacke, Daniel. *Die Nacht war kalt*. 2007. [soprano, clarinet, cello, piano; half una corda]

Tan, Dun. *Concerto for Pizzicato Piano and Ten Instruments*. 1995. [harmonics, pizzicato, glass bottle slide on strings, strike strings, string sweep, finger muting, others]

Ueno, Ken. . . . *blood blossoms* . . . 2002. [amplified sextet—bass clarinet, piano, percussion, electric guitar, cello, bass]

Ustvolskaya, Galina. *Composition No. 2 "Dies Irae."* [piano, eight contrabasses, and wooden cube]

Van der Aa, Michel. *Quadrivial*. 2000. [flute, violin, cello, and prepared piano; includes bowing and bowing stand]

Van Nostrand, Burr. *Fantasy Manual for Urban Survival*. 1972. [flute, cello, prepared piano]

Williams, Amy. *First Lines*. [flute and piano—includes hand muting, pizzicato, harmonics, other]

FOR TOY PIANO SOLO AND IN COMBINATION WITH OTHER INSTRUMENTS

Alessandrini, Patricia. *Schattengewächse*. 2013. [toy piano and electronics]

Baker, Elizabeth A. *Dream*. 1991. [mandolin and toy piano]

Banks, Rusty. *Babbling Tower-to-Tower*. 2011. [toy piano and four (or more) cell phones]

Barganier, Erich. *Kintsugi*. 2016. [toy piano and cello]

Bohn, James. *Chamone*. 2009. [toy piano, cello, and fixed electronics]

Bolleter, Ross. *Hymn to Ruin*. 2010. [ruined toy piano and ruined piano, one player]

Bresnick, Martin. *High Art*. 1983. [piccolo with toy piano]

Bunk, Lou. *Being and Becoming*. 2010. [toy piano and electronics; lateral tremolo on keys, bowing underside of toy piano]

Cage, John. *Suite for Toy Piano*. 1948. [solo toy piano]

Chen, Phyllis. *Chimers*. 2011. [toy piano, tuning forks, toy piano rods, toy glockenspiel, clarinet, and violin]

———. *Cobwebbed Carousel*. 2010. [toy piano, hand-cranked music box, and video]

———. *Three Lullabies*. 2014. [string orchestra, toy piano/music box/electronics]

Clark, Eric K. M. *Zin Lye*. 2006. [processed toy piano and percussion]

Crompton, Jeff. *Sonatina for Toy Piano*. 2016. [solo toy piano]

Crumb, George. *Put My Little Shoes Away*. 2008. [toy piano, toy percussion quartet, voice]

Curran, Alvin. *Inner Cities 3*. 1999. [piano and/or toy piano]

Davis, Nathan. *Mechanics of Escapement*. 2008. [toy piano and clock chimes]

Distler, Jed. *Landscapes for Peter Wyer*. 1994. [solo toy piano]

———. *Minute Ring (with apologies to Richard Wagner)*. 2011. [solo toy piano]

Di Vora, Lorenzo. *Naughty Child*. 2014. [solo toy piano]

Donofrio, Anthony. *For Lucy*. 2016. [solo toy piano]

Essl, Karlheinz. *Kalimba*. 2005. [toy piano and electronics]

———. *Pachinko*. 2014. [toy piano and computer]

———. *Under Wood*. 2012. [toy piano and chamber orchestra]

Finnissy, Michael. *Sonata for (Toy) Piano*. 2006–2007. [solo toy piano or piano]

Flaherty, Tom. *Airdancing*. 2015. [toy piano, piano, electronics]

Fleitz, Robert. *Shooting for the Moon, We Land amongst Stars*. 2016. [two performers on toy instruments]

Fujikura, Dai. *Breathless*. 2004. [toy piano and violin]

———. *Milliampere*. 2010. [solo toy piano]

Gibson, Sarah. *Aria*. 2014. [toy piano (one player) and piano (one player)]

Grant, Julian. *Etudes transcendentales pour le toy piano*. 2013. [solo toy piano]

Griswold, Erik. *Down the rabbit hole*. 2015. [solo toy piano]

———. *The Little Toy Piano Book*. 2014. [solo toy piano]

———. *Old MacDonald's Yellow Submarine*. 2004. [toy piano, prepared piano, music boxes, bicycle horns, bicycle bell, prepared melodica (all one player)]

Harper, Ryan. *A19*. 2015. [two toy pianos]

Hobbs, Christopher. *Working Notes*. 1969. [four toy pianos]

Joslin, James. *Für Enola*. 2011. [toy piano, musical top, jack-in-the-box]

Kawai, Takuji. *Okura*. 2012. [solo toy piano]

Kenefick, Zaq. *litany of those who would have could have been cats on a sundress*. 2016. [two toy pianos, simultaneously playing melodicas]

Keyt, Aaron. *Yu Feng, Seven Fugues for Toy Piano*. 2007.

Kieffer, Olivia. *Nobility of Homophones*. 2015. [toy piano]

———. *Nobility of Homophones II*. 2017. [toy piano duet]

———. *The Texture of Activity*. 2015–2016. [book of fifty-five short toy piano solos]

Kitzke, Jerome. *The Animist Child*. 1994. [toy piano and voice, one player]

Kotcheff, Thomas. *death, hocket, and roll*. 2014. [two toy pianos]

Lang, David. *miracle ear*. 1996. [toy piano and percussion, one player]

Lann, Vanessa. *Is a bell . . . a bell?* 2004. [two toy pianos, one player]

Lee, HyeKyung. *Dream Play*. 2005. [toy piano]

Liben, Laura. *She Herself Alone*. 1996, 2002. [toy piano and toy psaltery, one player]

Luppi, Fabio. *Soldati*. [solo toy piano]

Macklay, Sky. *The Big Wind Up*. 2016. [toy piano and toy viola]

Marasco, Anthony T. *Mid-Century Marfa*. 2013, rev. 2014. [toy piano, Totem harp, Plastorgan, computer audio, and electric fans]

Neal, Adam Scott. *Hammers*. 2015. [toy piano solo with knocks to the body, key lip pluck, others]

Negrón, Angélica. *Columpio*. 2008. [toy instruments and electronics]

———. *The Little Things*. 2011. [toy instruments and electronics]

Ochs, Hunter. *It's a Toy*. 2005. [toy piano and electronics]

Oorebeck, Christina Viola. *Edges*. 2015 [toy piano, toy piano tines, mini-plexiphone, recorded sounds; clusters, full-compass cluster on available freestanding tines; underpressure glissandi on black and on white keys]

Perich, Tristan. *qsqsqsqsqqqqqqqqq*. 2009. [three toy pianos and one-bit electronics]

Pertout, Adrián. *Estrellita*. 2012. [two thirty-seven-key toy pianos and an unlimited number of twenty-five-key toy pianos]

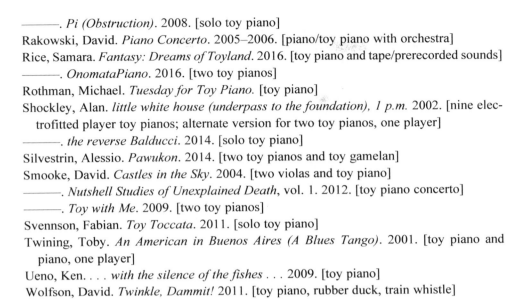

———. *Pi (Obstruction)*. 2008. [solo toy piano]

Rakowski, David. *Piano Concerto*. 2005–2006. [piano/toy piano with orchestra]

Rice, Samara. *Fantasy: Dreams of Toyland*. 2016. [toy piano and tape/prerecorded sounds]

———. *OnomataPiano*. 2016. [two toy pianos]

Rothman, Michael. *Tuesday for Toy Piano*. [toy piano]

Shockley, Alan. *little white house (underpass to the foundation), 1 p.m.* 2002. [nine electrofitted player toy pianos; alternate version for two toy pianos, one player]

———. *the reverse Balducci*. 2014. [solo toy piano]

Silvestrin, Alessio. *Pawukon*. 2014. [two toy pianos and toy gamelan]

Smooke, David. *Castles in the Sky*. 2004. [two violas and toy piano]

———. *Nutshell Studies of Unexplained Death*, vol. 1. 2012. [toy piano concerto]

———. *Toy with Me*. 2009. [two toy pianos]

Svennson, Fabian. *Toy Toccata*. 2011. [solo toy piano]

Twining, Toby. *An American in Buenos Aires (A Blues Tango)*. 2001. [toy piano and piano, one player]

Ueno, Ken. *. . . with the silence of the fishes . . .* 2009. [toy piano]

Wolfson, David. *Twinkle, Dammit!* 2011. [toy piano, rubber duck, train whistle]

Appendix B

Materials for Piano Preparation

A general list of common materials for string and surface preparations.

METAL

Coins
Screws (machine, wood; constructed of brass or steel)
Bolts (bolts, eye bolts, U-bolts, L-bolts)
Bolts with washers and/or nuts attached
Aluminum foil rested on strings or strips threaded over and under strings
Metal tacks in hammer tips (warning: this is likely to cause permanent damage
    to the hammers; safe alternatives are listed in chapter 9)
Metal bars set across (perpendicular to) strings (brass, steel, etc.)
Prayer bowl rested on strings
Finger cymbals rested on strings
Inverted cymbal or gong rested on strings
Metal chain rested on strings (light aluminum chain, thicker-gauge steel chain)

WOOD

Golf tees
Hardwood dowels rested across strings
Clothespins clipped to strings
Half clothespin used as wedge in strings
Bamboo wedge

RUBBER

Gaskets and insulation strips
Piano tuner's mutes
Pencil cap erasers (cut slit in base, snap over string 2 of triple-unison set)
Cushion erasers

PAPER

Paper strips threaded through strings
Paper sheets rested on strings
Cardstock/poster board rested on strings
Phone book on strings

TAPE

Painter's tape or masking tape attached to tops of strings, perpendicular to strings
Painter's tape or masking tape attached to top of strings, running parallel to strings (attached in discrete fashion to a single-unison set or attached so that edge of tape rattles against adjacent unisons)

GLASS

Glass sheet rested on strings
Glass bowl or tumbler rested on strings
Glass rod rested on strings
Glass tile rested on strings

PLASTIC

Plastic screws and bolts
Ping-pong balls rested on strings
Plexiglass sheet rubbed on strings
Plastic piece threaded through strings

MISCELLANEOUS

Poster putty pressed on strings to mute
Monofilament fishing line or horsehair bows
Wool strip threaded through strings, draped between hammers and strings
Slate

STANDARD TOOLS FOR PIANO PERFORMANCE

Brass or glass guitar slides
Brass setup gauges
Monofilament bows
Horsehair-and-tongue-depressor bows
EBow
Glass tumbler, glass bottles
Timpani and bass drum mallets
Yarn mallets
Super Ball mallets
Painter's tape
Poster putty (Blu-Tack)
Thin cotton gloves
Clean, soft towel (for cleaning up after inside-the-piano performance)
Guitar picks
Paper clips
Piano hammers
Piano tuner's mutes
Weighted cloth-covered mutes [BBs wrapped in multiple layers of t-shirt material or socks]

Appendix C

Grand Piano Interior Architecture and Stringing

This appendix gives the brace structure and internal layout for all grand piano models likely to be found in concert halls and other professional performing spaces. This is useful information for determining whether certain strummed effects will work and for determining the length and placement of mutes and other objects to be placed on the strings (glass rods, chains, paper, etc.). Also included for each instrument is a map of which notes have a single string, two unisons (two strings), or three unisons per key and where the copper-wound strings are used and where the steel strings begin. This is essential information for a composer using many extended techniques and for a pianist to know whether a piece is practical in a particular hall when it is equipped with a particular model of piano. If a piece asks for a winding scrape in the tenor register, depending on the particular note and piano model, the pianist may find that that note does not have copper-wound strings but flat steel strings, on which a scrape produces no real effect. Understanding how many strings have no dampers in the highest register of a particular model provides useful information for a pianist attempting the key-frame slide-muting technique, as, if the pianist needs all notes muted, the notes with no dampers are the ones that must be muted with felt or another (separate) preparation.

The Steinway Model D is the model of concert grand most larger concert halls feature, so I use a photo in figure C.1 and details of the Steinway D here to explain the information given for about forty-five models of piano from makers both small and large located all over the world.

Much of a grand piano's internal layout and much of the architecture that affects playing inside the instrument is structural in nature. On practically all modern grand pianos, there are long raised braces or struts that are cast as part of the metal plate, which is in turn attached to the soundboard. In figure C.1, you can see several of these braces extending from just beyond the keys at the very start of

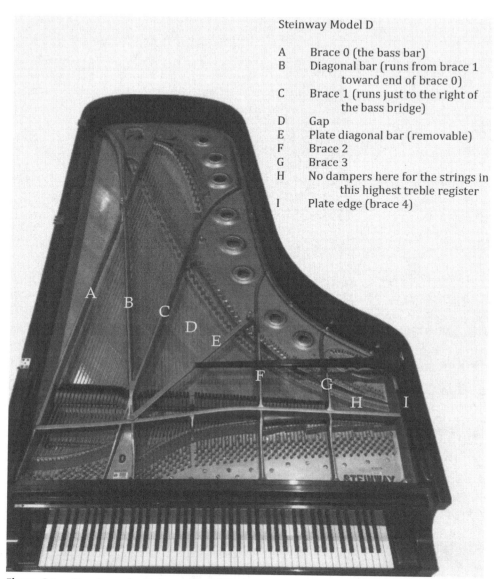

Steinway Model D

A	Brace 0 (the bass bar)
B	Diagonal bar (runs from brace 1 toward end of brace 0)
C	Brace 1 (runs just to the right of the bass bridge)
D	Gap
E	Plate diagonal bar (removable)
F	Brace 2
G	Brace 3
H	No dampers here for the strings in this highest treble register
I	Plate edge (brace 4)

Figure C.1. Structure of a Steinway Model D

the plate toward the tail or toward the bent side of the instrument. I number these braces from left to right and describe their placement for each model of piano detailed here. The brace that appears to the left of and runs parallel to the lowest bass string I number *0* because it does not interrupt the strings. (This brace is sometimes called the "bass bar." See chapter 4.) The next brace is 1. On the Model D and on many other models, this brace forms the right upright of a long *V*. You can see in figure C.1 that the left upright of this *V* actually crosses brace 0 close to the tail of the instrument. More significant for inside-the-piano techniques, the right upright of that *V* interrupts the strings at the dampers, preventing a smooth glissando of the notes that have that right upright of the *V* in their midst. The right upright of the *V* also marks the end of the bass bridge, so all the strings below that brace are attached to the bass bridge.

On the D (and on most of the larger models of grand pianos detailed here), all of the strings attached to the bass bridge are copper-wound steel-core strings, and all of the strings above the *V* (above brace 1) are flat steel strings and triple unisons, as well. Continuing to move from the bass to the treble, the next structural element visible on the D is a short diagonal metal piece running from the tuning-pin end of brace 1 and attached to the bridge-pin end of the next structural brace. This "plate diagonal bar" is a much thinner piece than the structural braces; it is attached on both ends with bolts and can be removed. This bar does not appear on most models of grand piano. Next on the Steinway Model D, there is a gap between two sets of unisons running parallel to the structural braces and running underneath approximately the middle of the removable diagonal brace. The next labeled structural part is brace 2, which is another interruptive brace, followed by brace 3. On the Model D, brace 3 separates the territory of strings provided with dampers from those strings without dampers—all the strings to the left of brace 3 have dampers; none of the strings to the right of brace 3 have dampers. Like brace 0, brace 4 on this model does not interrupt the strings but instead exists as the raised edge of the plate on the treble side.

In addition to these braces running parallel to the strings, almost all grand pianos have shorter cross-braces that run perpendicular to the strings near the tuning pins. In the treble register and the high treble, most grand piano models do not use agraffes but substitute a capo d'astro (also called a capo tasto) bar. Because this bar forms the termination of the sounding length of the string, it also reduces the player's access to the tuning-pin end of the treble strings. The dampers also cover a portion of the strings, and in the upper register, where the string lengths are much reduced, the dampers may cover a significant proportion of the overall string length. The combination of the capo d'astro and the dampers means for some instruments the pianist may have little to no access for playing sul ponticello techniques near the tuning-pin end of the strings. Fortunately, this does not affect the topmost region of strings, as those strings have no dampers. As a general rule of thumb, only the second-highest treble region of strings may limit the pianist's ability to play sul ponticello at the tuning-pin end of the strings (or to mute in that region and so forth). Fortunately, the strings are short enough throughout both of the top two regions of the piano that the player can still pluck sul ponticello or mute with the fingertips or with implements, even if she has no access to the tuning-pin end of the strings; these techniques simply need to be played at the bridge end of the strings. Nevertheless, for a few models here whose structures do cover the portion of strings below the dampers, I have listed that the model limits access.

ESSENTIAL INTERNAL DETAILS FOR STEINWAY MODEL D

Steinway D (8'11¾", 274 cm)

3 braces
   Brace 1 (right leg of *V*) E2/F2
   Gap G3/G♯3
   Brace 2 C♯5/D5
   Brace 3 G6/G♯6
Notes 1–20 [brace 1] 21–35 [gap] 36–53 [brace 2] 54–71 [brace 3] 72–88
Single unisons: A0–E1 (8 notes)
Double unisons: F1–A1 (5 notes)
Triple unisons (wound): A♯1–E2 (7 notes)
Triple unisons (steel): F2–C8 (68 notes)

No dampers for G♯6–C8 (17 notes)

Strings obscured by overstringing: F2–C3 (and minimally covered to F♯3)

GRAND PIANO BRACE STRUCTURES, STRING LAYOUTS, DAMPER DISTRIBUTION

Baldwin SD10 (9'0")

4 braces
   Brace 1 E2/F2
   Brace 2 G3/G♯3
   Brace 3 C♯5/D5
   Brace 4 G6/G♯6
Single (wound) unisons: A0–E1 (8 notes)
Double (wound) unisons: F1–A1 (5 notes)
Triple (wound) unisons: A♯1–E2 (7 notes)
Triple (steel) unisons: F2–C8 (68 notes)

No dampers for E6–C8 (21 notes)

Strings obscured by overstringing: F2–C♯3 (and minimally covered to F3)

Baldwin SF10 (7'0")

3 braces
    Brace 1 E2/F2
    Brace 2 C♯5/D5
    Brace 3 G6/G♯6
Single (wound) unisons: A0–E1 (8 notes)
Double (wound) unisons: F1–E2 and F2–C♯3 (21 notes)
Triple (steel) unisons: D3–C8 (59 notes)

No dampers for E6–C8 (21 notes)
Note the SF10 has 9 wound double unisons on the long bridge rather than the bass bridge.

Strings obscured by overstringing: F2–D3 (and minimally covered to A3)

Barenboim-Maene (284 cm)

4 braces
    Brace 1 E2/F2
    Brace 2 G3/G♯3
    Brace 3 C♯5/D5
    Brace 4 G6/G♯6
Single (wound) unisons: A0–E1 (8 notes)
Double (wound) unisons: F1–A1 (5 notes)
Triple (wound) unisons: A♯1–E2 (7 notes)
Triple (steel) unisons: F2–C8 (68 notes)

No dampers for G♯6–C8 (17 notes)

Bass strings are wound in brass rather than copper. Instrument is straight-strung, not overstrung, so no midrange strings are covered by bass strings. (Nevertheless, instrument has separate bass and long bridges.) Builder Chris Maene appears to be developing a 90-key version of this instrument, extending the bass to G0.

Bechstein Model B 212 (6'11")

3 braces
    Brace 1 A2/A♯2
    Brace 2 C5/C♯5
    Brace 3 F♯6/G6

Single (wound) unisons: A0–F1 (9 notes)
Double (wound) unisons: F#1–A2 (16 notes)
Triple (steel) unisons: A#2–C8 (63 notes)

No dampers for F#6–C8 (19 notes)

Strings obscured by overstringing: A#2–F#3 (and minimally covered to B3)

Bechstein Model C 234 (7'8")

4 braces
   Brace 1 E2/F2
   Brace 2 G#3/A3
   Brace 3 C5/C#5
   Brace 4 F#6/G6
Single (wound) unisons: A0–E1 (8 notes)
Double (wound) unisons: F1–E2 (12 notes)
Triple (steel) unisons: F2–C8 (68 notes)

No dampers for F#6–C8 (19 notes)
Strings obscured by overstringing: F2–C3 (and minimally covered to F#3)

Bechstein Model D 282 (9'3")

4 braces
   Brace 1 C#2/D2
   Brace 2 F#3/G3
   Brace 3 C5/C#5
   Brace 4 F#6/G6
Single (wound) unisons: A0–E1 (8 notes)
Double (wound) unisons: F1–A#1 (6 notes)
Triple (wound) unisons: B1–C#2 (3 notes)
Triple (steel) unisons: D2–C8 (71 notes)

No dampers for F#6–C8 (19 notes)
Strings obscured by overstringing: D2–B2 (and minimally covered to E3)

Blüthner Model 1 (9'2", 280 cm)

3 braces
   Brace 1 F2/F#2
   Brace 2 F4/F#4
   Brace 3 C#6/D6
Single (wound) unisons: A0–F#1 (10 notes)

Double (wound) unisons: G1–C2 (6 notes)
Triple (wound) unisons: C♯2–F2 (5 notes)
Triple (steel) unisons: F♯2–C♯6 (44 notes)
Quadruple (steel) unisons (4th string is aliquot string): D6–C8 (23 notes)
No dampers for E6–C8 (21 notes)

Strings obscured by overstringing: F♯2–D♯3 (and minimally covered to A3)

Blüthner Model 2 (7'8", 238 cm)

3 braces
   Brace 1 A2/A♯2
   Brace 2 F♯4/G4
   Brace 3 D6/D♯6
Single (wound) unisons: A0–E1 (8 notes)
Double (wound) unisons: F1–A2 (17 notes)
Triple (steel) unisons: A♯2–D6 (41 notes)
Quadruple (steel) unisons (4th string is aliquot string): D♯6–C8 (22 notes)

No dampers for F6–C8 (20 notes)
Strings obscured by overstringing: A♯2–F♯3 (and minimally covered to C4)

Bösendorfer 200 (6'7", 200 cm)

3 braces
   Brace 1 A♯2/B2
   Brace 2 G♯4/A4
   Brace 3 D♯6/E6
Single unisons: A0–F1 (9 notes)
Double unisons: F♯1–A♯2 (16 notes)
Triple unisons: B2–C8 (63 notes)

No dampers for G6–C8 (18 notes)
Strings obscured by overstringing: B2–G♯2 (and minimally covered to C3)

Bösendorfer 225 (7'4", 225 cm), 92 Keys

4 braces
   Brace 1 D♯2/E2
   Brace 2 B3/C4
   Brace 3 D5/D♯5
   Brace 4 F6/F♯6

Single (wound) unisons: F0–F1 (13 notes)

Double (wound) unisons: F#1–D#2 (10 notes)
Triple (wound) unisons: E2–C8 (notes)

No dampers for G#6–C8 (17 notes)

Strings obscured by overstringing: E2–D#3 (and minimally covered to B3)

Bösendorfer 280 (9'2", 280 cm)

4 braces
    Brace 1 E2/F2
    Brace 2 A#3/B3
    Brace 3 D5/D#5
    Brace 4 G#6/A6

Single (wound) unisons: A0–D#1 (7 notes)
Double (wound) unisons: E1–B1 (8 notes)
Double (wound) unisons: C2–E2 (5 notes)
Triple (steel) unisons: F2–C8 (68 notes)

No dampers for A6–C8 (16 notes)

Strings obscured by overstringing: F2–D3 (and minimally covered to G3)

Bösendorfer 290 "Imperial" Grand (9'6", 290 cm), 97 Keys

4 braces
    Brace 1 C#2/D2
    Brace 2 G#3/A3
    Brace 3 C#5/D5
    Brace 4 F#6/G6

Single (wound) unisons: C0–D#1 (16 notes)
Double (wound) unisons: E1–C#2 (10 notes)
Triple unisons: D2–C8 (71 notes)

No dampers for A6–C8 (15 notes)

Strings obscured by overstringing: D2–B2 (and minimally covered to F3)

Estonia Grand Model 274 (9'0", 274 cm)

4 braces
    Brace 1 E2/F2
    Brace 2 G3/G#3
    Brace 3 C#5/D5
    Brace 4 G6/G#6

Single (wound) unisons: A0–E1 (8 notes)
Double (wound) unisons: F1–E2 (12 notes)
Triple (steel) unisons: F2–C8 (68 notes)

No dampers for G#6–C8 (17 notes)

Strings obscured by overstringing: F2–C3 (and minimally covered to F#3)

Estonia Model 225 (225 cm)

3 braces, though, note, brace 1 forms a wider *V* with the diagonal bar than most
  other grand designs
  Brace 1 F#2/G2
  Brace 2 A#4/B4
  Brace 3 F#6/G6

Single (wound) unisons: A0–E1 (8 notes)
Double (wound) unisons: F1–D#2 (11 notes)
Triple (wound) unisons: E2–F#2 (3 notes)
Triple (steel) unisons: G2–C8 (66 notes)

No dampers for G6–C8 (18 notes)

Strings obscured by overstringing: G2–D#3 (and minimally covered to A3)

Fazioli F212 (212 cm)

3 braces
  Brace 1 G2/G#2
  Brace 2 G#4/A4
  Brace 3 D#6/E6

Single (wound) unisons: A0–E1 (8 notes)
Double (wound unisons: F1–G2 (15 notes)
Triple (steel) unisons: G#2–C8 (65 notes)

No dampers for F#6–C8 (19 notes)

Strings obscured by overstringing: G#2–F3 (and minimally covered to B3)

Fazioli F228 (228 cm)

3 braces
  Brace 1 F#2/G2
  Brace 2 F#4/G4
  Brace 3 D#6/E6

Single (wound) unisons: A0–E1 (8 notes)
Double (wound) unisons: F1–F♯2 (14 notes)
Triple (steel) unisons: G2–C8 (66 notes)

No dampers for G6–C8 (18 notes)

Strings obscured by overstringing: G2–D♯3 (and minimally covered to A3)

Fazioli F278 (278 cm)

3 braces plus a gap
  Brace 1 F2/F♯2
  Gap G3/G♯3
  Brace 2 C♯5/D5
  Brace 3 G6/G♯6

Single (wound) unisons: A0–E1 (8 notes)
Double (wound) unisons: F1–A1 (5 notes)
Triple (wound) unisons: A♯1–E2 (7 notes)
Triple (steel) unisons: F2–C8 (68 notes)

No dampers for G♯6–C8 (17 notes)

Strings obscured by overstringing: F♯2–D♯3 (and minimally covered to F♯3)

Fazioli F308 (10'2", 308 cm)

3 braces plus a gap
  Brace 1 D♯2/E2
  Gap G3/G♯3
  Brace 2 B4/C5
  Brace 3 F6/F♯6

Single (wound) unisons: A0–E1 (8 notes)
Double (wound) unisons: F1–A1 (5 notes)
Triple (wound) unisons: A♯1–D♯2 (6 notes)
Triple (steel) unisons: E2–C8 (69 notes)

No dampers for F♯6–C8 (19 notes)

Strings obscured by overstringing: E2–C♯3 (and minimally covered to F♯3)
The F308 includes a fourth pedal, a half-blow pedal, located to the left of the usual
  three pedals.

August Förster 215 (215 cm)

3 braces
    Brace 1 E2/F2
    Brace 2 D#5/E5
    Brace 3 G6/G#6

Single (wound) unisons: A0–F#1 (10 notes)
Double (wound) unisons: G1–E2 (10 notes)
Triple (steel) unisons: F2–C8 (68 notes)

No dampers for F6–C8 (20 notes)

Strings obscured by overstringing: F2–C#3 (and minimally covered to F3)

Note: The Förster Model 215 has a very broad section of middle strings uninterrupted by any brace or gap.

Kawai EX (9'0", 278 cm)

4 braces
    Brace 1 E2/F2
    Brace 2 G3/G#3
    Brace 3 C#5/D5
    Brace 4 G6/G#6

Single (wound) unisons: A0–E1 (8 notes)
Double (wound) unisons: F1–A1 (5 notes)
Triple (wound) unisons: A#1–E2 (7 notes)
Triple (steel) unisons: F2–C8 (68 notes)

No dampers for G6–C8 (18 notes)

Strings obscured by overstringing: F2–E3 (and minimally covered to G3)

Kawai RX-7 (7'6", 229 cm)

4 braces
    Brace 1 F#2/G2
    Brace 2 A#3/B3
    Brace 3 D5/D#5
    Brace 4 G#6/A6

Single (wound) unisons: A0–F#1 (10 notes)
Double (wound) unisons: G1–F#2 (12 notes)

Triple (steel) unisons: G2–C8 (66 notes)

No dampers for G6–C8 (18 notes)

Strings obscured by overstringing: G2–E3 (and minimally covered to A♯3)

Shigeru Kawai SK-6 (6'7", 200 cm)

4 braces
   Brace 1 F♯2/G2
   Brace 2 A♯3/B3
   Brace 3 D5/D♯5
   Brace 4 G♯6/A6

Single (wound) unisons: A0–F♯1 (10 notes)
Double (wound) unisons: G1–F♯2 (12 notes)
Triple (steel) unisons: G2–C8 (66 notes)

No dampers for F♯6–C8 (19 notes)

Strings obscured by overstringing: G2–F♯3 (and minimally covered to B3)

Shigeru Kawai SK-7 (7'6", 229 cm)

4 braces
   Brace 1 F♯2/G2
   Brace 2 A♯3/B3
   Brace 3 D5/D♯5
   Brace 4 G♯6/A6

Single (wound) unisons: A0–F♯1 (10 notes)
Double (wound) unisons: G1–F♯2 (12 notes)
Triple (steel) unisons: G2–C8 (66 notes)

No dampers for G6–C8 (18 notes)

Strings obscured by overstringing: G2–F3 (and minimally covered to A♯3)

Shigeru Kawai SK-EX (9'0", 278 cm)

4 braces
   Brace 1 E2/F2
   Brace 2 G3/G♯3
   Brace 3 C♯5/D5
   Brace 4 G6/G♯6

Single (wound) unisons: A0–E1 (8 notes)
Double (wound) unisons: F1–A1 (5 notes)
Triple (wound) unisons: A#1–E2 (7 notes)
Triple (steel) unisons: F2–C8 (68 notes)

No dampers for G6–C8 (18 notes)

Strings obscured by overstringing: F2–E3 (and minimally covered to G3)

Mason and Hamlin AA (6'4", 193.04 cm)

3 braces
   Brace 1 E2/F2
   Brace 2 B4 /C5
   Brace 3 E6/F6

Notes 1 [brace 1]–[brace 2]–[brace 3]–88

Single (wound) unisons: A0–E1 (8 notes)
Double (wound) unisons: F1–F#2 (14 notes)
Triple (wound) unisons: G2–C#3 (7 notes)
Triple (steel) unisons: D3–C8 (59 notes)

No dampers for F6–C8 (20 notes)

Strings obscured by overstringing: F2–F3 (and minimally covered to A#3)

Mason and Hamlin BB (6'11½", 212.09 cm)

4 braces
   Brace 1 F2/F#2
   Brace 2 G#3/A3
   Brace 3 D5/D#5
   Brace 4 G6/G#6

Single (wound) unisons: A0–E1 (8 notes)
Double (wound) unisons: F1–F2 (13 notes)
Triple (steel) unisons: F#2–C8 (67 notes)

No dampers for F#6–C8 (19 notes)

Strings obscured by overstringing: F#2–F3 (and minimally covered to G#3)

Like the larger CC, the BB has a full plate that extends all the way to the bass rim, so the only access to the soundboard is through small sound holes. In addition, from A3 up, the pianist has no access to the strings on the front side of the dampers, only behind the dampers. (This means that, for this range on this instrument, sul ponticello techniques can only be played at the far ends of these strings.)

Mason and Hamlin CC (9'4")

[There may be some differences between CC and new CC-94.]

4 braces
    Brace 1 F2/F♯2
    Brace 2 G3/G♯3
    Brace 3 C♯5/D5
    Brace 4 G6/G♯6

Single (wound) unisons: A0–F1 (9 notes)
Double (wound) unisons: F♯1–B1 (6 notes)
Triple (wound) unisons: C2–F2 (6 notes)
Triple (steel) unisons: F♯2–C8 (67 notes)

No dampers for D♯6–C8 (22 notes)

Strings obscured by overstringing: F♯2–D♯3 (and minimally covered to E3)
Note: CC-94 has a full plate that extends to the bass side rim, so the only access to the soundboard is through small sound holes.

Brace 1 combined with the diagonal bar forms an *X* shape and has an additional cross-brace to brace 2. This somewhat restricts access to the strings of the bass bridge.

Petrof 237 Monsoon (7'9", 237 cm)

2 braces and 2 gaps
    Brace 1 E2/F2
    Gap 1 G♯3/A3
    Brace 2 C♯5/D5
    Gap 2 F♯6/G6

Single (wound) unisons: A0–E1 (8 notes)
Double (wound) unisons: F1–E2 (12 notes)
Triple (steel) unisons: F2–C8 (68 notes)

No dampers for F♯6–C8 (19 notes)

Strings obscured by overstringing: F2–C♯3 (and minimally covered to G3)

Petrof Concert Grand (9'0")

4 braces
    Brace 1 E2/F2
    Brace 2 A3/A♯3
    Brace 3 D5/D♯5
    Brace 4 G6/G♯6

Single (wound) unisons: A0–D♯1 (7 notes)
Double (wound) unisons: E1–A1 (6 notes)
Triple (wound) unisons: A♯1–E2 (7 notes)
Triple (steel) unisons: F2–C8 (68 notes)

No dampers for G6–C8 (18 notes)

Strings obscured by overstringing: F2–D♯3 (and minimally covered to G3)

Sauter Omega 220 (7'3", 220 cm)

3 braces
    Brace 1 G2/G♯ 2
    Brace 2 G♯4/A4
    Brace 3 E6/F6

Notes 1–23 [brace 1] 24–48 [brace 2] 49–68 [brace 3] 69–88

Single (wound) unisons: A0–F1 (9 notes)
Double (wound) unisons: F♯1–G2 (14 notes)
Triple (steel) unisons: G♯2–C8 (65 notes)

No dampers for G6–C8 (18 notes)

Strings obscured by overstringing: G♯2–F3 (and minimally covered to B3)

Seiler SE-208 (208 cm)

3 braces
    Brace 1 A♯2/B2
    Brace 2 C5/C♯5
    Brace 3 F♯6/G6

Single (wound) unisons: A0–G1 (11 notes)
Double (wound) unisons: G♯1–A♯2 (15 notes)
Triple (steel) unisons: B2–C8 (62 notes)

No dampers for E6–C8 (21 notes)

Strings obscured by overstringing: B2–G♯3 (and minimally covered to C♯4)

Note: The cross-member between brace 2 and brace 3 (C♯5–F♯6) leaves only a tiny space for sul ponticello techniques before the dampers in this register. (However, these strings may be played sul ponticello at the bridge end of these strings.)

Steingraeber & Söhne C-212 (7'0", 212 cm)

3 braces
   Brace 1 A2/A♯2
   Brace 2 C5/C♯5
   Brace 3 F♯6/G6

Single unisons: A0–E1 (8 notes)
Double unisons: F1–A2 (17 notes)
Triple unisons: A♯2–C8 (63 notes)

No dampers for F♯6–C8 (19 notes)

Strings obscured by overstringing: A♯2–G3 (and minimally covered to B3)

Steingraeber & Söhne D-232 (7'7", 232 cm)

3 braces
   Brace 1 E2/F2
   Brace 2 D4/D♯4
   Brace 3 D6/D♯6

Single (wound) unisons: A0–E1 (8 notes)
Double (wound) unisons: F1–E2 (12 notes)
Triple (steel) unisons: F♯6–C8 (68 notes)

No dampers for F♯6–C8 (19 notes)

Strings obscured by overstringing: F2–D3 (and minimally covered to G3)

Steingraeber & Söhne E-272 (8'11", 272 cm)

4 braces
   Brace 1 D♯2/E2
   Brace 2 G♯3/A3
   Brace 3 D5/D♯5
   Brace 4 G♯6/A6

Single unisons (wound): A0–D1 (6 notes)
Double unisons (wound): D#1–A#1 (8 notes)
Triple unisons (wound): B1–D#2 (5 notes)
Triple unisons (steel):–C8 (69 notes)

No dampers for G6–C8 (18 notes) confirm

Strings obscured by overstringing: E2–D3 (and minimally covered to G3)

Steinway A (6'2")

3 braces
   Brace 1 E2/F2
   Brace 2 B4/C5
   Brace 3 E6/F6

Single (wound) unisons: A0–E1 (8 notes)
Double (wound) unisons: F1–E2 and F2–A2 (17 notes) (note that 5 of the wound
   double-unisons appear on the treble bridge, not the bass bridge)
Triple (steel) unisons: A#2–C8 (53 notes)

No dampers for F6–C8 (20 notes)

Strings obscured by overstringing: F2–D3 (and minimally covered to A#3)

Steinway B (6'11", 211 cm)

3 braces, plus two diagonal braces that branch off diagonally from brace 1
   Brace 1 E2/F2
   Brace 2 B4/C4
   Brace 3 E6/F6

Single (wound) unisons: A0–E1 (8 notes)
Double (wound) unisons: F1–E2 (12 notes)
Triple (steel) unisons: F2–C8 (68 notes)

No dampers for F6–C8 (20 notes)

Strings obscured by overstringing: F2–D3 (and minimally covered to A#3)

Steinway C (7'6", 227 cm)

3 braces plus a gap
   Brace 1 D#2/E2
   Gap F#3/G3

Brace 2 C5/C♯5
Brace 3 G6/G♯6

Single (wound) unisons: A0–E1 (8 notes)
Double (wound) unisons: F1–D♯2 (12 notes)
Triple (steel) unisons: E2–C8 (68 notes)

No dampers for G♯6–C8 (17 notes)

Strings obscured by overstringing: E2–C♯3 (and minimally covered to G3)

Steinway M (5'7")

3 braces
    Brace 1 A♯2/B2
    Brace 2 D5/D♯5
    Brace 3 G6/G♯6

Single (wound) unisons: A0–F♯1 (10 notes)
Double (wound) unisons: G1–A♯2 and B2–C3 (18 notes) (note that 2 of the wound
    double unisons appear on the treble bridge, not the bass bridge)
Triple (steel) unisons: C♯3–C8 (70 notes)

No dampers for E6–C8 (21 notes)

Strings obscured by overstringing: B2–G♯3 (and minimally covered to C4)

Note: The bass section is quite large on the M, and the first interruptive brace is a
    single brace rather than a *V*- or *U*-shaped brace as on many larger grands, giving
    very good access to the bass strings.

Stuart and Sons Concert Grand (9'6", 290 cm), 102 Keys

3 braces
    Brace 1 C♯2/D2
    Brace 2 D4/D♯4
    Brace 3 D♯6/E6

Single (wound) unisons: C0–E1 (17 notes)
Double (wound) unisons: F1–C♯2 (9 notes)
Triple (steel) unisons: D2–F8 (76 notes)

No dampers for A♯6–F8 (20 notes)

Strings obscured by overstringing: D2–A♯2 (and minimally covered to D♯3)

4 pedals: half-blow, una corda, sostenuto, damper

Stuart and Sons Concert Grand (300 cm), 108 Keys (C0–B8; forthcoming)

0 braces interrupting the string space!

Single (wound) unisons: C0–E1 (17 notes)
Double (wound) unisons: F1–C#2 (9 notes)
Triple (steel) unisons: D2–B8 (82 notes)

(These are projected details, as this next-generation Stuart grand has not been released yet.)

Yamaha C1 (6'1")

3 braces
  Brace 1 A#2/B2
  Brace 2 C#5/D5
  Brace 3 G6/G#6

Single (wound) unisons: A0–F#1 (10 notes)
Double (wound) unisons: G1–A#2 and B2–C#3 (19 notes) (note that 3 of the wound double unisons appear on the long bridge, not the bass bridge)
Triple (steel) unisons: D3–C8 (59 notes)

No dampers for F#6–C8 (19 notes)

Strings obscured by overstringing: B2–G#3 (and minimally covered to C#4)

Yamaha C6 (6'11")

3 braces
  Brace 1 G2/G#2
  Brace 2 A#4/B4
  Brace 3 F#6/G6

Single (wound) unisons: A0–F#1 (10 notes)
Double (wound) unisons: G1–G2 (13 notes)
Triple (steel) unisons: G#2–C8 (65 notes)

No dampers for F#6–C8 (19 notes)

Strings obscured by overstringing: G#2–F3 (and minimally covered to A3)

Yamaha C7 (7'6")

3 braces
  Brace 1 G2/G#2
  Brace 2 A#4/B4
  Brace 3 F#6/G6

Single (wound) unisons: A0–F#1 (10 notes)
Double (wound) unisons: G1–G2 (13 notes)
Triple (steel) unisons: G#2–C8 (55 notes)

No dampers for G6–C8 (18 notes)

Strings obscured by overstringing: G#2–E3 (and minimally covered to A3)

Yamaha CFX (9'0", 275 cm)

3 braces plus a gap
   Brace 1 E2/F2
   Gap G3/G#3
   Brace 2 C#5/D5
   Brace 3 G6/G#6
Single (wound) unisons: A0–E1 (8 notes)
Double (wound) unisons: F1–A1 (5 notes)
Triple (wound) unisons: A#1–E2 (7 notes)
Triple (steel) unisons: F2–C8 (69 notes)

No dampers for G#6–C8 (17 notes)

Strings obscured by overstringing: F2–C#3 (and minimally covered to F#3)

Notes

CHAPTER 1. BASICS OF THE PIANO AND ITS NOTATION

1. Throughout the text I use the American Standard Pitch Notation (also called Scientific Pitch Notation, or SPN), which combines a note name with a number for the octave designation. In this system middle C is C4, and the lowest note on an eighty-eight-key piano is A0.

2. Nevertheless, such anomalies are out there. I have played one seventy-three-key spinet. As a graduate student, I was once snowed in in Corbin, Kentucky. After a couple days, I went searching for a piano to practice on, located a spinet in a banquet room of the hotel where I was staying, opened the fallboard, and discovered that not only was this instrument horribly out of tune but it also didn't have the "right" number of keys!

3. Joseph Banowetz, *The Pianist's Guide to Pedaling* (Bloomington: Indiana University Press, 1985), 9.

CHAPTER 2. THE HISTORY AND MECHANISM OF THE INSTRUMENT

1. Wendy Powers, "The Piano: The Pianofortes of Bartolomeo Cristofori (1655–1731)," *Heilbrunn Timeline of Art History, Metropolitan Museum of Art*, October 2003, http://www.metmuseum.org/toah/hd/cris/hd_cris.htm.

2. Jeremy Siepmann, *The Piano: The Complete Illustrated Guide to the World's Most Popular Musical Instrument* (Milwaukee: Hal Leonard and Carlton Books, 1996), 17.

3. Edwin M. Good, *Giraffes, Black Dragons, and Other Pianos: A Technological History from Cristofori to the Modern Concert Grand*, 2nd ed. (Stanford, CA: Stanford University Press, 2002), 49–50.

4. Martha Novak Clinkscale, *Makers of the Piano*, vol. 2: *1820–1860* (Oxford: Oxford University Press, 1999), 118; "Erard Piano History," *Piano Romantiques*, accessed March 21, 2016, http://www.pianosromantiques.com/erardhistory.html.

5. Robert Adelson, Alain Roudier, Jenny Nex, Laure Barthel, and Michel Foussard, *The History of the Erard Piano and Harp in Letters and Documents, 1785–1959* (Cambridge: Cambridge University Press, 2015), 93.

6. Good, *Giraffes*, 167.

7. Robert Palmieri, ed., *The Piano: An Encyclopedia*, 2nd ed. (New York: Routledge, 2003), 95.

8. Alfred Dolge, *Pianos and Their Makers* (Covina, CA: Covina, 1911), 99.

9. Denzil Wraight, "Recent Approaches in Understanding Cristofori's Fortepiano," *Early Music* 34, no. 4 (November 2006): 638.

10. Keith G. Grafing, Alpheus Babcock, Thomas Loud, and Emilius N. Scherr, "Alpheus Babcock's Cast-Iron Piano Frames," *Galpin Society Journal* 27 (1974): 118.

11. Palmieri, *Piano*, 69.

12. Ibid., 20.

13. Ibid. Other piano makers have looked for ways to move the bass strings closer to the center of the soundboard for improved resonance.

14. Good, *Giraffes*, 162.

15. Ibid., 252.

16. Phillip R. Belt, *The Piano: The New Grove Musical Instruments Series* (New York: W. W. Norton, 1988), 158.

17. R. Larry Todd, *Nineteenth-Century Piano Music* (New York: Schirmer Books, 1990), 53.

18. I have seen Bösendorfer 275 grand pianos (nine-foot concert grands) from as late as the late 1970s with only two pedals.

19. Mario Igrec, *Pianos Inside Out* (Mandeville, LA: In Tune Press, 2013), 36.

20. Belt, *Piano*, 158.

21. "Bluthner," *Universal Piano Services*, 2017, accessed July 16, 2017, https://www.universalpianoservices.com/brands/bluthner.html.

22. In fall 2016, Taylor debuted his "hyper-piano" inspired by these double-manual instruments. This new instrument has a double-manual keyboard controller and two concert grand pianos serving as slaves to it. The pianist plays on the controller's keyboards, sending signals to robotic fingers that then play the two "slave" pianos. Catherine Capellaro, "The Grand Design," *Isthmus*, September 22, 2016, accessed July 26, 2017, https://isthmus.com/news/snapshot/christopher-taylor-invented-hyper-piano-uw-music.

23. "Pinchi Pedalpiano System," *Organi Pinchi*, 2017, accessed July 16, 2017, http://www.pinchi.com/pezzi-unici.

24. "The Millennium III ABS-Carbon Action," *Kawai*, 2015, accessed July 26. 2017, http://www.kawaius.com/technology/abs-c_action.html.

25. "Sordino: The Revival of an Old Tonality," *Steingraeber and Sohne*, accessed July 16, 2017, http://www.steingraeber.de/grand_pianos/sordino_724.html.

26. "Innovation," *Phoenix*, accessed July 16, 2017, http://www.phoenixpianos.co.uk/innovation.

27. "About Phoenix Pianos," *Phoenix*, accessed July 16, 2017, http://www.phoenixpianos.co.uk/about-phoenix-pianos-3.

28. Steingraeber & Söhne, "Mozart Rail: The Performance of a Fortepiano, Today," accessed February 15, 2018, www.steingraeber.de/en/innovationen/mozart-zug/.

29. In e-mail correspondence on June 16, 2017, and July 10, 2017, Stuart explained that "barless" frames were actually first offered by Broadwood in the 1880s and that the first Stuart and Sons upright piano built in 1990 also featured a barless frame. His stance as a piano maker is that the modern piano should offer nine octaves and have a barless frame to grant the pianist greater access to the strings.

30. "Harmonic Pedal: Examples," *Pédale Harmonique*, 2008, accessed July 16, 2017, http://www.harmonicpianopedal.com/comment_en.php.

31. Wayne Stahnke, "CEUS and My Imperial Piano," *Bösendorfer*, 2015, accessed July 25, 2017, http://www.company7.com/bosendorfer/ceus.html.

32. Independent developers have created other optical sensor systems for installation in ordinary pianos. The EPiCK optical sensor bar offers another route to adding sensors to a piano, allowing the user to turn a piano into a MIDI controller.

33. "K-2 ATX Upright Piano," *Kawai*, accessed July 26, 2017, http://www.kawai .co.uk/k2atx.htm.

CHAPTER 3. ON THE KEYS AND ON THE PEDALS

1. Luk Vaes, "Extended Piano Techniques in Theory, History, and Performance Practice" (Doctoral dissertation, Leiden University, Leiden, Netherlands), 204.

2. Henry Cowell, *Henry Cowell: Piano Music* (Washington, DC: Smithsonian Folkways, 1994), track 20.

3. Jelly Roll Morton, *Jelly Roll Morton: The Library of Congress Recordings*, vol. 1, CD (Solo Art, 1990). In this 1938 recording, Morton's elbow clusters are prominent.

4. Vivian Perlis and Libby Van Cleve, *Composers' Voices from Ives to Ellington: An Oral History of American Music* (New Haven, CT: Yale University Press, 2005), 160–61.

5. Ibid., 161. Over the years, Cowell told this story of his first engagement with clusters in different ways. Michael Hicks makes a solid case for dating *Tides of Manaunaun* later than Cowell's sometimes claim of 1912 in his article "Cowell's Clusters," *Musical Quarterly* 77, no. 3 (Autumn 1993): 428–58.

6. George Crumb, *Makrokosmos*, vol. 1, 17.

7. Charles Ives, Piano Sonata, no. 2, "Concord, Mass., 1840–60," score, 25.

8. Edward M. Ripin and Phillip R. Belt, *The Piano* (New York: W. W. Norton, 1988), 72.

9. Vaes, "Extended Piano Techniques," 416–17.

10. Leta E. Miller and Frederic Lieberman, *Composing a World: Lou Harrison, Musical Wayfarer* (Urbana: University of Illinois Press, 2004), 135.

11. Ibid., 136.

12. Thanks to Aron Kallay for alerting me to this piece (and who described the end of the piece as "impossible to play"). Kallay was the pianist for the premiere of this piece, after the manuscript was discovered in the Harrison archive.

13. Among other mid-eighteenth-century works that include notation for glissando, Luk Vaes discusses a sonata by Domenico Scarlatti with a repeated eight-note run on the white keys marked *"con dedo solo"* ("with one finger") in the score. Vaes, "Extended Piano Techniques," 124.

14. Herbert Henck, *Experimentelle Pianistik: Improvisation, Interpretation, Komposition* (Mainz, Germany: Schott, 1994), 92–93.

15. Drew Baker, "Stress Position," *Drew Baker Composer*, 2008, accessed May 30, 2017, drewbakermusic.com/stress-position.

16. Ken Ueno, "Performance Notes" to *Volcano* (New Jack Modernism, 2011).

17. Vaes, "Extended Piano Techniques," 71.

18. Marco Stroppa, *Miniature Estrose*, 42. Stroppa goes on to say, "This type of sound is more effective when the dampers have had some wear, but it nonetheless remains fairly delicate."

19. Ibid.

20. Edwin M. Good, *Giraffes, Black Dragons, and Other Pianos: A Technological History from Cristofori to the Modern Concert Grand*, 1st ed. (Stanford, CA: Stanford University Press, 1982), 106. Good explains that, in opus 101, Beethoven's score at one point asks for "progressively more strings."

CHAPTER 4. INSIDE THE PIANO:
PLUCKING, STRUMMING, SCRAPING, RUBBING

1. The College and University Technicians Committee of the Piano Technicians Guild's "Protocol for Extended Techniques Piano Performance" suggests that the pianist may also add a "reasonable amount (not too much) of powdered talc" to the hands before playing on the strings a moderate amount. The protocol suggests, for extensive contact with the strings, the player should wear thin gloves.

2. Hudicek, in her dissertation on extended techniques suggests another alternative to the screwdriver—a wooden popsicle stick. She also records that pianist Herbert Henck suggests using a wooden or rubber wedge to separate the strings before then placing a metal object between the strings. Laurie Marie Hudicek, "Off Key: A Comprehensive Guide to Unconventional Piano Techniques" (D.M.A. dissertation, University of Maryland, College Park, 2002), 144–45.

3. Piano Technicians Guild, "Protocol."

4. The maker itself explains that this bar can be safely removed when the piano is in its usual position. Hudicek in her dissertation also received confirmation of this from a few different piano technicians, including, she says, "two from Steinway Hall." Hudicek, "Off Key," 295.

5. I have chosen two Fazioli models close in size to each other for this comparison but could just as easily use two models by Steinway or Baldwin or some other maker and find at least as many distinctions. And, there tend to be even greater distinctions when compar-

ing grands of much greater size differences; on the insides at least, a Steinway Model O and a Steinway D present vastly different landscapes.

6. New music pianist Adam Tendler, though he says he has marked note names on small paper flags on every damper on his piano at home, says he is always hesitant to mark the dampers because of how delicate they are. He looks for alternative locations for marking when he is prepping a piano for performance. Conversation with the author, June 8, 2017.

7. The Piano Tuners Guild document allows using chalk for marking the plain steel strings but not the wound strings or the dampers. Chalk leaves residue, however, both on and around the surfaces where it is used and may require a lot of cleanup. The technicians I have consulted with all say not to use it.

8. David Burge, *Twentieth-Century Piano Music* (New York: Schirmer Books, 1990), 217.

9. Margaret Leng Tan, conversation with the author, July 30, 2017.

10. Margaret Leng Tan, conversation with the author, August 18, 2017.

11. A glissando across the strings while the dampers remain seated on the strings is certainly possible, but because the weight of the dampers does not allow the strings to ring, such a glissando produces very little sound—just the brittle chink of the fingernail or plectrum against each constituent string of the glissando.

12. Catherine R. Carr, "Riding *The Winds of Destiny*: An Oral History of George Crumb's Fourth Song Cycle in the *American Songbook Collection*" (D.M.A. document, University of Oklahoma, 2006), 69–70.

13. Ibid., 70–71.

14. This movement has a very slow tempo, and some of the chords extend over multiple measures. Theoretically, the pianist could watch the dampers move and use those movements to coordinate the strumming, but as some of the chordal moves change or add only a note or two, the pianist might miss some of the damper movements. I selected two notes otherwise not in use in the movement and programmed the mechanism to "play" silent quarter notes on those throughout the movement. Those two dampers lifting on every quarter note provide a visual metronome. The score asks that the pianist mute the strings of the two metronome notes using piano tuner's mutes to make sure those notes do not get accidently sounded by either the metronome movement or by the player's strumming the notes in the same register.

15. Henry Cowell, *The Banshee* (Los Angeles: W. A. Quincke, 1930), 8.

16. Ibid.

17. There is no real equivalent to pizzicato sul tasto on the piano. On the bowed string instruments, a portion of the string is over the primary resonator: the body of the instrument. The remainder of the speaking string length is over the fingerboard, so articulating the string over the fingerboard and not over the primary resonator produces a different sound. For the piano, the entire speaking length of every string is over the soundboard, so there is no place to pluck the string away from the primary resonator.

18. On bowed string instruments, there is only one bridge end of the string for bowing or plucking sul ponticello. The other end of the stopped string is at the nut and at the end of

the fingerboard and not over the body of the instrument. Articulating strings here is difficult to do and would not produce the same sound as articulating the strings near the bridge.

19. Stacey Barelos, "*Sinister Resonance* (1930)," *Henry Cowell—Piano Music*, accessed June 17, 2017, www.cowellpiano.com/SinRes.html.

20. Ibid.

21. Ryan Frechette, "The Ping Pong Piano: New 21st Century Timbres," *Music History Collaborative Blog*, April 6, 2015, accessed June 1, 2017, https://musichistoryfsu.wordpress.com/2015/04/06/the-ping-pong-piano-new-21st-century-timbres-2.

22. Alvin Lucier, liner notes to *Alvin Lucier: Theme* (Lovely Music, 1999).

CHAPTER 5. MUTING

1. The Piano Technicians Guild recommends using Blu-Tack on the strings over many other materials that might be placed in contact with them.

2. Piano technicians often refer to this assembly simply as "the action." Because this assembly includes the full action, the keys, and the key frame to which they are attached, I refer to the full assembly as the key frame in the hope that this is less confusing than calling it the action.

3. Many thanks to my piano technician, Mr. Ed Whitting, for showing me the basic principles of this method of muting. He told me that Pierre Boulez had once asked him to mute every string of a piano for him, and at the time, he had done so by pressing a felt strip between all the strings on the instrument. If he had been asked to do it now, he'd suggest the key-frame sliding technique.

CHAPTER 6. HARMONICS

1. If the composer wishes to use some of these covered tenor-register string nodes, the performer needs to access these nodes before the performance and stop the string at the node using one of the fixed harmonic preparation techniques detailed later. This means that the fundamentals for the strings so prepared are unavailable to the player until the player can pause and remove the preparations.

2. Laurie Marie Hudicek, "Off Key: A Comprehensive Guide to Unconventional Piano Techniques" (D.M.A. dissertation, University of Maryland, College Park, 2002), 65.

3. George Crumb, "Performance Notes," in *Gnomic Variations* (New York: C. F. Peters, 1982), 6.

4. I notate this example as a tremolo. Though the resultant sound here is a trill between a B♭ and a B♭ almost a one-third-tone flat, on the keys the pianist is playing a tremolo of a minor seventh, which looks on the page and would feel to the hand like a tremolo, not a trill.

5. E-mail correspondence with the author, June 15, 2017.

CHAPTER 7. THE PIANO IS A BIG BOX,
AND THE PIANIST IS A NOISE-MAKING ANIMAL

1. Mason and Hamlin's concert and semiconcert grand pianos extend the plate from the bass strings all the way to the rim of the piano, so these instruments only really give access to the soundboard through the sound holes.

2. Edward F. Kravitt, "The Joining of Words and Music in Late Romantic Melodrama," *Musical Quarterly* 62, no. 4 (October 1976): 575.

3. Richard Buskin, "Jerry Lee Lewis: 'Whole Lotta Shakin' Goin' On,'" *Sound on Sound*, June 2011, accessed June 12, 2017, http://www.soundonsound.com/people/jerry-lee-lewis-whole-lotta-shakin-goin.

4. La Monte Young, *Piano Piece for David Tudor #1*, in *An Anthology of Chance Operations, Concept Art, Anti-Art, Indeterminacy, Improvisation, Meaningless Work, Natural Disaster, Plans of Action, Mathematics, Poetry, Essay*, ed. La Monte Young and Jackson Mac Low (New York: Heiner Friedrich, 1962–1963).

5. Ibid.

6. Thanks to pianist Guy Livingston for alerting me to van Bergerijk's work and describing some of the "obstacles" the composer uses.

CHAPTER 8. BOWING

1. Curtis Curtis-Smith, "Notes Concerning the Second, Third and Fourth Pieces," in *Rhapsodies*, ii.

2. Though Curtis-Smith's instructions in the front of the score say bow length may be up to sixty inches, *Rhapsodies* itself asks for a sixty-six-inch bow.

3. Curtis-Smith, *Rhapsodies*, vi. Emphasis in original.

4. Tom Huizenga, "The Bowed Piano: Fishing for a New Sound," *Morning Edition*, National Public Radio, February 5, 2008. In an interview with Daniel Varela, Scott identifies the work as one by Curtis-Smith.

5. David Burge, *Contemporary Piano*, page included with the score to Curtis-Smith, *Rhapsodies*.

6. "Stephen Scott: Interview by Daniel Varela," *Perfect Sound Forever*, March 2005, accessed July 21, 2017, http://www.furious.com/perfect/stephenscott.html.

CHAPTER 9. PREPARATIONS

1. Edwin M. Good, *Giraffes, Black Dragons, and Other Pianos: A Technological History from Cristofori to the Modern Concert Grand*, 1st ed. (Stanford, CA: Stanford University Press, 1982), 110.

2. Kyle Gann, "If You Build It, They Will Come!" *American Mavericks*, 2005, accessed July 26, 2017, http://musicmavericks.publicradio.org/features/essay_gann05.html. Gann is fully aware that many composers and performers experimented with piano preparations before Cage, but it is also impossible to overstate the influence of Cage's works on subsequent prepared-piano works.

3. There are a few notable (though limited production) exceptions: The grand pianos constructed by Stephen Paulello in France and the very limited production of Barenboim-Maene pianos constructed by Chris Maene in Belgium are both straight-strung instruments.

4. John Cage, foreword to *The Well-Prepared Piano*, 2nd ed., by Richard Bunger (San Pedro, CA: Litoral Arts Press, 1981).

5. Crumb's score specifies that the rod should rest on all the strings from C4 to F5. A single glass rod cannot cover these strings on a Steinway D, as on this model a brace runs between C♯5 and D5. (The Steinway B and some of the other, smaller models work better for this particular passage and preparation. The B has no brace interrupting this register.) Crumb does suggest that a small glass plate can be substituted for the rod; another solution for performance on such models as the D that have an interruptive brace in just the wrong place is to use two lengths of glass rod, tied to each other with a small length of string that can run over the brace.

6. The score specifies a "very light metal chain (e.g., of aluminum)." George Crumb, *Makrokosmos*, book 1, 5.

7. Hauschka at NPR, "Mount Hood."

8. Bunger, *The Well-Prepared Piano*, 2nd Edition, 88.

9. Thanks to Elizabeth Baker for sharing this preparation with me.

10. Cage, foreword.

11. Ibid.

12. James Pritchett, liner notes to John Cage and Philipp Vandré, *The Piano Works 2: Sonatas and Interludes for Prepared Piano* (Mode, 1996).

13. Christian Wolff, "Preparations," in *For Prepared Piano* (New York: C. F. Peters, 1952), 2.

14. Richard Bunger, *The Well-Prepared Piano* (Colorado Springs: Colorado College Music Press, 1973), 37.

15. Bunger discusses this briefly in *Well-Prepared Piano*, 37.

16. Richard Bunger, *Two Pieces for Prepared Piano* (New York: Highgate Press, 1977), 2.

17. Bunger, *Well-Prepared Piano*, 18.

18. Ibid, 69.

19. William Duckworth, *The Time Curve Preludes* (New York: Henmar Press, 1979).

20. Neely Bruce, "Duckworth Weights," *Neely's Blog*, June 2, 2014, accessed July 26, 2017, http://neelybruceblogs.blogspot.com/2014/06/duckworth-weights.html.

CHAPTER 10. THE TOY PIANO

1. "History," *Schoenhut*, accessed March 1, 2016, http://www.toypiano.com/about_his tory.asp.

2. Ibid. According to the Schoenhut website, by the time of Albert Schoenhut's death in 1912, the company he had founded was the largest toy company in the United States.

3. Schoenhut and the piano manufacturer Kawai have constructed miniature strung pianos, instruments using hammers striking metal strings much like a full-size piano, and that have dampers and pedals. These are actual pianos, though single-strung and with a reduced scale (most models have forty-four or forty-nine keys). Though sometimes mislabeled, these instruments are not generally considered toy pianos, and they, along with electronic keyboards constructed to look like traditional toy pianos (and sometimes marketed as "toy pianos," as well), are not discussed here.

4. Thomas Kotcheff, e-mail to the author, June 14, 2017.

5. David Smooke, "Extended Toy Piano," *New Music Box*, November 15, 2011, http://www.newmusicbox.org/articles/extended-toy-piano.

6. Xenia Pestova, "Toy Pianos, Poor Tools: Virtuosity and Imagination in a Limited Context," *Tempo* 71, no. 281 (July 2017): 31.

7. The Schoenhut company has produced a short document on toy piano tuning. This suggests that the copper wire may be attached to the rod more permanently by applying a drop of super glue. "Toy Piano Tuning Instructions," *Schoenhut*, 2012, accessed March 1, 2016, http://www.toypiano.com/instructions/piano_tuning_instructions.pdf.

8. I borrow the term *dead-stroke* to refer to this, as this is the term percussionists use to refer to striking a drum or keyboard percussion instrument with the beater and then immediately dampening the sound by keeping the beater against the head or bar it has just struck.

Bibliography

Abbinanti, Frank. "Sections of *Exergue 1 / Evocations / Dialogue with Timbre*." *Contemporary Music Review* 23, nos. 3–4 (September–December 2004): 81–90.

Akbulut, Åirin. "The Use of Extended Piano Techniques at Conservatories in Turkey." *Procedia—Social and Behavioral Sciences* 2, no. 2 (2010): 3080–87.

Anderson, Simon Peter. "The Prepared Piano Music of John Cage: Towards an Understanding of Sounds and Preparations." Master's thesis, University of Huddersfield, 2012.

Baker, Elizabeth A., and Fofi Panagiotouros, eds. *Toyager: A Toy Piano Method*. Saint Petersburg, FL: Elizabeth A. Baker, 2016.

Banowetz, Joseph. *The Pianist's Guide to Pedaling*. Bloomington: Indiana University Press, 1985.

Beal, Amy C. "How Johanna Beyer Spent Her Days." Web-published essay draft, 2007; rev. 2011): 1–46. http://music.ucsc.edu/faculty/amy-beal.

———. *Johanna Beyer*. Urbana: University of Illinois Press, 2015.

Beckman, Seth Victor. "The Traditional and the Avant-Garde in Late Twentieth-Century Music: A Study of Three Piano Compositions by Frederic Rzewski (1938–)." Ph.D. dissertation, Ball State University, 1996.

Belt, Phillip R. *The Piano: The New Grove Musical Instruments Series*. New York: W. W. Norton, 1988.

Bloland, Per. "The Electromagnetically Prepared Piano and Its Compositional Implications." In *International Computer Music Conference*, pp. 125–28. Copenhagen, Denmark, 2007.

Britt, Neil Cameron. "Actuated Acoustic Instruments: Relationships and Mind-Sets." Ph.D. dissertation, Princeton University, January 2014.

Brougham, Henrietta, Christopher Fox, and Ian Pace. *Uncommon Ground: The Music of Michael Finnissy*. Aldershot, UK: Ashgate, 1997.

Bruce, David. "Ian Pace Interview." *Composition: Today*. April 19, 2005. http://www.compositiontoday.com/interviews/ian_pace.asp.

Bruns, Steven. "George Crumb: *Makrokosmos I and II*." Note to the album.

Bruns, Steven, Ofer Ben-Amots, and Michael Grace. *George Crumb and The Alchemy of Sound*. Colorado Springs, CO: Colorado College Music Press, 2005.

Bunger, Richard. *The Well-Prepared Piano*. Colorado Springs, CO: Colorado College Music Press, 1973.

———. *The Well-Prepared Piano*, 2nd ed. San Pedro, CA: Litoral Arts Press, 1981.

Burge, David. "An Approach to the Performance of Twentieth-Century Music." *Clavier* (March/April 1963): 10–17.

———. "The Quest for New Repertoire Categories: A Call for Renewed Emphasis on Twentieth-Century Compositions." *Piano Quarterly* 40 (Spring 1992): 55–56.

———. *Twentieth-Century Piano Music*. New York: Schirmer Books, 1990.

Burtner, Matthew. "Making Noise: Extended Techniques after Experimentalism." *New Music Box*. March 1, 2005. http://www.newmusicbox.org/articles/making-noise-extended-techniques-after-experimentalism.

Cage, John. "How the Piano Came to Be Prepared." In *Empty Words: Writings '73–'78 by John Cage*. Middletown, CT: Wesleyan University Press, 1979.

Cahill, Sarah. "The Inside Story." *Piano and Keyboard* 203 (March–April 2000): 32–35.

Carr, Catherine R. "Riding *The Winds of Destiny*: An Oral History of George Crumb's Fourth Song Cycle in the *American Songbook Collection*." D.M.A. document, University of Oklahoma, 2006.

Casadel, Delia. "George Crumb Hears the Heartbeat of America." *Los Angeles Times*, November 14, 2010.

Clinkscale, Martha Novak. *Makers of the Piano*. Vol. 2: *1820–1860*. Oxford: Oxford University Press, 1999.

Clough, Allison Rachelle. "A Performance Guide for Selected Works for Piano by Henry Cowell." D.M.A. thesis, University of Alabama, 2013.

Cope, David. *New Directions in Music*, 7th ed. Prospect Heights, IL: Waveland Press, 2001.

Cowell, Henry. *New Musical Resources*. Cambridge University Press, 1930.

Craenen, Paul. *Composing under the Skin: The Music-Making Body at the Composer's Desk*. Leuven University Press,

Dianova, Tzenka. *John Cage's Prepared Piano: The Nuts and Bolts*. Victoria, BC: Mutasis Books, 2008.

Dimpker, Christian. *Extended Notation: The Depiction of the Unconventional*. Berlin: LIT Verlag, 2013

Dolan, Emily I. "Portrait: Andrew McPherson and the Magnetic Resonator Piano." In *Keyboard Perspectives: Yearbook of the Westfield Center for Historical Keyboard Studies*, vol. 8 (2015): 173–84.

Dolge, Alfred. *Pianos and Their Makers*. Covina, CA: Covina Publishing, 1911.

Drury, Stephen. "A View from the Piano Bench or Playing John Zorn's *Carny* for Fun and Profit." *Perspectives of New Music* 32, no. 1 (Winter 1994): 194–201.

Dullea, Mary Josephine. "Performing Extended Techniques in Contemporary Piano Repertoire: Perspectives on Performance Practice, Notation and the Collaborative Process in the Use of the Inside of the Piano and Non-conventional Methods." Ph.D. dissertation, Ulster University, 2011.

Eckardt, Jason. "Broadening Knowledge: An Interview with Ursula Oppens." *American Music Review* 38, no. 1 (Fall 2008): 6.

Edgar, Michelle. "From Early Coaching at Aspen to a Zest for the Contemporary: An Interview with Ursula Oppens." *Clavier* 42, no. 5 (May–June 2003): 6.

Ehle, Robert. "Twentieth Century Music and the Piano." *Piano Quarterly*, no. 96 (Winter 1976–1977): 28–31.

Ettenauer, Isabel. "A Short Introduction to the Music for Toy Piano by Karlheinz Essl." *Fowl Feathered Review*, no. 4 (Summer 2013): 74–81.

Fischer, Victoria. "Articulation Notation in the Piano Music of Béla Bartók: Evolution and Interpretation." *Studia Musicolologica Academiae Scientiarum Hungaricae* 36, nos. 3–4 (1995): 285–301.

Fox, Christopher. "Under the Lens: Michael Finnissy's *History of Photography in Sound*." *Musical Times* 143, no. 1879: 26–35.

Frechette, Ryan. "The Ping Pong Piano: New 21st-Century Timbres." *Music History Collaborative Blog*. April 6, 2015. https://musichistoryfsu.wordpress.com/2015/04/06/the-ping-pong-piano-new-21st-century-timbres-2.

Gartner, Kenneth. "The Expansion of Pianism since 1945." Ph.D. dissertation, New York University, 1979.

Good, Edwin M. *Giraffes, Black Dragons, and Other Pianos: A Technological History from Cristofori to the Modern Concert Grand*. 1st ed. Stanford, CA: Stanford University Press, 1982.

———. *Giraffes, Black Dragons, and Other Pianos: A Technological History from Cristofori to the Modern Concert Grand*. 2nd ed. Stanford, CA: Stanford University Press, 2002.

Grafing, Keith G., Alpheus Babcock, Thomas Loud, and Emilius N. Scherr. "Alpheus Babcock's Cast-Iron Piano Frames." *Galpin Society Journal* 27 (1874): 118–24.

Grant, Neva. "Musical Innovation: A Grander Grand Piano." *Morning Edition, NPR*. January 18, 2011. http://www.npr.org/2011/01/18/132945634/musical-innovation-a-grander-grand-piano.

Harbinson, William G. "Performer Indeterminacy and Boulez's Third Sonata." *Tempo*, no. 169 (June 1989): 16–20.

Henck, Herbert. *Experimentelle Pianistik: Improvisation, Interpretation, Komposition*. Mainz, Germany: Schott, 1994.

Hicks, Michael. "Cowell's Clusters." *Musical Quarterly* 77, no. 3 (Autumn 1993): 428–58.

———. *Henry Cowell, Bohemian*. Urbana: University of Illinois Press, 2002.

Hiser, Kelly Ann. "'An Enduring Cycle': Revaluing the Life and Music of Johanna Beyer." Master's thesis, University of Miami, 2009.

Hudicek, Laurie Marie. "Off Key: A Comprehensive Guide to Unconventional Piano Techniques." D.M.A. dissertation, University of Maryland, College Park, 2002.

Huizenga, Tom. "The Bowed Piano: Fishing for a New Sound." *Morning Edition, NPR*. February 5, 2008. http://www.npr.org/templates/story/story.php?storyId=18666248.

Igrec, Mario. *Pianos Inside Out*. Mandeville, LA: In Tune Press, 2013.

Isacoff, Stuart. *A Natural History of the Piano: The Instrument, the Music, the Musicians—From Mozart to Modern Jazz and Everything in Between*. New York: Alfred A. Knopf, 2011.

Ishii, Reiko. "The Development of Extended Piano Techniques in Twentieth-Century American Music." D.M.A. dissertation, Florida State University, 2005.

Jackson, Claire. "Pimp My Instrument: The Advantage to Filling a Piano with Ping Pong Balls." *Guardian* Music Blog. May 29, 2009. https://www.theguardian.com/music/musicblog/2009/may/29/pimp-my-instrument.

Kim, Hyangmee. "A Performer's Guide to George Crumb's *Makrokosmos IV (Celestial Mechanics)*." D.M.A. dissertation, University of North Texas, 2008.

Kozinn, Allan. "A Performer Drawn to the Piano's Wild Side." *New York Times*, November 19, 2004.

Kravitt, Edward F. "The Joining of Words and Music in Late Romantic Melodrama." *Musical Quarterly* 62, no. 4 (October 1976): 571–90.

Lee, Richard Andrew. "The Interaction of Linear and Vertical Time in Minimalist and Postminimalist Piano Music." D.M.A. dissertation, University of Missouri–Kansas City, 2010.

Loesser, Arthur. *Men, Women, and Pianos*. Mineola, NY: Dover, 1990.

Loffredo, Antonietta. "Curious Instruments before the Toy Piano." In festival program for Florida International Toy Piano Festival, January 2016.

MacVean, Mary. "The Piano's Status in U.S. Living Rooms Is Declining." *Los Angeles Times*, May 16, 2009.

Marks, Adam. "The Virtuosic Era of the Vocalizing Pianist." Ph.D. dissertation, New York University, 2012.

Maroney, Denman F. "Hyperpiano: Extended Piano Performance Techniques." *Downbeat* (March 1999).

McGowan, Dale, and Ursula Oppens. "The Feast of 'Saint Ursula': A Conversation with Ursula Oppens." *American Music Teacher* 49, no. 4 (February–March 2000): 38–40.

McKay, John Robert. "Notational Practices in Selected Piano Works of the Twentieth Century." D.M.A. dissertation, Eastman School of Music, 1977.

Midgette, Anne. "Pianos: Beyond the Steinway Monoculture." *Washington Post*, September 5, 2015. https://www.washingtonpost.com/entertainment/music/the-piano-keys -of-the-future/2015/09/03/9bbbbfee-354c-11e5-94ce-834ad8f5c50e_story.html?utm_ term=.a391f8855f62.

Miller, Leta E., and Frederic Lieberman. *Composing a World: Lou Harrison, Musical Wayfarer*. Urbana: University of Illinois Press, 2004.

Nonken, Marilyn. *The Spectral Piano: From Liszt, Scriabin, and Debussy to the Digital Age*. Cambridge: Cambridge University Press, 2014.

Oppens, Ursula, in conversation with Marilyn Nonken. "Being Expressive of What's There." *Contemporary Music Review* 21, no. 1 (2002): 61–69.

Oteri, Frank J. "George Crumb: Jumping off the Page to Become Sound." *New Music Box.* August 1, 2002. http://www.newmusicbox.org/articles/george-crumb-jumping-off-the-page-to-become-sound.

———. "Stephen Scott: The Inside Story." *New Music Box.* March 1, 2005. http://www.newmusicbox.org/articles/the-inside-story-stephen-scott-talks-with-frank-j-oteri-stephen-scott.

Pace, Ian. "Ferneyhough Hero: Scholarship as Promotion." *Music and Letters* 96, no. 1 (February 2015): 99–112.

———. "An Interview between Ian Pace and Michael Finnissy." *Notations,* vol. 1: Music and Evolution (February 2009): 13–16.

———. "Lachenmann's *Serynade*: Issues for performer and listener." *Contemporary Music Review* 24, no. 1 (February 2005): 101–12.

———. "Maintaining Disorder: Some Technical and Aesthetic Issues Involved in the Performance of Ligeti's Études for Piano." *Contemporary Music Review* 31, nos. 2–3 (April–June 2012): 177–201.

———. "Notation, Time and the Performer's Relationship to the Score in Contemporary Music." In *Collected Work: Unfolding Time: Studies in Temporality in Twentieth-Century Music.* Collected Writings of the Orpheus Institute, no. 8. Leuven, Belgium: Leuven University Press, 2009.

———. "The Panorama of Michael Finnissy (I)." *Tempo,* no. 196 (April 1996): 25–35.

———. "The Panorama of Michael Finnissy (II)." *Tempo,* no. 201 (July 1997): 7–16.

Palmieri, Robert, ed. *The Piano: An Encyclopedia.* 2nd ed. New York: Routledge, 2003.

Perlis, Vivian, and Libby Van Cleve. *Composers' Voices from Ives to Ellington: An Oral History of American Music.* New Haven, CT: Yale University Press, 2005.

Pestova, Xenia. "Toy Pianos, Poor Tools: Virtuosity and Imagination in a Limited Context." *Tempo* 71, no. 281 (July 2017): 27–38.

Pollens, Stewart. *The Early Pianofortes.* Cambridge, MA: Cambridge University Press, 1995.

Proulx, Jen-Francois. "A Pedagogical Guide to Extended Piano Techniques." D.M.A. thesis. Temple University, Philadelphia, Pennsylvania, 2009.

Read, Gardner. *Compendium of Modern Instrumental Techniques.* Westport, CT: Greenwood Press, 1993.

———. *Contemporary Instrumental Techniques.* New York: Schirmer Books, 1976.

Reblitz, Arthur A. *Piano Servicing, Tuning, and Rebuilding. For the Professional, the Student, and the Hobbyist.* Lanham, MD: Vestal Press, 1993.

Robair, Gino. "Interview: Sarah Cahill." *Keyboard Magazine.* December 16, 2016. http://www.keyboardmag.com/artists/1236/interview-sarah-cahill/61215.

———. "Unleash the Hidden Bank of Sounds in Your Acoustic Piano." *Keyboard Magazine.* October 18, 2013. http://www.keyboardmag.com/acoustic-piano/1189/unleash-the-hidden-bank-of-sounds-in-your-acoustic-piano/29461.

Saxon, Kenneth Neal. "A New Kaleidoscope: Extended Piano Techniques, 1910–1975." D.M.A. dissertation, University of Alabama, 2000.

Service, Tom. "Expressivity and Critique in Lachenmann's *Serynade*." *Contemporary Music Review* 24, no. 1 (2005): 77–88.

Stearns, David Patrick. "At 87, Avant-Garde Philly Composer George Crumb Pushes New Boundaries." *Philliy.com*. May 11, 2017. http://www.philly.com/philly/columnists/ david_patrick_stearns/at-87-avant-garde-philly-composer-george-crumb-pushes-new -boundaries-20170511.html.

Stone, Kurt. *Music Notation in the Twentieth Century, A Practical Guidebook*. New York: W. W. Norton, 1980.

Takahashi, Yuji. "The Piano and Its Transformations." *Perspectives of New Music* 30, no. 2 (Summer 1992): 86–89.

Todd, R. Larry. *Nineteenth-Century Piano Music*. New York: Schirmer Books, 1990.

Toop, Richard. "Brian Ferneyhough's *Lemma-Icon-Epigram*." *Perspectives of New Music* 28, no. 2 (Summer 1990): 52–100.

Tyranny, "Blue" Gene. "88 Keys to Freedom: Segues through the History of American Piano Music." *New Music Box*. October 1, 2003. http://www.newmusicbox.org/article .nmbx?id=2219.

Vaes, Luk. "Extended Piano Techniques in Theory, History, and Performance Practice." Ph.D. dissertation, Leiden University, Leiden, Netherlands, 2009.

Van Cleve, Libby. *Oboe Unbound: Contemporary Techniques*. Lanham, MD: Scarecrow Press, 2004.

Wang, Chien-Wei. "Examples of Extended Techniques in Twentieth-Century Piano Etudes by Selected Pianist-Composers." D.M.A. essay, University of Miami, 2010.

Williams, Maggie. "Child's Play." *International Piano* (March–April 2007). http://www .isabelettenauer.com/en/reactions/childs-play-international-piano.

Wilson, Samuel. "Building an Instrument, Building an Instrumentalist: Helmut Lachenmann's *Serynade*." *Contemporary Music Review* 32, no. 5 (2013): 425–36.

Wraight, Denzil. "Recent Approaches in Understanding Cristofori's Fortepiano." *Early Music* 34, no. 4 (November 2006): 635–44.

Yang, Chia-Shan. "Exploring New Techniques in Contemporary Piano Music: A Guide for the Intermediate-Grade Student." D.M.A. dissertation, University of Washington, 2004.

Sources and Permissions

Every effort has been made to obtain permissions for works under copyright. Any necessary adjustments to permissions statements are made upon notification to the author or publisher.

Works by the author

Shockley, Alan. *black narcissus*, 1996. "an image in the water." [p. 11, mm. 17–19]
———. *bristlecone and pitch*, 2014. [p. 3, mm. 62–64]
———. *I feel open to . . .* , 2011. [p. 4, mm. 23–25]
———. *Hoc florentes arbor*, 2017. [p. 4, first system]
———. *wndhm (1785)*: ii (two-piano realization), 2016. [p. 3, mm. 33–35]

Works in the Public Domain or with Excerpts Replicated within Fair Use Restrictions

Alkan, Charles-Valentin. *Une fusée, Introduction et Impromptu*, op. 55. Paris: Simon Richault, 1859. [last page, third system]
Bartók, Béla. Suite, op. 14. Vienna: Universal, 1918. [movement 2, last system]
Cage, John. *Suite for Toy Piano*. New York: Henmar Press, 1960. [mm. 1–5]
Chopin, Frédéric. Nocturne in D-flat, op. 27, no. 2. Leipzig: Breitkopf and Härtel, 1837. [mm. 62–64]
Finnissy, Michael. *English Country Tunes*. London: United Music Publishing, 1986. [p. 13, m. 1]
———. *Sonata for (Toy) Piano*. Karlsruhe: Edition Tre Media, 2006–2007. [mm. 1–3]
Gubaidulina, Sofia. *Piano Sonata*. New York: Associated Music Publishers, 1977. [p. 3, mm. 1–2]
Kolb, Barbara. *Appello*, 4: "And I Remembered the Cry of the Peacocks—Wallace Stevens." New York: Boosey and Hawkes, 1978. [p. 17, last measure]

     Sources and Permissions

Liszt, Franz. "La campanella" from *Grandes* Études *de Paganini*, S. 141, no. 3, 1851.

Messiaen, Olivier. *Mode de valeurs et d'intensités.* Paris: Durand, 1950. [p. 7, mm. 51–53]

Rzewski, Frederic. *De Profundis.* Brussels: Sound Pool Music, 1992. [p. 3, mm. 32–35]

————. *The People United Will Never Be Defeated!* Tokyo: ZEN-ON Music, 1979. [p. 22, mm. 5–6]

Schoenberg, Arnold. *Drei Klavierstücke*, op. 11, no. 1. Vienna: Universal Edition, 1910. [mm. 14–16]

Wiggins, Thomas "Blind Tom." De Roode, R., arranger. *The Battle of Manassas.* Cleveland, S. Brainard's Sons, 1913.

Works Reprinted by Permission

Baker, Drew. *Stress Position*, 2008. [m. 57] Used by permission of the composer.

Berio, Luciano. *Erdenklavier.* London: Universal Edition, 1974. [first system] Copyright Universal Edition. All rights reserved. Reprinted by permission.

Boulez, Pierre. *Structures: 2 pianos à 4 mains.* Vienna: Universal Edition, 1955–1967. [Section Ic, mm. 4–7] Used by permission of Universal Edition.

Cage, John. *Totem Ancestor.* New York: Henmar Press, 1942. [Portion of "Table of Preparations"] Copyright Henmar Press licensed by C. F. Peters.

Cowell, Henry. *Aeolian Harp.* Associated Music Publishers, 1930. [mm. 9–11] Copyright 1930 (renewed) by Associated Music Publishers, Inc. (BMI), international copyright secured. All rights reserved. Reprinted by permission.

————. *Antinomy.* Associated Music Publishers, 1922. [last three measures]. Copyright 1922 (renewed) by Associated Music Publishers, Inc. (BMI), international copyright secured. All rights reserved. Reprinted by permission.

————. *The Tides of Manaunaun.* Associated Music Publishers, 1922. [mm. 1–3 and excerpt from notation key] Copyright 1922 (renewed) by Associated Music Publishers, Inc. (BMI), international copyright secured. All rights reserved. Reprinted by permission.

Crumb, George. *Gnomic Variations.* New York: C. F. Peters, 1982. [p. 11, "Var. 6-largamente, retoricamente," end of first system] Copyright C. F. Peters. All rights reserved. Reprinted by permission of the composer.

————. *Makrokosmos*, book 1, New York: C. F. Peters, 1974. [no. 10, "Spring Fire," and p. 11, beginning of first system; p. 17, second system] Copyright 1974 by C. F. Peters. All rights reserved. Reprinted by permission of the composer.

————. *Makrokosmos*, book 2. New York: C. F. Peters, 1973. ["Agnus Dei," first measure] Copyright C. F. Peters. All rights reserved. Reprinted by permission of the composer.

————. *Vox Balaenae.* New York: C. F. Peters, 1972. [p. 8, mm. 1–3, "Sea Theme," and p. 10, middle of second system] Copyright C. F. Peters. All rights reserved. Reprinted by permission of the composer.

Ferneyhough, Brian. *Opus Contra Naturam.* London: Edition Peters, 2000. [mm. 14–15] Copyright C. F. Peters.

Holloway-Nahum, Aaron. *Remember Me?* [p. 61, mm. 507–8, and p. 63, mm. 517–21] Used by permission of the composer.

Iannotta, Clara. *Troglodyte Angels Clank By*. [piano part, mm. 177–82] Reprinted by permission of the composer.

Kotcheff, Thomas. *death, hocket, and roll*. [m. 50] Used by permission of the composer.

Lachenmann, Helmut. *Guero*. Köln: Musikverlage Hans Gerig, 1972. [p. 1, second system] Copyright 1972 by Musikverlage Hans Gerig, Köln. 1980 assigned to Breitkopf and Härtel, Wiesbaden.

Lin, Mu-Xuan. *Pale Fire*. [mm. 1–3 and mm. 23–25] Used by permission of the composer.

Ornstein, Leo. *Danse sauvage*. London: Schott, 1915. [mm. 7–8] Used with kind permission of European American Music Distributors Company, sole U.S. and Canadian agent for Schott Music, Ltd., London.

Rice, Samara. *OnomataPiano*, 2016. [opening (unnumbered measure)] Used by permission of the composer.

Sciarrino, Salvatore. *Due Notturni Crudeli*. [p. 10, beginning of second system] Milan: Ricordi, 2001.

Sciarrino, Salvatore. *Sonatina*. [p. 7, first system] Milan: Ricordi, 1975.

Stockhausen, Karlheinz. *Klavierstück X*. Vienna: Universal Edition, 1961. [p. 11, first system] Copyright 1961 Universal Edition. All rights reserved. Reprinted by permission.

Stroppa, Marco. *Miniature Estrose*. Milan: Ricordi, 2009. ["Innige Cavatina," p. 91, m. 79] Copyright Ricordi.

Svensson, Johan. *Study for Piano No. 2*. [m. 1.] Used by permission of the composer.

Ueno, Ken. *Volcano*. New Jack Modernism Music, 2011. [mm. 11–13] Used by permission of the composer.

Valitutto, Richard. *assemblages* "papier-mâché." [m. 19] Used by permission of the composer.

Index

About the Author

Alan Shockley (Ph.D., Princeton University) is the director of composition and theory and an associate professor in the Bob Cole Conservatory of Music at California State University, Long Beach. As a composer, he has held residencies at the MacDowell Colony, the Atlantic Center, the Virginia Center for the Arts, Italy's Centro Studi Ligure, and France's Centre d'Art Marnay Art Centre (CAMAC), among others, and he has received grants from the American Music Center, Pittsburgh ProArts, the Andrew W. Mellon Foundation, and the Heinz Foundation. A dedicated scholar and educator, Shockley's teaching interests have led him to join Kronos Quartet on a panel on intersections between technology and music and to present in a Princeton University atelier alongside Anonymous 4. Shockley's essays on and reviews of contemporary music and intersections between music and modernist fiction can be found in journals and collections published by several of the leading presses. His book, *Music in the Words: Musical Form and Counterpoint in the Twentieth-Century Novel*, was released in 2009.

0 1341 1716311 0